Billy Bishop VC

This book is dedicated to my home team: Judy, Clayton and Christine, Karl and Christina, Cara, Elaine and Tessa, Brendan and Christian Kilduff, and Pearl – also to my friend and mentor, the late Clayton Knight, OBE, who was also a friend of Billy Bishop's.

Other books by Peter Kilduff

The Red Baron
That's My Bloody Plane
Germany's Last Knight of the Air
U.S. Carriers at War
A-4 Skyhawk
Germany's First Air Force 1914-1918
Richthofen – Beyond the Legend of the Red Baron
Over the Battlefronts
The Red Baron Combat Wing
The Illustrated Red Baron
Talking With the Red Baron
Red Baron – The Life and Death of an Ace
Black Fokker Leader
Hermann Göring – Fighter Ace
Iron Man Rudolf Berthold: Germany's Indomitable World War I Fighter Ace

Billy Bishop VC

Lone Wolf Hunter
The RAF Ace Re-examined

Peter Kilduff

Grub Street · London

Published by
Grub Street
4 Rainham Close
London
SW11 6SS

ISBN-13:9781909808133

Printed and bound by Berforts Information Press Ltd

Grub Street Publishing uses only FSC (Forest Stewardship Council) paper for its books.

Contents

Foreword

'History must speak for itself. A historian is content
if he has been able to shed more light.'
– William L. Shirer[1]

By the time the Armistice was signed, on 11 November 1918, William Avery Bishop – popularly known as Billy – was being hailed as the British Empire's highest-scoring fighter ace of World War I. Officially credited with being victorious in seventy-two aerial combats[2], Bishop became the third-ranking ace of the Great War belligerent nations. He trailed only Germany's Manfred Freiherr von Richthofen (with eighty confirmed aerial victories) and France's René Fonck (seventy-five confirmed victories). Richthofen and many other prominent fighter aces were well known for leading squadrons into combat, but Bishop and Fonck were among the fighter pilots who achieved most of their victories while flying alone.

In Bishop's case, that 'lone wolf' tactic, which he practiced even as a squadron commander, freed him to chase targets over German-held territory without having to look after less experienced pilots. But that approach to aerial combat was more dangerous, making him more vulnerable to adversaries' attacks. And, with sparse corroboration of his air fighting claims, Bishop's modus operandi later left him open to questions about the veracity of his combat reports.

This book will demonstrate, however, that qualifications for air combat successes were not carefully defined during the 1914-1918 war and 'victories' were awarded subjectively on both sides of the battle lines; often those decisions were made by superiors far removed from the fighting. Consequently, matching victors and victims is often difficult to do accurately. Assessing German losses is hindered by the scarcity of official records due to the intentional burning of many Luftstreitkräfte [German Air Force] documents in the field during the November 1918 retreat and the near destruction of the Reichsarchiv [Imperial German Archives] outside Berlin by a British bomber on 14 April 1945[3].

Surviving German World War I records consist of a small number of Luftstreitkräfte pilot and aircrew combat reports, air unit histories, and incomplete sets of Kommandeur der Flieger [Officer in Charge of Aviation] weekly reports for various army corps. To make this book as comprehensive as possible, this author drew on Luftstreitkräfte records available in various German archives and other sources. That research included a thorough examination of the most complete broad-view sources of German air operations, the *Nachrichtenblatt* weekly intelligence summaries for the army and a compilation of similar material for the Imperial Navy. Largely devoted to Western Front operations, both publications reported selectively on individuals and units – and, as will be pointed out, there are flaws in those reports. Post-war memoirs of German airmen filled some of the gaps, but were often very subjective.

Also to be considered from the German side is faulty record-keeping or even obfuscation. One such occurrence was cited by 74 Squadron pilot and thirty-seven-victory ace Wing Commander Ira T. Jones, DSO, MC, DFC, MM[4]. Between the wars he was attached to the Royal Air Force Historical Section and worked with German counterparts, exchanging archival and other material to help each side bring balance to official histories of their respective military air arms between 1914 and 1918. After some time, he told official RAF Historian H.A. Jones (no relation) that he questioned the 'credence' of German information provided[5] and cited the following example:

'On 19 June 1918, Major … Billy Bishop … who was then commanding 85 Squadron, shot down five Huns before breakfast and Captain [Arthur] Cobby, DSO, MC, DFC, [of] 1 Australian Squadron, shot down one Hun after tea. These were the only victories claimed on that day by the Royal Air Force.

'In reply to our query, the German Air Ministry said they had lost neither pilots nor aircraft on 19 June. I know for a fact that that statement was a lie. Captain Cobby's victim was lying, riddled with bullets in [my squadron's] hangar at Clairmarais North Aerodrome, near St. Omer, on the evening in question.'[6]

Cobby's claim remains reinforced by a war souvenir: the tail-skid of Jagdstaffel 7 pilot Unteroffizier [Corporal] Max Mertens' Pfalz D.IIIa in the Australian War Memorial in Canberra[7]. Also, a German aviation necrology compiled by Major a.D. Wilhelm Zickerick, published in 1920[8] and updated in a more recent English-language version[9], lists nine air casualties for the day. That total included two Western Front deaths, one of which was Uffz Mertens.[10] The 'Zickerick necrology' covers aviation personnel who died on any given day and does not infer that their deaths were combat related. The day's RAF War Diary entry confirms I.T. Jones' contention that Bishop claimed five victories at about 9:58 am, which will be discussed later in this book, and Cobby's one victory at 6:45 pm.[11]

Various British reports refer to a wide range of air combat events, of which Captain Cobby's victory claim is easy to match with a known German loss. Yet, whatever happened that day, the RAF awarded full aerial victory credits to Major Bishop, Captain Cobby and the crew of a Bristol F.2B crewmen two-seat fighter.[12] This book examines each of Bishop's seventy-two credited aerial victory claims to determine which ones can be identified through available British and German archival sources – and to explain when other RFC/RAF victory claims cannot be matched with German casualties.

As this author has learned in over forty-five years of such research, it is less complicated to reasonably identify British air casualties claimed by German airmen. First, most such incidents occurred over German-held territory, where confirming evidence could be retrieved. Second, the relative wealth of Allied materials found in such resources as the UK's National Archive at Kew greatly aids current researchers in identifying Royal Flying Corps/Royal Air Force/Royal Naval Air Service casualties, as well as victors in combats. Those men are named in British squadron combat reports, squadron record books, RFC/RAF War Diary daily entries, RFC/RAF weekly Communiqués (with RNAS men's activities detailed in comparable reports and publications), nearly complete daily compilations of British air losses (listing pilot/crew identifications, aircraft types and serial numbers and brief loss-related texts), and much casualty and personal information that appeared in such publicly available sources as *Flight* magazine.

The multi-volume RAF history *The War in the Air*, chiefly written by H.A. Jones and published from 1922 to 1937, contains a wealth of material, including documentation from the Reichsarchiv. Personal memoirs in books and articles – including those by and about Billy Bishop and his contemporaries – offered subjective but first-hand views of events that occurred almost a century ago.

However, thefts of British archival documents added to the ravages of war. In the late 1980s, a rapacious thief stole a vast number of original RFC/RNAS/RAF documents then held by the Public Record Office (PRO) – now called The National Archive (TNA). That despicable occurrence, the scope of which was reportedly 'over 15,000 First and Second World War Air Ministry and War Office records from the Public Record Office',[13] has become another impediment to studying World War I aviation history. Researchers now seeking access to various British air unit records are greeted by a cover note attached to the files, dated 2 September and 7 October 1991, stating:

> 'Papers from records in this class and six other classes of public records relating to air operations in the Wars of 1914-1918 and 1939-1945 … were discovered in 1989 and 1990 to be missing. Investigations led to the conviction of a PRO reader on charges of theft and criminal damage; and many of the papers were subsequently recovered.'[14]

Many, perhaps, but not all – and there is no telling what is missing.

Billy Bishop himself created a problem with his historical legacy. As he retold his war stories over the years, he embellished some of them in ways that conflicted with known facts. Consequently, this book draws heavily on World War I-era documents and reports, as well as Bishop's letters to his fiancée (and later wife) Margaret Eaton Burden. To be sure, the letters contain inflated drama or, conversely, assurance that 'things aren't all that bad', as many a young man in his early twenties would say or write to impress or comfort the most important woman in his life. Bishop's two books – *Winged Warfare* (1918) and *Winged Peace* (1944) – also contain some useful information. But the official, often terse, World War I combat-related documents are straightforward and unadorned.

Long after Billy Bishop's death, his achievements were questioned by the 1982 film 'The Kid Who Couldn't Miss', a docudrama produced by the National Film Board of Canada. It combines fact and fiction to question Bishop's World War I accomplishments – e.g., alleging that his 2 June 1917 attack on a German airfield was entirely fabricated. (See Chapter Eight.) Viewed as assaulting one of Canada's greatest military heroes, the film became the subject of extensive hearings in the Canadian parliament; much material about the uproar can be found online.

In 1995, retired RCAF Wing Commander Philip Markham, a noted aviation historian, published his article 'The Early Morning Hours of 2 June 1917' in the American journal *Over the Front*. That text was followed by articles and comments about Bishop's World War I career in the *Cross & Cockade International* journal in Britain (included in this book's Bibliography). Then, in 2002, Canadian history writer Brereton Greenhous published *The Making of Billy Bishop – The First World War Exploits of Billy Bishop, VC*. He used some

– but not all – of the Bishop letters that appear in this volume, noting that he had 'mixed feelings about using them to question and partially destroy the reputation of their originator'. [15]

This book considers dispassionately Billy Bishop's life and military aviation achievements. It seeks to understand the Canadian flying ace, who some people are so quick to criticise and denigrate. Conjecture is inevitable, but this author has tried to use it minimally and let the facts speak for themselves. This author's views on Billy Bishop reflect a principle of the 20th Century American journalist and historian William L. Shirer, who wrote: 'History must speak for itself. A historian is content if he has been able to shed more light.'[16]

While researching and writing this book, this author received help from many friends and colleagues and notes with gratitude the kind efforts, encouragement and information provided by the following people and their institutions: Lt.-Col. David Bashow, OMM, CD, RCAF (Ret.) and Editor-in-Chief of *Canadian Military Journal*; Carl J. Bobrow, Museum Specialist, Collections Processing Unit, National Air and Space Museum/Smithsonian Institution; the late Dr. Gustav Bock for sharing his monumental German aviation historical research; Valerie Casbourn, Assistant Archivist, Canadian Directorate of History and Heritage; Director and Chief Curator Virginia Eichhorn and Museums Curator Mindy Gill at the Billy Bishop Home and Museum; Ann Y. Evans, Springs Close Family Archives; Kate Jackson, Assistant Archivist, Grey Roots Museum & Archives; Major Mathias Joost, RCAF, Operational Records Team, Directorate of History and Heritage; Stephanie Jozwiak, Referat, Bundesarchiv Militärarchiv Freiburg; Dr. Kristine Larsen, Professor of Physics and Astronomy, Central Connecticut State University; Dr. Wolfgang Mährle, Oberarchivrat, Hauptstaatsarchiv Stuttgart; author Dan McCaffery; Johannes Moosdiele, M.A., Archivrat, Bayerisches Hauptstaatsarchiv Militärarchiv München; Murdo Morrison, Editor of *Flight International* magazine; Public Editor Sylvia Stead and Stephanie Chambers at the *Toronto Globe and Mail*; Pat Watson, New Britain Public Library; and Kimberly Farrington and Ewa Wolynska of the Elihu Burritt Library of Central Connecticut State University exemplify the valued help I have received from my alma mater.

Photographs have been important to this research and the author is grateful to friends and colleagues who have generously shared images for this book: Colin Huston, Trevor Henshaw, Dr. Volker Koos, Dan McCaffery, Colin A. Owers, Alex Revell, and Greg VanWyngarden, who has also been helpful in other aspects of the research project that led to this book.

Other friends and colleagues who have helped in many ways include: Rainer Absmeier, Trudy Baumann, Dr. Lance J. Bronnenkant, Trevor Henshaw, Paul S. Leaman, Oberleutnant Sebastian Rosenboom, Gunnar Söderbaum, Dr. James Streckfuss and Lothair Vanoverbeke.

Sincere thanks also go to this cadre of friends: Ronny Bar for his excellent colour artwork portraying aircraft flown by Billy Bishop, Judy and Karl Kilduff and my long-time friend and mentor David E. Smith for their helpful review of and comments on the manuscript, my cultural mentor Klaus Littwin for helping locate important research sources, my commercial pilot friend James F. Miller for helping me understand various aspects of powered flight, and Stewart K. Taylor for sharing his encyclopaedic knowledge of Canadian personnel and flight operations in World War I.

Finally, a review of this book's bibliography will show that a number of seminal World War I aviation history research books have been published by Grub Street, a fact that makes this author pleased to be affiliated with this publisher.

Peter Kilduff
New Britain, Connecticut
August 2014

CHAPTER ONE

The Lone Wolf Strikes

'Ambition was born in my breast, and … along with this new ambition there was born in me as well a distinct dislike for all two-seated German flying machines… Many people think of the two-seater as a superior fighting machine because of its greater gun-power. But to me [it] always seemed [to be] fair prey and an easy target …'
– William A. Bishop[1]

Tuesday, 28 May 1918 was a mostly sunny day[2], heralding the arrival of summer. In the sky over Ypres, Belgium, a dark mottled German two-seat biplane circled the war-ravaged old city, occasionally swooping low over buildings and roads pummelled into the Flemish soil during nearly four years of artillery and troop assaults. With fierce Allied resistance to another German assault now underway, it was too dangerous for the aeroplane continually to orbit overhead, where it could be seen against the sky.

Every time the two-seater rose up, it headed north west, so the aerial observer could view

The Rumpler C.VII was Germany's premier high-altitude reconnaissance aeroplane. Powered by a 240-hp super-compressed Maybach engine, the two-seater could reach altitudes approaching 24,000 feet. (Greg VanWyngarden)

Line-up of Royal Aircraft Factory S.E.5a fighters assigned to 85 Squadron, RAF. Billy Bishop flew the aeroplane in the foreground – C.1904 – in the last thirteen aerial combats in which he was credited with aerial victories. (Greg VanWyngarden)

British artillery units firing at German positions. Through high-powered binoculars, he looked for big red muzzle flashes. Like a high-altitude sniper armed with a wireless telegraph, once he spotted his quarry, he tapped out its location to a ground station, which directed artillery units against the British gun emplacement. The observer sent messages confirming target hits or to adjust their fire.

Eyes in the Sky

The experienced observer, twenty-three-year-old Leutnant der Reserve [Second-Lieutenant, Reserves] Hanns-Gerd Rabe, knew that Allied single-seat fighters would be looking for his aeroplane. He and his pilot, Unteroffizier [Corporal] Peter Johannes, scanned the skies for tell-tale distant specks – Allied aircraft bent on shooting them down in order to save lives among their own ground forces.

Johannes drew Rabe's attention to a small, growing spot in the distance. It turned out to be a lone British single-seat aeroplane. Rabe later recalled:

'It was quite far off, so I was not worried about one Tommy fighterplane. Then he seemed to have disappeared, perhaps to find a more opportune target.

'I returned to looking at the target area with my binoculars, watching for the next shell to hit. Suddenly an S.E.5a fighter aeroplane came between me and the target and filled my view. It was gaining fast and through the binoculars I could see the aeroplane as if I were next to it. The first thing I noticed was the white octagon insignia on the fuselage side and a big white letter next to it. I recognised the symbols from a report I had read recently. *Mein Gott!* It was Bishop, the British Richthofen!

'We had to make a fast dive for our lines. The engine was not yet at full power, so I leaned over to my pilot and yelled: "Dive for home! Right now or we are done for!"

'He gave full power and pushed the machine over into a streaking dive eastwards. I looked through the binoculars at Mr. Bishop, who became smaller and

Fl.-Abt (A) 253 observer Ltn.d.Res Hanns-Gerd Rabe (left) and his pilot, Uffz Peter Johannes (middle), also flew low-level reconnaissance missions in Hannover Cl.IIIa 2714/18. The 'bird' insignia on the fuselage alludes to the name Rabe [Raven]. Aircraft mechanic Noll is at right. (Author's Collection)

smaller, and I was overjoyed that we had managed to elude this master fighter pilot. If given a choice, I would always avoid combat and the possible loss of the exposed photographic plates and notes I had made earlier in the flight.'[3]

Wary of tricks, Rabe tightly gripped the stock of his machine gun. He was ready to fend off any aeroplane that attacked from behind or – even worse – from above, with the sun at its back, making it difficult to see. Likewise, Johannes readied his forward-firing machine gun in case any adversary impeded their retreat.

Rabe's decision was vindicated that evening, when he and Johannes were back at Flieger-Abteilung (A) 253's airfield at Pont à Marcq, France, some seventeen miles south east of Ypres. Their comrades agreed that the lone British attacker must have been the (then) forty-eight-victory fighter ace Major William A. Bishop, VC, DSO and Bar, MC, and that there was no shame in declining to fight such a formidable opponent.[4]

Major William A. Bishop, VC, DSO and Bar, MC, was a forty-eight-victory ace when he pursued Ltn.d.Res Rabe and Uffz Johannes on 28 May 1918. (Directorate of History and Heritage, Department of National Defence photo RE-16579-1)

The Albatros D.III enjoyed a long service life. Seen here is an aeroplane built by the company's subsidiary OAW (East German Albatros Works) in Schneidemühl and decorated in summer 1918 national insignia. (Dr. Volker Koos)

At age twenty-four, Billy Bishop enjoyed a formidable reputation among German airmen, who whispered his name with fear.[5] But later that morning, Billy – as he was called by most people – was still angry with himself for failing to shoot down the two-seater.

After lunch Bishop flew another solo hunting mission, heading eastward toward Courtemarck, where he attacked two Albatros biplane fighters. At day's end, his usual high spirits were restored by his latest successes and he easily dismissed the opponent that got away. He wrote about it to his wife:

'I went up to the lines this morning and only succeeded in frightening a fat two-seater to death. He ran for all he was worth, so I didn't follow. This afternoon, however, was my lucky moment. I spied nine Albatros [fighters] under me … The two back ones were higher than the rest, so I went after them. They saw me when I was 150 yards away. I opened fire on one, twenty rounds, and passed on to the second one, who was doing a climbing turn. I [put] thirty rounds into him and then zoomed and saw the second one burst into flames. Then looking over, the first one, 600 feet lower, [was] also in flames. I then left well enough alone and cleared off, easily getting away from the remainder.'[6]

Conflicting Reports
That letter is the most detailed surviving account of Billy's combat activities on 28 May 1918. Copies of combat reports about his morning and afternoon patrols have not been found in the UK National Archives or in any other such known resource in Britain or Canada. He was credited with scoring his forty-ninth and fiftieth aerial victories[7] in that day's entry in the Royal Air Force War Diary. They were among twenty-eight EA [enemy

aeroplanes] credited as having been shot down by RAF airmen that day.[8] Yet, the German weekly *Nachrichtenblatt* [air intelligence summary] for the period listed only eight losses – three aircraft reported missing and five shot down across the entire Western Front.[9] A post-war German aviation necrology,[10] however, lists twenty-three air-related deaths on 28 May 1918; of that number nineteen occurred over the Western Front.[11]

Determining which of those casualties Billy Bishop caused is complicated by reports from the German 4th Army air staff, over whose sector the Canadian pilot's combats occurred. Hauptmann [Captain] Helmuth Wilberg, who was the 4th Army's officer in charge of aviation, reported five casualties within his area that day. His listing included Gefreiter [Lance-Corporal] Peisker, a pilot with the Pfalz D.IIIa-equipped fighter unit Jagdstaffel 7, who was reported as being 'lightly injured while making an emergency landing'.[12] But Jasta 7's commanding officer, Ltn.d.Res Josef Jacobs, had not mentioned Gefr Peisker's incident in his war diary; rather, he recorded that another pilot, Uffz Sicho, 'had been shot up by an S.E.5a and was wounded in the arm and upper leg'.[13] Jacobs stated that Sicho's wounds resulted from an early morning encounter with 'five S.E.5s who were [fighting] with a formation of Albatros D.V' aircraft.[14]

The preceding assemblage of casualty information does not help identify which German aircraft or unit Billy encountered, but it demonstrates the confusing array of facts to be considered in arriving at a hypothesis. Further, in his letter that evening, Billy Bishop said he saw both Albatros fighters on fire. Possibly, one or both German pilots managed to extinguish the flames or make a 'controlled crash' that wrecked the aircraft but did not kill the pilots.

One remarkable aspect about aerial combat during World War I is that, often, opponents were able to recognise each other. Easily the best-known example is the series of red (or mostly red) fighter aircraft flown by Germany's top-scoring fighter ace, Rittmeister [Cavalry Captain] Manfred Freiherr von Richthofen, the pilot to whom Ltn.d.Res Rabe alluded when he recognised Bishop pursuing him on 28 May. In addition to being easily identified in the air, Richthofen's distinctive aircraft helped create a bogey-man image, which at least put his opponents on edge. Similarly, Billy's rapid rise to high-scoring ace status made him of high interest to his German counterparts. Shared word-of-mouth descriptions of Allied squadron markings (often revealed in prisoner of war interrogations) and the sight of a fighter aircraft, whose pilot was so bold as to operate like a lone wolf, convinced Rabe that a single S.E.5a bearing a white octagon and large white number on the fuselage must have been Billy Bishop's. Rabe's letter home, describing the date, time of day and location of his encounter matched the incident that Bishop described to his wife. That historical evidence led this author to conclude that Rabe and Bishop most likely had an aerial encounter over Ypres.

There are many facets to Billy Bishop's story. Before delving into the air combat role for which he is best known, the man and events that shaped him should be considered.

Family History

Billy Bishop was descended from people with strong convictions and the courage to act on them. An example of those qualities is his Puritan ancestor John Seaman, who left England in 1630, during the tumultuous reign of King Charles I, for a more stable life in North

Billy Bishop's parents, Will and Margaret, at home in Owen Sound, Ontario. The elder Bishop was clerk of the High Court and registrar of the Surrogate Court for Grey County and always dressed accordingly. (Billy Bishop Home and Museum)

America. Seaman sailed aboard one of eleven ships led by John Winthrop to the Massachusetts Bay Colony. From there, Seaman set out for neighbouring Connecticut and then to Long Island, where he found success.[15]

Well over a century later, when increasing numbers of American colonists sought independence from England, Bishop's maternal great-great-grandfather, Caleb Seaman II, remained loyal to the British crown. Following the American Revolution and the subsequent British troop withdrawal in 1783, Seaman was continually harassed about his sentiments. Consequently, six years later, he and his wife and their two children moved to Canada, where Caleb became a blacksmith near the village of Rockville.[16]

Caleb's son Nehemiah married the daughter of another loyalist-émigré family, Margaret McCready. Their daughter, Eliza Ann Seaman, married Hiram Kilbourn in 1838 and, as a result of that union, the Bishop name entered the family history. After the Kilbourns moved[17] to 'the boom town of Owen Sound … [a] port on Georgian Bay, the world's largest fresh-water bay',[18] they established a tannery. As the business grew, in 1853 they hired nineteen-year-old leatherworker Eleazar Wilson Bishop. He fell in love with the Kilbourns' sixteen-year-old daughter and only child, Sarah Sophia; the following year the couple ran away to be married.

Eleazar Bishop tried several business ventures and went broke. Then, his wife took charge of supporting the family, eventually six children. Sarah worked all day long at cooking, cleaning, sewing and other domestic work. Eleazar and Sarah's oldest son, William Avery Bishop, showed such promise that his mother saved money to send him to Osgoode Hall (now part of York University), one of Canada's leading law schools. But before Will Bishop, as he was known, left to pursue his studies he became engaged to Margaret Louise Greene.[19]

The red brick house at 948 Third Avenue West in Owen Sound, where Billy Bishop lived until he entered the Royal Military College. The house is now the Billy Bishop Home and Museum, which kindly provided this pre-World War I photograph.

The couple set out on a much more successful life path than Will's parents had. Arthur Bishop noted:

'Margaret Louise ... and Will Bishop ... grew up together. They were married soon after Will returned to practice [law] in Owen Sound and Will staked his future by building an elegant Victorian home for his bride. They moved into it just before their first son ... was born in 1884.' [20]

Thursday's Child

That child was named Reginald Worth Bishop, and went by Worth; a good student who set a good example for other siblings to come. A 1903 graduate of Canada's Royal Military College, Worth was successful in his military and civilian endeavours.[21] A second son, Kilbourne, was born in 1886, but died at age seven. On Thursday, 8 February 1894, 'their third son was born, an eleven-pound baby with a full head of blond hair and bright blue eyes. True to the line in an old fortune telling children's rhyme – 'Thursday's child has far to go' [22]– the younger Bishop boy had quite a future ahead of him. He was named after his father, William Avery[23], but he was not listed as 'Junior'; rather, he was called Billy. The following year, the Bishops' last child was born; baptised as Mary Louise, she became known as Louie.[24]

Will Bishop became involved in Liberal Party politics in the 1896 national election and, two years later, he was appointed as clerk of the High Court and registrar of the Surrogate Court for Grey County.[25] Will Bishop had an office in the local court house and, following the custom of the time, he wore formal attire. His younger son looked and acted very much like Will and so Margaret Louise dressed Billy in similar finery.

The youngster's well-dressed look was noticed by male schoolmates who singled out boys who were 'different' from them. The more aggressive lads criticised Billy's fine clothes and his disdain for competitive team sports; rather, he enjoyed 'shooting, riding and swimming'.[26] He 'was undoubtedly the only pre-teenaged boy in Owen Sound who enjoyed attending [dancing] classes ...'[27]

Consequently, Billy 'developed formidable fighting skills and won the respect of his peers with his fists in numerous schoolyard scraps'.[28] Indeed, he augmented his physical toughening with hand-eye coordination skills that would serve him well as a fighter pilot. His father bought Billy a membership in the local YMCA, where executing good shots in the billiard room challenged his manual dexterity.

Next, the teenager received a .22-calibre rifle and practiced marksmanship, a skill that would help him when he became an air fighter. Spurred by the incentive of twenty-five cents for every squirrel he shot, Billy learned the art of deflection shooting – aiming his gun beyond a moving target to anticipate its movement – and earned quite a few dollars for his talent.

Billy Bishop and his sister, Mary Louise, were very close, as this childhood view shows.
(Billy Bishop Home and Museum)

A Budding Aviator

In 1910, sixteen-year-old Billy Bishop built and tested his own 'flying machine', actually an unpowered glider. Based on newspaper photos of contemporary aircraft, he constructed a craft out of a crate and other wood, cardboard and bed sheets, all held together with heavy string. After his 'flight', the local newspaper charitably called Billy's craft 'a real credit to the inventive mind of this lad'. [29]

Arthur Bishop's book offered a more critical view:

'[Billy] hauled it off to the roof of the family home, took his place in the orange-crate cockpit, and skidded down the steep roof into space. His descent was more a nose-dive than a flight. The twenty-eight-foot fall demolished the machine, but Billy scrambled out of the wreckage with no more than a bruised knee and a scratched ear … [The] incident …[became] the first of many violent contacts between the earth's surface and aircraft piloted by William Avery Bishop, near disasters which became known simply as "Bishop landings". [30]

Immediately after the incident, his sister Louie helped clean him up and dispose of the wreckage. But she sought compensation. One of her friends was hosting a girl from To-ronto and asked whether Billy, who was popular with the local young ladies, would take the guest to a local dance. Billy agreed to consider the out-of-town girl. Louie invited her friend and the other girl, Margaret Burden, over for refreshments on the veranda, where Billy viewed the new girl from behind dining room curtains.

The Girl from Toronto

Billy liked what he saw and, as if struck by lightning, became totally smitten by Margaret. From that point forward, he spent all of his free time with her. Early Bishop biographer Alan Hynd described the quickly blossoming love between the young couple:

'Billy was an outdoor boy, and he used to point out to her [the] gaily coloured birds that a … girl never saw in the city. [Margaret] talked about him so much that the

Billy Bishop presenting a dapper look in his Royal Military College cadet uniform. (DHH/DND photo RE-21098)

two families eventually became acquainted. Fall came, and she went away. But she didn't forget, and neither did he.'[31]

In this case, however, the course of young love had to overcome a big obstacle. Margaret was born into one of country's wealthiest families. Her grandfather was Timothy Eaton, founder of the Canadian retail empire that bore his name. As Arthur Bishop described his parents' early situation:

'It was a strangely democratic confrontation of the grandson of the least successful merchant of Owen Sound and the granddaughter of the most successful merchant of all Canada … At the time that Eleazar's grandson took Timothy's granddaughter dancing, Eleazar had not earned a dollar for many a year – and Timothy had ceased counting his millions.'[32]

Margaret's parents, Charles and Margaret Burden, did not encourage a romantic attachment between their daughter and the unpromising lad from Owen Sound. Indeed, her father tried to break up the relationship several times. [33]

Billy Bishop had little to offer Margaret. He was an unenthusiastic student with no plans for the future. In a discussion with the boy's parents, the local high school principal once described Billy in an unwittingly prescient way: 'As far as I can see, the only thing your son is good at is fighting.'[34] But Billy was in love and made up his mind to win Margaret's heart – and allay her parents' fears that he would not amount to much.

The Royal Military College

Billy demonstrated his serious intent, on 8 February 1911 – his seventeenth birthday – when he applied for admission to the Royal Military College of Canada. The RMC trained future officers and conferred a degree that would benefit them when they left military service.

Billy Bishop's RMC tenure from August 1911 until September 1914 has been portrayed unfavourably in some published accounts. However, J. Ross McKenzie, curator of the RMC Museum, drew on existing college records to produce a 1990 essay[35] that offers more accurate views of Billy's cadet days, as follows.

Billy is said to have lived in the shadow of his older brother, Worth, who reportedly achieved 'the highest standing of any cadet in the history of [the] RMC' up to that time.[36] College records show that Worth Bishop 'did reasonably well' and placed 'ten out of twenty-six on graduation.'[37]

Billy was accepted as RMC Gentleman Cadet No. 943, 'having placed forty-second out of the forty-three men who passed the entrance exam.'[38] According to Arthur Bishop, on the evening of Monday, 28 August 1911,[39] 'Billy and forty [sic] other nervous recruits entered the ancient complex of stone buildings on the banks of the St. Lawrence [River] … across the harbour from the city of Kingston, Ontario'. [40]

At that time, the 'RMC had a three-year programme and … classes were known from junior to senior as the 3rd Class, 2nd Class and 1st Class.'[41] In addition to military drill exercises, the college provided classes in 'mathematics, physics, English, French, civil and military engineering, and military tactics', as well as such extracurricular activities as 'boxing, football, hockey, gymnastics, aquatics … cricket and horsemanship …'[42]

RMC offered the advantages of a civilian university, with the prospect of an interesting career. But the college's rigid discipline and stern life were as cold as the institution's century-old stone walls. An RMC history points out from Billy Bishop's experience that 'each first-year man was soundly trounced every Saturday night on the theory that seniors, however vigilant, must have overlooked some recruit crimes during the week. Bishop [said he] was "profoundly distressed by the indignities" of his first year at the college, which included being compelled to eat a live spider.' [43]

Billy dared not raise his very effective fists against his tormentors, a breach of conduct that would have resulted in his expulsion from the college. But he ended an altogether dreary first year by being 'suspended … a punishment short of expulsion, [which] was rarely used'. [44] McKenzie's examination of the records showed that during Billy's 1911-1912 academic year he was caught cheating on a year-end examination. It was a serious charge and 'college authorities would not hesitate to expel cadets [for it]', McKenzie noted. But, 'while [Bishop's] transgression was serious, [he] was obviously deemed worthy of a second chance'. [45]

Surely, Billy felt too ashamed to return home for a summer respite. Instead, he prevailed upon his brother to help find a temporary job. At the time Worth Bishop was a government engineer on a canal navigation system and secured a spot for Billy as a timekeeper. The work gave the younger man time to reflect on his first year away from home. It also provided Worth an opportunity to counsel Billy to improve his performance at the RMC.[46]

While he had been granted provisional second-year status, Billy had to spend another year at the college. If he failed the test again, his RMC days would be over. True to his word, Billy worked harder and bolstered his academic record. McKenzie notes: 'In his repeated 3rd Class year, the academic year 1912-1913, Bishop showed marked improvement, he placed twenty-third out of forty-two, a respectable showing'.[47]

Billy Bishop's third year at RMC has been characterised as 'an epic of rules broken and discipline scorned. His regular sorties – legal and illegal – into Kingston town to rendezvous with girls became the talk of the stone frigate.'[48] That account includes allegations of lying to a superior officer and using crib notes on a final examination, which, if true, could have resulted in Billy Bishop's expulsion. Yet, RMC Museum Curator McKenzie, who had unique access to various college administrative paperwork, pointed out: 'There is absolutely nothing to suggest that a "cheating" incident took place in [May] 1914. Bishop's marks did drop, however. He placed thirty-third out of thirty-four. Not quite the goat, but close …' [49]

McKenzie's research shows that at the end of the 1913-1914 academic year Billy Bishop was not eligible for graduation. Yet, as McKenzie noted: '… even though he was one year behind … his original classmates … Billy was still apparently one of the gang …' [50]

Further, addressing accounts that Billy Bishop did not return to RMC, McKenzie points to records that show that Billy reported back on '28 August 1914, as did all but one member of the new 1st Class'. Further, '[Billy] Bishop, now a senior, was appointed [by the college commandant] a lance-corporal; of his other classmates, three received no appointment at all. One week later … he was appointed to corporal … [Thus], despite his poor academic showing, Bishop was given some rank. He was deemed worthy of trust. Nothing here suggests he was under a cloud …' [51]

By that time, events in Europe since the assassination of Austro-Hungarian Archduke Franz Ferdinand and his wife Sophie in June 1914 had escalated to a state of war. The Triple Entente of Britain, France and Russia faced the Central Powers led by the German and Austro-Hungarian Empires.

As young men in all the belligerent nations flocked to recruiting stations, at the RMC fifteen of Billy's classmates left the college on Wednesday, 16 September to accept special commissions in the British Army. Twelve days later, the RMC commandant, Colonel (later Brigadier-General) Lancelot R. Carleton, DSO[52], forwarded Billy's application to join the war effort:

'I have the honour to request that Gentleman Cadet W.A. Bishop may have leave to withdraw from the college as he is applying for a commission in the 9th Mississauga Horse, at the request of the officer commanding that Corps, and has his father's consent.' [53]

On Wednesday, 30 September, Billy was recorded as being discharged from the RMC 'at parents' request',[54] a term that McKenzie explains 'seems to have been used in the [RMC] ledger for every departure from the college except for those resulting from graduation, academic failure, or expulsion … The timing of Bishop's departure from RMC is therefore not at all suspicious. His low academic standing no doubt ensured he wasn't [granted] one of the special commissions, but the departure of his friends may well have stirred him to act on his own.'[55]

At the beginning of World War I, 'Canada was woefully short of officers', Arthur Bishop wrote. He noted that his father's 'military training, albeit incomplete, and his ability to ride a horse, won him quick acceptance' into a local military unit. [56] The same day he was discharged from the RMC, former Cadet No. 943 William Avery Bishop was commissioned as a lieutenant in the Mississauga Horse[57], a Toronto-based cavalry detachment of the 2nd Canadian Division.

He could not have imagined that this action would propel him to the British Empire's highest honours and world fame.

CHAPTER TWO

Long Journey to the Front

'I suppose we'll get used to all manner of sordid things
in this horrible business.' – William A. Bishop[1]

Between the time Billy Bishop left the Royal Military College in Kingston, Ontario and joined the Mississauga Horse detachment, he visited Margaret Burden at her home in Toronto to explain why he needed to join the war effort. She understood that his military exercises were over and now he wanted to go overseas and – even though she could hardly imagine the horrible war that awaited him – she accepted the news bravely. 'Of course you're going to enlist, Billy,' she said. 'I would expect it of you – and I know it's what you want to do anyway. I just pray that the war will not last too long.' [2]

However, Billy (also called 'Bish') did not ship out with the Mississauga Horse.[3] Due to pneumonia and an allergy that defied identification, he ended up in a military hospital. After returning to duty, in January 1915, he was transferred to the 7th Canadian Mounted Rifles, commanded by Lieutenant-Colonel Elton Ibbotson Leonard, an RMC classmate of Worth Bishop's. Billy's shooting and weapons maintenance skills probably led him to be placed in charge of the unit's machine guns.[4]

In addition to his technical talents, Billy's genial nature made him popular with 7th CMR enlisted men. George Stirrett, then a corporal in the unit, later recalled:

'Bish was a nice fellow for an officer! He treated us more like buddies than subordinates ... We slept in a drafty barn and, one night, he reached into the straw and pulled out a bottle of brandy and shared it with us. He'd smuggled it out of [Col.] Leonard's headquarters! Maybe it was because he was the youngest officer in the camp, but he was well liked by the fellows who had to take orders from him.' [5]

Stirrett also recalled Billy's talent with a drum-fed Lewis machine gun:

'Bish would just riddle a target that the rest of us could barely see. The instructors would keep putting it further back, until it was just a tiny black dot, and he'd shoot it to ribbons ... he put every damn' bullet on target. He never missed. I ... recall the instructor shaking his head and saying, "If Bishop doesn't kill himself in training, he'll win the war by himself."' [6]

Later the regiment was moved to London, Ontario, where all of its horses were sent out to Canadian troops already in Europe. Billy was selecting a new horse for himself, on Tues-

Lieutenant W.A. Bishop, fourth from right, with other officers of the 7th Canadian Mounted Rifles in London, Ontario, prior to sailing for England.
(DHH/DND photo RE-22063)

day, 6 April 1915, when he had a bad accident. While recuperating in Victoria Hospital, he described it to Margaret:

'One of my new horses reared and fell back on me … it really is a wonder it didn't crush me to death. It made rather a mess of my head and face, as it shoved my head right into the ground. My nose is, of course, broken and quite swollen and I can't see out of one eye … [My] face is scraped a bit and my head [is] a series of bumps and bruises. My body is pretty well bruised, too, and I have two broken ribs. I'm all stuck up in plasters and bandages … so not very cheerful. Don't worry, dearest, the doctor says I shall probably be able to move around by Monday [8 April].' [7]

Much improved, the following week, Billy wrote:

'This morning I … had a glorious ride. I am in charge of the equitation class now and merely ride out and instruct [the men]. Any time I feel like it I take a good little canter off by myself, and my mare is feeling fine. I talked to her all morning about you and she sends her very best love to you.' [8]

Billy Bishop wrote to Margaret throughout his wartime service. His letters, typed copies of which are preserved in Canada's Directorate of History and Heritage, Department of National Defence, offer his thoughts and aspirations with a degree of candour not found in other sources. They also show the maturing effect that the course of the war had on him. He became impatient with and bored by the slow pace of events in April and May. But twenty-one-year-old Billy had little concept of the massive logistics involved as Great

Britain marshalled men and matériel from throughout her empire to fight in the first truly worldwide military conflict in history.

Billy and Margaret Engaged
Before he left Canada, Billy secured the hope of a future for him and Margaret by formally proposing to her. The event is not recorded among his letters, but their son Arthur recounted the moment as it was remembered within the family:

Billy Bishop and Margaret Burden in Toronto
at the time of their engagement.
(DHH/DND photo RE-22064)

> 'She accepted him, but at the romantic moment when he should have slipped the [engagement] ring on her finger he realised in panic he had forgotten to buy a ring. Margaret was gracious about the oversight. "Your RMC ring will do for now," she said.' [9]

Finally, on 8 June, the 7th Canadian Mounted Rifles were transported from London, Ontario to Montreal to board *SS Caledonia*, a 9,223-ton British passenger ship built in 1904 and, a decade later, converted into a troop ship to carry over 3,000 men and 200-plus horses.[10] Billy Bishop's impressions of his first sea voyage began with mixed feelings:

> 'As we pulled out of Montreal, crowds cheered and waved like mad. Every whistle within miles blew furiously and our men sang "God Save the King" and cheered back. It was very impressive ...' [11]

Just over a week later, Billy experienced a harsh reality of war. He wrote:

> 'Three horses died during the night, making a total of eight lost so far. And we will lose a lot more during the next couple of days, as there are a lot of the poor beasts sick. They stand as long as they can, then we move away the next horse and put straw in the double stall thus made, and the poor devil lies down and usually passes away. In about fifteen minutes, overboard he goes. The ship swings sharply to avoid the carcass touching the screw and then rights itself. It is horribly cold-blooded. I often wonder what the other horses think. However, I suppose we'll get used to all manner of sordid things in this horrible business.' [12]

In England at Last
The danger of German submarines increased as *SS Caledonia* drew closer to England. On

the final night of the ship's voyage, Tuesday, 22 June, heavy fog blanketed the sea lanes approaching south-west England. After near collisions among Canadian convoy ships preparing to dock, *Caledonia* took a position off shore at about 4:00 am on the 23rd. Twelve hours later the ship tied up at Plymouth. That evening Billy wrote:

> 'The people here certainly know how to welcome you. As the ship was towed into the harbour to the naval yards, crowds formed and cheered wildly. Then, after we got on the train [to Canterbury], all through England, every person who sighted us dropped whatever they were doing to wave and cheer. It was great …' [13]

Billy was young enough to enjoy the adulation of his early days in England, but the 7th CMR's brief stay in Canterbury also had a sobering effect. It also provided his first look at combat aeroplanes:

> 'Yesterday [13 July] we could hear firing all day from France and see clouds of smoke rising up. There was a big battle on and the sky was full of aeroplanes. The Channel was cleared of fishing boats … by a fleet of destroyers and last night everybody in the villages round about stayed in their houses as a Zeppelin [airship] raid was expected … I'd like to see one of the things.' [14]

That was as close as Billy Bishop got to combat action. After almost two months in England, he and his comrades grew impatient with routine patrol 'rides' in good weather and bad. And, towards the end of July, Billy found he was not as hearty as he thought himself to be, as described in a letter from Helena Hospital in London:

> 'Don't be worried when you see that I am in hospital, as I came here yesterday [Saturday, 24 July] and expect to leave tomorrow or perhaps Tuesday … The chill I got on our bivouac knocked me partially out of working order and, as a tent is a poor place to get over a chill, they sent me here for a few days … It is a very nice hospital and at the present full of wounded officers. Poor chaps, a lot are being sent home for good every day.' [15]

Drawn to the RFC

Some two years later, writing his first memoir, Billy recalled a defining moment in his life in the summer of 1915:

> 'It was the mud that made me take to flying. I had fully expected that going into battle would mean for me [to be in] the saddle of a galloping charger, instead of the snug little cock-pit of a modern aeroplane. The mud, on a certain day in … 1915, changed my whole career in the war …
>
> '[That day] I had succeeded in getting myself mired to the knees when suddenly, from somewhere out of the storm, appeared a trim little aeroplane. It landed hesitatingly in a nearby field as if scorning to brush its wings against so sordid a landscape; then [was] away again into the clean grey mists.

'How long I stood there, gazing into the distance, I do not know, but when I turned to slog my way back through the mud my mind was made up. I knew there was only one place to be on such a day – up above the clouds and in the summer sunshine. I was going into the battle that way. I was going to meet the enemy in the air.' [16]

Billy Bishop set out to achieve this goal by looking for Royal Flying Corps officers who could tell him 'how a man went about the business of getting away from horses, baled hay and mud – in short, how he acquired wings'. Billy's resolve soon paid off. He wrote to Margaret during a trip to London:

'Back in town again and for a reason which will surprise you very much. I got a note from an officer … on the staff of the Royal Flying Corps whom I had met [at the Grand Hotel] in Folkestone, asking me to call him at the War Office today. I had no idea what it was about, but I came hot foot, as a summons to the WO is something to make a poor subaltern tremble. Anyway … he enlightened me … [about] a vacancy in the RFC for an observing officer. (There are two kinds, pilots and observing officers.) And he offered it to me IF I can get transferred from the Canadians. I am to call him again at 12:45 and see Lord Cecil, whoever he is … and will know more then.' [17]

Billy's appointment was with Lord Hugh Cecil, youngest son of three-term British Prime Minister Lord Robert Cecil and a well-connected Member of Parliament. The forty-six-year-old politician held a deceptive-sounding lieutenant's commission in the RFC, but it was more like a lord lieutenant's position. As Billy learned, one of Lord Cecil's government duties was to be in charge of RFC aircrew recruitment. [18]

That night, Billy wrote to Margaret:

'[Lord] Cecil and he offered me a commission in the Royal Flying Corps just as soon as I can get my application through Canadian Divisional HQ. I go back to camp on Monday [9 August] and will see the colonel at once about getting my application signed … Oh, it is great luck, and to think a chance acquaintance should be of such importance to me. Incidentally, the pay in the RFC is much higher than any other branch of the service, extra pay being given for every flight you make.' [19]

Billy did not tell Margaret that he wanted to become a pilot and was told that it could take as long as a year to qualify. While that was too long for the man of action Billy felt himself to be, there was 'a great need for observers'.[20] That would be a good place to start.

Billy was overjoyed when Colonel Leonard readily agreed to approve his transfer to the RFC. The future aviator dashed off a note to Margaret, seeking her moral support and endorsement for what he thought was a 'really wonderful [opportunity] and don't worry your pretty head, not a risky one at all. One is so seldom really up in the air and truly the casualties are very small. Oh, Darling, say you are glad that I'm doing it.'[21]

Zeppelins Overhead

On the night of 12-13 August 1915 the air war came close to Billy Bishop and the 7th Canadian Mounted Rifles when two German dirigibles – the Zeppelin-built craft L.10 and L.11 – carried out a raid along the Suffolk and Kent coastline.[22] Billy heard airship engines and anti-aircraft fire directed at the marauders. He wrote to Margaret:

'I was just sitting down to write to you last night when we got a note from dispatch riders that the Zeppelins were coming. Every light was put out and we crawled into bed in the dark. We heard the Zeppelins buzzing up in the air and a lot of explosions caused by shells fired at them, and by a few bombs they dropped, but none came within a couple of miles of us, so after a bit, off to sleep I went. This morning we [will] go out and won't come back until tomorrow night. I hate these night manoeuvres.' [23]

Four nights later, the Zeppelins L.10, L.11 and L.14 carried out raids over England, with L.11 paying particular attention to Canterbury and surrounding areas.[24] Billy related the effects on the ground:

'About midnight there was another Zepp raid and all kinds of excitement. They bombed the ordnance stores near us and of all the unearthly rows I have ever heard, that was the worst. [We] must have had twenty guns firing at four [sic] Zepps and I don't think they hit one, for as far as we know they got back safely to Germany. The natives around here are scared stiff … but chances of being hit by Zepps are practically nil.'[25]

Billy was soon distracted from the Zeppelin menace by a War Office letter requiring another RFC physical examination. The letter also indicated he would begin observer's training soon, and possibly be posted overseas within a short time. Thinking mainly of his own route to success, Billy was overly candid when he wrote to Margaret that 'everybody who has been to the Front says we are fools to wish we were over there. But it is our goal and we are anxious to get there.' [26]

Observer Training

Ten days later, on 1 September, Billy left his regiment in Kent and reported for observer training at the Netheravon flying school on Salisbury Plain. The first course was in Morse code, which neophyte observers needed to know in order to transmit messages to the ground using wireless telegraphy devices in their aeroplanes. Billy noted that the primary mission was to carry out 'artillery observation and direct … the guns on their targets. The only answer we could receive … from the gunners was given by means of strips of cotton laid on the ground, each of which had a cryptic meaning of its own.' [27]

Netheravon was equipped with Avro 504 two-seat biplanes, which were 'remembered as a delightful trainer of the war period or as a friendly aeroplane popping into and out of improbable fields'[28] later on. Used during early wartime raids over German territory, Avro 504 aircraft were fairly rugged, as Billy noted:

'This morning we had [an Avro] machine smashed but, fortunately, no one was hurt. All morning we fooled around [at] the aerodrome but, as the weather was uncertain, only a few [students] went up. Then we all got into cars and went over to Upavon, about eight miles from here, to see a German aeroplane which had been captured. They are not as reliable machines as ours, but they are beautifully built.

'This morning a squadron also left for France. I wish I were with them. But my turn won't take long, they tell me. I am in 21 Squadron,[29] A Flight, 4 Wing.'[30]

Avro 504 (serial number 789) was fitted with an 80-hp Gnôme rotary engine.
Billy Bishop made his first flight with 21 Squadron, RFC, in an aeroplane of this type.
(*Cross & Cockade International*)

First Time in the Air
Billy wrote to Margaret about his first aviation training 'ride':

'Last night I had a flight in an Avro, around Salisbury, Amesbury and Salisbury Plain at a height of 3,000 feet. It was glorious and I loved every minute of it. There is certainly no sport like it in the world. Rushing along [at] about eighty miles an hour, a way up so that people look like mere specks, and the only way one can detect them is by seeing a movement. It must be wonderful up about 12,000 feet.' [31]

Billy became so enthusiastic about the Avro 504 and was so thoroughly committed to flying that he even tempted Margaret to go up:

'This morning I was up for a long flight with a chap named Robinson … from Toronto, and this afternoon I was up again, but we ran out of petrol and had a forced landing in a grain field, and rather smashed the grain up a bit, because [it] was all stacked. Another machine flew out and brought some mechanics. We then took their machine and flew home. Honestly, Darling, it is the most wonderful invention, this flying. Someday, I shall take you up and you will love it, too.'[32]

Anything to do with flying commanded Billy's rapt attention. Especially when it concerned preparations for war:

'Today, fourteen more machines left for the Front. It was a wonderful sight ... to see them one after another [join] up after rushing off the ground ... Then, when they had attained their [altitude], off they all flew in a long line for France, which they will reach about 4:00 this afternoon ...' [33]

Other times, Billy was simply overjoyed to be flying:

'[Today, 6 September] I had two glorious flights ... with my flight-commander, an Australian named Rutledge. This is the greatest game in the world, every moment full of intense excitement. A man ceases to be human when he is way up. The earth is merely a map and you feel that to you nothing is impossible.' [34]

And he was always concerned about Margaret. After several days of writing exuberantly, he became more serious and expressed his feelings for her:

'In one of your letters you said you were afraid of the RFC. Darling Margaret, it is really no more dangerous than any other branch; for, although it may be more dangerous before we get to the Front, it is not so dangerous after we get there ... [The] danger of being hit by a shell is very slight, [as] it is so hard to judge an aeroplane's height ... [35]
    'I am working very hard ... [as an observer]. I have to be everything from a detective to a wireless operator. I loathe the latter and, funny to say, I seem to have a talent in that line ... Don't be nervous about my flying. It is not half as dangerous as it would seem. In fact, one type of machine called the B.E.2c glides to earth automatically if anything goes wrong and [it] is as safe as a church.' [36]

The Royal Aircraft Factory B.E.2c two-seat biplane became well known as a very stable aircraft. But, even though he had not yet flown in one, Billy was expansive in his praise of it. Perhaps he was influenced by an oft-told – and true – account that circulated at his airfield about Major (later Air Vice-Marshal Sir) Sefton Brancker, who, the previous June, flew the first B.E.2c from the factory at Farnborough to Netheravon. Brancker reported that, after climbing to 2,000 feet altitude, he 'did not touch the controls again until he was at twenty feet on the approach to Netheravon ... [and] during his flight he wrote a reconnaissance report of the country over which he flew.' [37]

Aerial Gunnery Training

On Saturday, 2 October 1915, Billy moved a step closer to realising his air combat ambitions when he reported to the Duke of York School outside of Dover. With Margaret ever in his thoughts, he wrote:

'We are being trained especially for air duels, which I hear is a great honour … I hope luck is with me, for that game is all pure luck.

'Life without you is strangely like flying between two clouds, with a burst of sunshine coming through in front, just bright enough to lead one out. You are like that to me, Darling, a light that I am making for.' [38]

At Dover, Billy flew almost daily when the weather was 'at all decent'. He went out over the Channel and along the coast to Folkestone, firing a machine gun from the back seat of a training aeroplane, over the water. As he wrote to Margaret: 'I am getting quite expert at it. I am looking forward to the first time I shall have a chance to try it with a German aeroplane for a target.' [39]

By the end of October, Billy completed machine-gun and artillery-ranging practice and began flying over the frontlines in France. He wrote to Margaret about a flight from Dover across the Channel to St. Omer, where he and his pilot were directed to a battle zone:

'We had a two-hour reconnaissance over the lines and, believe me … I am not ashamed to say it, I was glad when it was over. Then we came back here [Netheravon], landing first at Dover [to refuel]. The whole trip … took about four hours. The RFC [personnel] who are stationed in France seemed to like it there, but they dread the bad weather coming. During the winter … [there] will be a continual series of machines … going over for the day, as that way has proved [to be] so successful. [It is] so crowded in France that it is hard to find suitable places for a large number of machines.' [40]

After his first combat mission Billy seems to have matured quickly. He proudly told Margaret: 'Today I was put in charge of all the observers for the 4th Wing. It is a promotion, but a rotten job, as I have to train all the new observers coming in and lecture, etc.' [41] Following this initial complaint, however, he wrote: 'I like my new work immensely and it makes a lot of time on the ground interesting, whereas it was dull before, when I wasn't flying.' [42]

As he noted after one particularly successful day:

'It was beautiful weather and we flew over to Lark Hill [north of Amesbury] to work with some artillery there. It is always a gamble, working with artillery … as the wireless so often doesn't work, and there is no way of knowing it in the air. Consequently, one might send down dozens of messages and then after flying for hours, land to find that [none] … were received … Tonight the colonel[43] told me a favourable report on my work had come from Lark Hill, so I'm quite happy.' [44]

Bishop's First Crash

On Wednesday, 24 November, Billy and his new pilot, a Captain Wadham, had another successful artillery-ranging exercise over Lark Hill, but experienced a mishap upon returning to Netheravon. Billy wrote:

> '[While] landing we had a real live crash and "did in" the machine. Both of us got off very lightly. I got my foot bruised a bit and now have a very artistic limp, of which I am very proud. The pilot was also very lucky and got a few little bruises.'[45]

Billy seems to have been none the worse for wear. Three days later he gladly accepted a ride in a new aircraft and described it to Margaret:

> 'This morning [27 November] I had what was probably the most thrilling time of my life. I flew over to the Central Flying School [at Upavon] with one of the instructors … A new machine had just come in and had to be tested, so up we went in it. To test a machine means, of course, to put it into the hardest tests possible. We went up to 13,000 feet and dove straight down [to] 11,000 feet. When we flattened out we were going about 300 miles an hour, so you may imagine the sensation to see the earth approaching you at that rate. Then we flew up again and got the machine facing vertically upward and shut off the engine [to induce a tail-slide[46]]. She came down backwards about 800 feet and then he righted her again. Then he looped the loop, [and] after that he banked her up vertical and we side-slipped about 1,000 feet.[47] Then we came down [and landed]. He certainly is a wonderful pilot and the whole show created quite a sensation.'[48]

Unfortunately, Billy Bishop did not identify the pilot or type of aircraft that combined to provide him such an experience. Many new aircraft types passed through the Central Flying School during the war, and an educated guess as to which one arrived at Upavon on 27 November 1915 would be the Armstrong Whitworth F.K.3. Neither designer Frederick Koolhoven's proposed improvement of the well-regarded B.E.2c nor any other World War I aircraft attained a speed of 300 mph, although 'the F.K.3 was … faster and had a higher ceiling'[49] than the B.E.2c. Billy had no way of knowing how high or fast the test aircraft went, but that did not prevent him from wanting to impress Margaret with his latest wartime experience.

Some things never change and, for the rest of the war, Billy Bishop would seek to 'prove' – if only to himself – that he would be the bravest and best combatant and the worthiest man in Margaret Burden's life.

CHAPTER THREE

Bad Aircraft and Bad Luck

'I'm very keen for a scrap in the air, for I feel quite confident that I shall
be able to take care of myself alright with a machine gun.'
– William A. Bishop[1]

As early winter dragged on, Billy Bishop had sky-high hopes that 21 Squadron would soon
be assigned to a frontline aerodrome in France. And it was wonderful news to him – a first
step in that direction – when the squadron was equipped with the latest two-seat reconnaissance, bombing and escort aircraft: the Royal Aircraft Factory R.E.7.[2] After Billy saw
the first new aeroplanes at Netheravon, he wrote to Margaret Burden:

'We are to be ready to fly over [to France] by December 24th [1915]. But the way
things happen in the Flying Corps, it will probably be a fortnight after that before we

Royal Aircraft Factory R.E.7 (serial number 2353), one of 100 of the type
produced by the Siddeley-Deasy Motor Co. Ltd. Billy Bishop flew to France in
this type aircraft and then flew in it as an observer with 21 Squadron.
(*Cross & Cockade International*)

go … Our new service machines, R.E.7s, are arriving now every day. They are lovely things, the biggest machines made, [and] awfully powerful and comparatively safe. They will carry a 600-lb bomb.'[3]

But squadron aircrews soon became apprehensive about the R.E.7's air defensive capability. At the time, Germany's Fokker E.I monoplane was the only front-engine 'single-seat … fighter fitted with a mechanism to allow machine-gun fire through the propeller'[4] arc without damaging the blades. In response to this threat, the R.E.7 observer was placed in the front seat with a side-mounted flexible .303-calibre Lewis machine gun. But his field of fire was limited by bracing wires between the wings, as well as by struts supporting the upper wing over the fuselage. In short, the observer was unable to use the Lewis gun effectively.[5] The pilot, placed in the more spacious rear seat, was armed with a rifle or pistol.[6] In the R.E.8 and other later British aircraft, pilots sat in front and observers occupied rear cockpits.

Preparing for Battle

For the moment, however, all squadron members were focused on the much-awaited deployment to the Western Front. Once the new aeroplanes were gathered at Netheravon, aircrews made training flights on every good day in a season better known for poor flying weather. Despite the R.E.7's limitations, Billy remained optimistic:

'Yesterday was glorious and at noon Johnson [a pilot] and I set out in [a] new machine for a long cross-country [flight]. We went half-way [to] the other side of London … and then on account of dense fog we turned back … [It was] quite a long flight and after attaining a height of 10,000 feet … it took twenty minutes to come down in a steep spiral.

'The Major [Frederick W. Richey[7]] is in France, making final arrangements … Lord, I'll be glad to get over [there], I'm very keen for a scrap in the air, for I feel quite confident that I shall be able to take care of myself all right with a machine gun …'[8]

A year earlier the popular feeling was that the war would be over by Christmas 1914. But the vast battleground that Billy saw on his first flight to St. Omer in late-October 1915 convinced him that the conflict would last for a long time. At the moment he sought a lively holiday party as a proper send off. His thoughts conveyed to Margaret on Christmas Day 1915 may have been overly candid, but he surely felt he could give her a realistic picture of life in London without inferring he participated in it:

'Merry Xmas, much merrier [where you are] than it is here. I came up [to London] last night and went to the Carlton for supper … [Another officer and I] are going to the Regent Palace Hotel and watch the [carefree] life there. I might say it is about the most cosmopolitan spot in England. It is full of people on what are called here "weekend honeymoons" and the grill and restaurant are full of love girls and men who are picking them up. It is one of the most amusing spots in town and the only place that doesn't look like a cemetery …'[9]

When 21 Squadron did not embark for France at Christmastime, New Year's Day became the next speculation point. Billy stopped worrying about it. He had already been awarded his observer's insignia, which conveyed a certain air of authority among the student observers. But, military bureaucracy being somewhat slow, the well-earned honour was not officially recognised until 15 November 1916, but 'with seniority from 18 January 1916'.[10]

To begin the new year. Major Richey ordered all squadron members to remain at Netheravon while preparing for their departure to France; each R.E.7 had to be flown for six-hours' duration. On Sunday, 9 January 1916, Billy was up in an aeroplane for only an hour when:

> '[A] dense mist closed in and we ran for home, only being able to see about 200 yards in front of us. Suddenly another machine appeared, heading straight for us. Oh Lord, I was scared; I thought we were gone. But he dived and we zoomed, and we missed [each other] by a few feet. I'm shaking yet ...'[11]

Off to France

At long last, at 7:00 am on Saturday, 15 January, all of 21 Squadron's equipment was packed into what Billy described as 'about sixty lorries, tenders and touring cars, and a flock of motorcycles'. They all headed toward Avonmouth, on the Severn estuary, at the mouth of the River Avon. The following day a transport ship loaded with the unit's equipment sailed

Billy Bishop wearing his RFC tunic and winged-O observer's insignia. (War Amputations of Canada)

out into the ocean and then swung eastward for France. Meanwhile, Billy led a contingent of men to Southampton to join up with other squadron members for the same journey in another ship. [12]

By Tuesday, the 18th, Billy had endured a rough sea voyage and was billeted at 'a nice little hotel [in Rouen], quite Bohemian sort of place, but very nice and clean'. In his first letter from France he wrote: 'Talk about mud! Salisbury is like a dried up desert compared to this [region]. But nobody cares as long as we are here. It is too funny for words, talking pigeon French and trying to be understood.'[13]

The following day, 21 Squadron had the distinction of being the 'only unit to go to France equipped [entirely] with R.E.7s'.[14] The unit arrived at Boisdinghem[15] in northern France, west of St. Omer on Sunday, 23 January 1916. Later that day, Billy wrote to Margaret from a hospital near the aerodrome, where he had been admitted after becoming very sick while accompanying squadron equipment to the new location:

'The doctor refused to let me go on by road, so I came here yesterday by train and, after seeing … Major [Richey], I came to this hospital. Continual wet feet, I suppose, knocked me out, so here I am for today and tomorrow … From my window I can see aeroplanes circling around, very high up. They are patrol machines … waiting in case a German crosses the lines, to attack him. It is absolutely a perfect day, not a cloud in the sky. I wish I were outside, [and in] another day or so I shall be. It is such a wonderful chance, flying over here; the opportunity of a lifetime, to see the whole show from miles above.

'Darling, I am a long, long way from you now, but perhaps nearer than [when] I was in England … for a lucky shot may send me back to you.

'Our new aerodrome is about six miles from here, and between twenty and twenty-five miles from the lines. I haven't seen our billets, but they say they are very nice, so we are in luck, as some are awful, from what I hear.'[16]

Royal Flying Corps general headquarters (GHQ) was also located at Boisdinghem and it required 'special strategic and patrol work … [which] was the duty of two squadrons (12 and 21) retained at Flying Corps headquarters'.[17] By Wednesday, 26 January, Billy was out of the hospital and preparing for his frontline duties. But, first, he settled into his living quarters – in expropriated civilian houses – about which he wrote:

'We are in billets here, two [officers] in a room … My billet is just across the road from our flight mess, which is in a room in another house. In it we have a fire [-place] and a gramophone, which is a great comfort in the lonely evenings. Our aerodrome is quite a good one and is only about a hundred yards away, so we are quite well placed.' [18]

The Fokker Scourge
Now close to the frontlines, Billy began to hear more about air combat and learn about his future adversaries. One piece of chilling news was the 12 January loss of an R.E.7 flown by 12 Squadron[19] – most likely shot down by the early German fighter ace Leutnant [Second-Lieutenant] Oswald Boelcke[20] in a Fokker monoplane. According to an RFC report, the R.E.7 had been escorting a reconnaissance patrol[21] when it was attacked by the superior German aeroplane. Two days later, RFC general headquarters issued an order, 'which brought about, at a stroke, one of the drastic changes in the air war – formation flying …'[22] It stated:

'Until the Royal Flying Corps are in possession of a machine as good as or better than the German Fokker it seems that a change in tactics employed becomes necessary. It is hoped very shortly to obtain a machine which will successfully engage the Fokkers … In the meantime, it must be laid down as a hard and fast rule that a [British] machine proceeding on reconnaissance must be escorted by at least three other fighting machines. These machines must fly in close formation and a reconnaissance should not be continued if any of the machines become detached … From recent experience it seems that the Germans are now employing their aeroplanes in

Oberleutnant Oswald Boelcke, an early, highly successful Fokker Eindecker pilot, with his aeroplane. Note the forward-firing synchronized machine gun protruding over the cowl. (Dr. Lance J. Bronnenkant)

groups of three or four, and these numbers are frequently encountered by our aeroplanes. Flying in close formation must be practiced by all pilots.'[23]

Frontline personnel had to submit correspondence to a local area censor – and, indeed, Billy was assigned to that duty on occasion. Consequently, he did not share all of the news with Margaret, but did mention other information he learned about life at the Front:

'An arrangement has been made with the German flying corps and our own, by which if a [British] machine goes down behind the German lines, as soon as possible a German machine will come back and drop a message telling whether the pilot and observer are killed or wounded and [if the latter] how badly. If killed they [will] enclose a photograph of the grave and we [will] do the same for them. It is awfully nice to be on such good terms with one's enemies, and everyone here speaks very highly of all the German flyers. They seem to all be of a fine crowd.'[24]

Flying in the R.E.7
Billy Bishop showed no fear of German aircraft when he and Lt Roger Neville, later a five-victory fighter ace[25], made a flight over the lines in their R.E.7. Billy wrote:

One RFC response to the 'Fokker scourge' was the rear-engined Airco D.H.2 which allowed the pilot an unobstructed forward field to use his machine gun. The aeroplane seen here was captured on 9 August 1915. (Dr. Volker Koos)

'We are having a lot of trouble getting our machines to leave the ground. It is so muddy that the wheels sink right in and if the machine is at all heavily loaded it simply won't rise … we are really in an awful state, not knowing what to do about it. We simply have to get up somehow, and the sun so seldom appears that the ground stays wet.' [26]

Years later, Billy amplified that early memory:

'[We] gunned across our own aerodrome at least a dozen times, trying to get off into the wind, then taxied back to try again, before anyone realised that we were asking too much of the aircraft. Consultation between senior officers followed and it was decided to move to the larger field at St. Omer … in hopes that with a larger run the R.E.7 might consent to struggle into the air. Before this decision was taken we had even tried to take off without the bomb and failed.

'So the young observer and four machine guns were ferried to St. Omer by truck, while the pilot brought the R.E.7 across country minus its bomb. At St. Omer, with myself and four Lewis guns added, we got off, the guns being mounted on four pegs on the forward cockpit rim. The bomb was simply left behind, since the 'plane utterly refused to lift it.'[27]

Billy's repeated mention of problems with the 500-lb bomb ignored the fact that the first R.E.7s, powered by a 120-horsepower engine, could not carry such a heavy explosive device. According to British aviation historian J.M. Bruce, that aeroplane was intended to fly bearing 'one 336-lb Royal Aircraft Factory bomb or two 112-lb bombs augmented by 20-lb bombs'.[28] As for the aeroplane itself, Roger Neville considered it 'hopeless' and 'outdated before it arrived in France'. He also stated that the designation 'R.E. stood for Reconnaissance Experimental and the 7 meant, according to cynics, that the previous six had failed to get off the ground'.[29]

Commenting on this mission, Billy later heaped further abuse on the aeroplane:

'[Eventually it] … got into the air, although hours must have elapsed as we circled around and around St. Omer until we had attained an altitude of 6,000 feet and could set off toward the lines. There I had my first taste of ack-ack [anti-aircraft] fire and I remember it was hard to take, though later I felt completely [like] a hero for having come through this visit to the baptismal font of war …

'Ack-ack or no ack-ack, however, we slipped across the enemy lines, visited the German batteries, the locations of which [our] artillery wanted to take down, took photographs (praying the while nobody would catch us at it and want to discuss the matter), and sneaked home …' [30]

There is a question, however, as to whether that undated mission with Roger Neville was Billy Bishop's first flight over the lines in an R.E.7. Such a difficult flight in that aeroplane no doubt occurred and Neville is mentioned in subsequent correspondence. But on Saturday, 29 January, Billy flew with a Lieutenant Hunt on an artillery-spotting sortie that may have been his initial combat flight from Boisdinghem. He described that mission to Margaret in terms much more charitable to the R.E.7:

'At last my flying in France has really commenced. Yesterday [the weather] quite suddenly cleared up and off I went with Hunt. Very funny, too, [as] it was the same job … I had here last October, only much more exciting this time. At one time, while doing some dodging to keep altering the aim of the guns, we attained such a terrific speed that the engine could hardly be heard on account of the screaming of the [aeroplane's bracing] wires. We were diving almost vertically, with the engine full on, so it is little wonder. However I enjoyed it much more than I did last time.'[31]

Introduction to 'Archie'

Adding to the minor mystery of the first R.E.7 combat flight – an example of the difficulty in understanding conflicting accounts about Billy's various activities – a letter a few days later contained his first mention to Margaret of German anti-aircraft fire:

'Today … it was clear as a bell with a terrific wind blowing, but we all went [up] on various expeditions. Mine was a three-hour look [around for] Hun machines.

Thank God I didn't see any.

'[At one point] a strange machine appeared above and behind us. He evidently thought we were Huns, but fortunately discovered the [British cockades] on our [wings] in time. I was just about to open fire on him with two machine guns, as I couldn't see his markings, either. But after that we both swerved and missed each other. And ... about two minutes after [that], we were both targets of "Archibald" [anti-aircraft fire] from behind the German lines. Fully fifty shells were bursting in the air at one time, near us ... A friend of mine from Netheravon was shot down an hour later by a Fokker ... near the same place. I'm glad [the German pilot] didn't see us.'[32]

Alerted to the approach of Allied airmen, German Flieger-Abwehr-Kanone [Flak] crews run to their anti-aircraft guns in an effort to stop the intruders. (Bayerisches Hauptstaatsarchiv Militärarchiv München/Staudinger photo 017850)

It is worth noting that 'Archibald' – or, more commonly, 'Archie' – became the accepted British term for any of several anti-aircraft gun types to fire explosive rounds that detonated at the expected altitude of opposing aircraft. The word appears often in 1914-1918 War literature and lore. The official history of the Royal Air Force in World War I, *The War in the Air*, referenced in this book's bibliography, noted that the name 'Archie' came: 'from a light-hearted British pilot, who, when he was fired at in the air, quoted a popular music-hall refrain – "Archibald, certainly not!"'[33]

No British air casualties were recorded that day. Indeed, the RFC daily report noted only that '[3rd] Army reconnaissance escort machines were attacked by a Fokker which, however, made no attempt to come closer than 500 yards.'[34] One has to wonder whether

Billy's friend had been luckier than reported or whether the report Billy heard had been based on misinformation – or imagination.

Almost a week later, Billy recounted another R.E.7 flight for Margaret's benefit:

'This morning … Neville and I went over the lines. There were machines all over the place, about twelve in sight at one time. I nearly had nervous prostration trying to watch them all at once. It is so hard to tell whether they are friend or foe, [they] approach so rapidly. One has to keep training his guns on every machine that approaches. On the way home a big Hun Battleplane started to chase us, so I trained my guns on him, and waited for him to get [within] range, which is about 400 yards. It is only a waste of ammunition to fire from farther away, with machines going about 100 miles an hour. Then, just as he got in the right place, one of our Battleplanes came swooping down and he turned and fled, with the two of us after him. Then the "Archies" started on us and [were] getting very accurate, [and so] Neville and I headed for home full tilt. They wasted a lot of ammunition on us and didn't touch us at all. This all occurred two miles on the German side …

'Then after we got back, I realised for the first time that [today] is my twenty-second birthday. Dearest, I greet you.' [35]

Billy Bishop and Roger Neville may have been involved briefly with the German aircraft mentioned in the 8 February RFC War Diary report: 'The 2nd Army reconnaissance [mission] was attacked by two Fokkers and two Aviatiks. They were driven off. Hostile anti-aircraft guns were also very active, [a] 2nd Army reconnaissance machine being damaged.'[36]

A popular German postcard of the time depicted an Aviatik C.I of the type that Billy Bishop and Roger Neville drove off. (Author's Collection)

But that encounter was mild compared to what the weather did to Billy the following day:

'This morning I went up for a three-and-a-half hour patrol and it [was] the coldest day I have seen here … I got my right cheek quite badly [frost-bitten]. It has swelled up and blistered and burst, which they say is a good thing, but … it is extremely painful. The worst of it is that it will stop my flying for some days. I am spending the night in hospital on condition they will let me go tomorrow, because if I stay any longer they will cable home and then you will all worry, which there is no cause to do at all…'[37]

A flight of R.E.7s outside their tent hangars preparing for a mission over German lines. (Stewart K. Taylor)

More Misfortunes
Despite his protestations, Billy had to remain in hospital a day longer than he had planned. When he returned to duty he saw another demonstration of natural forces:

'Yesterday … we were chasing Boches[38] all day long. The wind was right for them, i.e., blowing from our side of the lines to theirs and giving them a chance to get back [to their own lines] quickly. Quite a lot [of them] came over, probably because there seems to be a general [German] liveliness all along the line …
    'Today there was a sixty-mile-an-hour gale blowing at 3,000 feet. It was hopeless to fly much higher … and so the day was spent in wireless work near the aero-drome.'[39]

Earlier that morning, the War Diary reported, 'the gale overturned all the iron hangars of 20 Squadron at Clairmarais, wrecking three F.E.2 [two-seaters] and seriously damaging three lorries.'[40]
    The next day all RFC flying was cancelled due to damage caused by the gale-force winds.[41] But 21 Squadron was not affected – much to Billy's dismay:
    'This has been a terrible day, raining and blowing like mad. All the tents on the aerodrome have been blown down and are in shreds. Fortunately, our [aircraft] are

in hangars so they are safe, though we wish they had been blown to shreds, too, because they are really the [ones] easiest hit out here and are not a success, being too cumbersome. When we smash these [R.E.7s] we shall probably get better ones, of another type, and faster.' [42]

The strain of combat took a toll on Billy, as Roger Neville observed:

'After he had been in operations in France for a time he became noticeably more moody and frustrated, the limitations of the R.E.7 as a combat machine became more and more apparent … [He] was boiling with rage because he could not fire back without danger of shooting off the R.E.7's tail-plane or his pilot's head. He was a very fine shot … Yet inevitably all his keenness made pilots wonder when his enthusiasm was going to overcome his judgement.' [43]

The R.E.7's operational problems led 21 Squadron to be withdrawn from frontline work. The unit's next assignment was flying aerial defence missions over St. Omer, site of the GHQ of General Sir Douglas Haig, commander-in-chief of the British Expeditionary Force. Over a quarter-century later Billy recalled 'flying in … the freezing mist of a Pas de Calais February … Fortunately, the enemy did not seem to know we were there … Presumably, we would have tried to join issue with the Hun if he had come along and, I imagine, [would] have been shot down ingloriously for our pains …' [44]

On 9 March 1916, six of 21 Squadron's F.E.7s joined in a bombing raid behind German lines and it was a miracle that none of the unit's crews were among the mission's casualties. [45] Billy's letter to Margaret revealed mood swings that accompanied his combat fatigue; apparently, he was so distraught that he could not even bear to use the perpendicular pronoun in describing his misery:

'In the air you feel only intense excitement. You cheer and laugh and keep your spirits up. You are all right just after you have landed as you search your machine for bullet and shrapnel holes. But two hours later, when you are quietly sitting in your billet, you feel a sudden loneliness. You want to lie down and cry.' [46]

That low point was followed and, no doubt, compounded by a series of mishaps over the coming weeks. Near the aerodrome, Billy was driving a small motor vehicle when he 'collided with an army lorry and was severely shaken up'. [47] Days later, he was inspecting his aeroplane when 'a supporting cable struck his head and left him unconscious for two days'. [48] Then a recently-extracted tooth became infected, resulting in another hospital stay. And, when Roger Neville pranged an aeroplane while landing, Billy slammed forward and 'cracked his knee against a metal bracket'. [49]

Another traumatic event occurred on Tuesday, 2 May 1916, after he took a Channel steamer from Boulogne to Folkestone for a much-needed three-week leave. As he left the ship to go ashore, Billy 'slipped on the gangplank and stumbled forward on the concrete pier with three other men on top of him'. [50] He landed on the same knee injured in the recent crash with Neville.

During Billy's subsequent stay at the RFC Hospital in Bryanston Square in London, on Friday, 26 May, he received formal notification that 'the general officer commanding London district has been directed to cause a medical board to be assembled shortly to report upon the state of your health'.[51]

The order portended an extended stay in London. It would either mark the end of his flying career or provide an opportunity for him to find someone to help him enter a pilot training programme.

CHAPTER FOUR

From Albion to Zeppelins

'You were put into a swivel chair, spun around, and suddenly invited
to spring to attention. If you did not fall flat on your face, it was
presumed that you were a healthy individual and fit to fly.'
– William A. Bishop[1]

Billy Bishop's hospitalisation on 11 May 1916[2] proved to be a multiple blessing. As he later pointed out, 'the doctors found that, in addition to the cracked knee … I had a severely strained heart – which was comfortingly blamed on the tension of the long patrols and on the continual changes in altitude and temperature.'[3] And, as he later wrote about his time in London: 'I found [an] opportunity to pull a few strings, talk to a few people I knew, and finally wangle my way to flying school.'[4] In fact, while at the Royal Flying Corps Hospital he became friends with a well-connected dowager in her early seventies and it was she who pulled the right strings and talked to the right people on his behalf. Surely, she and her connections rescued his military flying career.

Lady St. Helier
Known as Lady St. Helier,[5] the twice married and twice widowed aristocrat was among wealthy British society members who used their resources and contacts to aid the war effort.[6] Arthur Bishop described his father's first impression of the person who – after his mother and Margaret Burden – became the third most important woman in Billy's life:

'[Lady St. Helier was] lean with sparse hair severely drawn back to show unusually large ears. Her most remarkable features were her wide-set luminous eyes that appeared [to be] much younger than the rest of her, eyes that penetrated and probed and yet were kindly and reassuring …'[7]

The *Times* obituary about her suggested ways in which she could have helped the confident and ambitious man that Billy Bishop was becoming:

'Lady St. Helier … did for several years work as a woman alderman of the London County Council, but her chief [claim] to fame is to be found in the multitude of her friendships and in the wide hospitality which she exercised in London … She was a hostess of genius and her house … was the meeting place of a varied succession of men and women … [She] had a rare double gift: she could make close friends and keep them, and at the same time she could attract new people, people of mark, many of them birds of passage, and thus make her table and her drawing-room a scene of constant variety … To all she was a delightful hostess, while those who were admitted to her intimacy found in her a wide knowledge of persons and things, a bright intelligence, and a critical power without the slightest tinge of ill-nature.

'It is immensely to Lady St. Helier's credit that, with all her popularity, she was no social butterfly; she had serious interests and worked at them wisely … During the war she did noble service … paying long and almost daily visits to the great hospital near Epsom,[8] which the council had transformed for the use of the soldiers. In a sense she must have regarded this strenuous war service as a tribute to the memory of her only son, a young [Grenadier] Guardsman who died of [enteric] fever at Poona [in Western India] …'[9]

By an interesting coincidence, Billy was the same age as Lady St. Helier's son, Francis Jeune, when he died in 1904 at age twenty-two. During their first meeting, however, she remarked about a different connection between them: 'I saw your name on the register and I was sure that someone named William Bishop, from Canada, must be the son of my friend Will Bishop. And when I looked at you I was sure of it; you look very much like him.'[10]

Billy was confused and responded only: 'My father's name is Will, but he lives in Owen Sound, a small town in Ontario …'[11]

To which Lady St. Helier replied: 'Then you are Will Bishop's son.' She went on to recount a visit to Canada, where she attended a reception hosted by Sir Wilfrid Laurier, Can-

Billy Bishop and Margaret Burden during Billy's home leave in 1916. Billy proudly wore the chest insignia of a 'Flying Officer (Observer)'. (DHH/DND photo RE-22066-3)

ada's seventh prime minister. She recalled being introduced to Billy's father. Months later, when Billy inquired about the event, the elder Bishop barely remembered meeting Lady St. Helier.[12] But a warm connection had been made in London and Billy benefitted from it.

Lady St. Helier lived in a four-storey mansion at 52 Portland Place, a prestigious address on a broad and sumptuous boulevard of Georgian townhouses running south from Regents Park into the heart of London. Above 'the entertainment floors she had staying visitors whom she called her "lodgers"'.[13] In mid-June, when Billy was discharged from the RFC hospital, he joined the 'lodgers'. Arthur Bishop clarified the relationship:

'A strong bond of affection had grown between the young Canadian country boy and one of Britain's most sophisticated noblewomen during her regular visits to the hospital. … In a rare sentimental moment this indomitable woman told Bishop: "You are the kind of grandson my son would have given me if he had lived."

'Her voice was choked. She was close to tears. It was the first time Bishop had seen her show anything but cheerfulness and self-assurance. He tried to comfort her in the only way he knew, by saying with an impertinent grin: "Yes, Granny." From then on he called her "Granny" – and she introduced him to her vast array of friends as "my grandson"'. [14]

Home Leave

Billy respectfully appreciated being taken under Lady St. Helier's wing and for the opportunity to meet members of British society he knew only by reputation. But he was still convalescing from various injuries and, while residing in the stately home, he was being worn out by the partying. Lady St. Helier soon sensed that he needed to rest, despite his protesting that he had done nothing to deserve a further respite. A week later Billy was again summoned to a medical board and was granted home leave.[15]

Soon, Billy was aboard a ship heading for Canada. Once ashore, he was only one person in a sea of military uniforms as he travelled from Halifax, Nova Scotia to Montreal and then to Toronto. His final destination – Owen Sound – was the sweetest of all, as he fell into the warm embrace of his family. The local newspaper characterisation of his injuries as wounds caused people to treat him like a hero. The drawback, he said, was that if his comrades in 21 Squadron ever heard about his inaccurate press notices, he would 'never hear the end of it'.[16]

Best of all, Margaret's father, perhaps seeing Billy in a new and more favourable light, consented to Billy's formal proposal of marriage to Margaret. The young couple agreed to postpone their wedding, as Billy was determined to become a pilot and 'did not consider it fair to Margaret to make her a widow almost as soon as she became a wife'.[17]And this time Billy presented Margaret with a real engagement ring.

Back to England

In early September 1916, Billy Bishop returned to England. He hoped to be assigned to pilot training, but learned at the War Office that he needed to appear again before a medical board to determine his fitness for active duty. This board was stricter than the previous one and denied his request. Further, his service records had gone missing, which meant he could not apply for pilot's training. He had to bide his time until his medical condition improved and, even then, the best he could hope for was a return to 21 Squadron.

Powerless against the RFC bureaucracy, Billy could only complain about his bad luck to Lady St. Helier. She had the answer, of course. She raised the matter with her friends Lord Hugh Cecil, who had originally arranged for Billy's transfer to the RFC, and with Rt.Hon. Winston Churchill, the former First Lord of the Admiralty and soon to become Minister of Munitions. Billy was bowled over to learn that his patroness knew Churchill. She explained that Churchill's wife, Clementine, was her great-niece and, in fact, Lady St. Helier had introduced the couple. Further, Lord Cecil had been Churchill's best man.[18]

Days later, Billy was back at the War Office. He remembered a much different atmosphere this time:

'Stiff formality was swept aside. Bureaucratic procedure became friendly co-operation. The brick walls of English protocol suddenly developed open arms. My [previously lost] papers appeared from nowhere ...'[19]

Billy was, of course, required to pass a pre-flight physical examination. He recalled it as a model of simplicity:

'After the doctor had listened to your heart and banged your lungs and persuaded you to say "aah" and "ninety-nine", you were put into a swivel chair, spun around, and suddenly invited to spring to attention. If you did not fall flat on your face, it was presumed that you were a healthy individual and fit to fly. You also did things like walking a chalk line with your eyes shut. That was about all there was to it.'[20]

Pilot Training

On Sunday, 1 October 1916, Billy Bishop reported to Brasenose College at the University of Oxford to begin a four-week course of ground-school training. Billy's observer training and his flight experiences put him ahead of most of his classmates in the lectures and he passed the course handily.

In November, Billy was back at Central Flying School in Upavon to train in a French-designed Maurice Farman Série 11 two-seat biplane. One seat for the instructor and one for the student, with both linked by dual controls to enable the former to correct the latter's movements in flight, as needed. Formally known as the MF.11, the rear-engined aeroplane was based on a pre-war design.[21] The first entry in Billy Bishop's flight logbook,[22] dated 4 November 1916, records a ten-minute orientation flight with a Lieutenant Wood in MF.11 (serial number) 5885. The number indicates it was from a thirty-aircraft batch produced by the Aircraft Manufacturing Company.[23]

Billy recalled his training in the MF.11, which was derisively called the 'Rumpty' by many due to the rumbling sound the engine made as it taxied across the aerodrome:

'I did not get along very well while flying dual [control] with my instructor. Sometimes I would be roundly cursed for my ham-handedness as I almost froze to the controls in my anxiety to do well. That would send me to the other extreme and on

A Maurice Farman Série 11 two-seat biplane of the type in which Billy Bishop made his first solo flight at the Central Flying School in Upavon. (Colin A. Owers)

the next attempt I would be "timid-handed" – and, if you go timid with a "Rumpty", the lady is very likely to fly you into the ground … for your lack of attention to her …'[24]

On Wednesday, 15 November, the day that Billy Bishop was formally notified he had been 'seconded for duty as a flying officer (observer)',[25] he made his first solo flight – in a 'Rumpty'. He had logged in just over eleven hours of dual instruction flight time[26], and recalled:

'There is not a pilot above ground who won't tell you that this is the greatest day in any flying man's life … I had become a knight in shining armour – to myself.

'All the trappings were present for such a great occasion, even to the ambulance parked outside the hangar to bring me back alive, I hoped … [But] right then I had that awful dentist's-anteroom feeling in the pit of my stomach. I climbed in [to the aeroplane] and waved a hand to the mechanics at the chocks … All I had to do was hold the hand up. Its natural shakes in themselves constituted a very rapid wave. But I taxied out and nosed into the wind and ran [the aeroplane] like mad across the field … [and] staggered into the air, climbing steadily, and kept going in straight line. Now I felt like a king!'[27]

Billy had only to make a take-off and landing to complete this flight – no turns. He felt comfortable with leaving the ground alone and, after some minutes, he was ready to return to the aerodrome. As he described it:

'Finally I levelled off and executed to perfection everything I had been told to do in order to make a perfect landing. The only thing … wrong was that I executed it [at] forty feet above the ground. Fortunately for my career in the Royal Flying Corps I noticed this in time, put the nose down and made another perfect landing, this time

An early Royal Aircraft Factory B.E.2c, the first combat-type aeroplane in which
Billy Bishop became qualified to fly. (Colin A. Owers)

only eight feet above the grass tops. [The aeroplane] simply fell the rest of the way,
banged [its] sturdy undercarriage onto the field and groaned to a stop …'[28]

To round out Billy's experiences at Upavon, he also qualified on B.E.2c 4702,[29] a single-seat
version of the broadly-used B.E. aeroplane series. He felt he was ready for a bigger challenge and, as he wrote to Margaret, he nearly got it:

'The night before last [27 November] there was a Zeppelin raid, and up [I] went …
Only the Zepps didn't come over our way at all, so down we came again. Yesterday
I went up twice in a B.E.2c and managed to get in an hour and twenty minutes alto-
gether. That brings my time solo [in the B.E.2c] to five hours and fifty-five minutes.
If the weather would only clear today I would get in another hour …'[30]

During the night of 27-28 November 1916 six Zeppelin dirigibles – L.14, L.21, L.22, L.24,
L.34 and L.36 – attacked targets from Norfolk to Durham; two were lost to British aeroplanes.[31] Various British air units were alerted to their presence; hence, Billy's logbook
shows that he flew B.E.2d (serial number) 6306[32], a relatively new and improved aeroplane,
that evening. As noted, however, he was too far away and unable to reach any of the German airships.

Night Flying
Billy received a better opportunity to learn more about attacking Zeppelins a few days
later when he was assigned to 11 Reserve Squadron[33] – also known as 11 Reserve (Home
Defence) Training Squadron[34] – at Northolt, a night-flying base north west of London.
He had done well at Upavon but, as Arthur Bishop explained, his father 'immediately ran

afoul of the strict discipline with which Northolt's commanding officer, Major Barry F. Moore, ran his station'.[35]

On Friday, 1 December, Billy made two forced landings in a B.E.2c at the aerodrome and, on 5 December, while landing at Rochford in another B.E.2c, his engine failed and he crashed into a tree.[36] He caused considerable damage to an aeroplane that, at the time, cost the British government £1,549[37] – which in 2014 value translates into about £115,741 or $190,968 (US).

Over the next few weeks, Billy Bishop and Major Moore had 'matters' to discuss: On 8 December 1916, Billy logged in 'two good landings and two bad landings' in a B.E.2c; on 19 December he had a forced landing at Northolt; and, on Sunday, 7 January 1917, the 'pièce de résistance' – he made what is described in his flight logbook as six 'joyrides' with enlisted ground personnel over the aerodrome.

Once again, Billy stood on the brink of disaster when a 'saviour' appeared in the form of Tryggve Gran, a Norwegian aviation pioneer and Antarctic explorer, who had relinquished a commission in his neutral nation's navy for a more adventurous billet as an officer in Britain's Royal Flying Corps.[38] Gran was the only instructor at 11 Reserve Squadron who liked Billy well enough to step forward on his behalf.

According to Arthur Bishop:

'Many years later, Squadron Commander (then Captain) Tryggve Gran … gave a softened version of the twenty-two-year-old Canadian's conduct at Northolt: "[Billy] was full of joie de vivre and high jinks, and hated discipline, with the result that he was always in conflict with squadron regulations."' [39]

As a result of Gran's intercession with Major Moore, Billy was given only a vociferous chewing-out and sent[40] to 37 (Home Defence) Squadron, to which he had been formally assigned as of 8 December 1916.[41] One of six night-fighter units 'placed in a line between Dover and Edinburgh'[42] to interdict German aerial raiders, the squadron was led by an early wartime pilot, Major William B. Hargrave,[43] and was equipped with single-seat Royal Aircraft Factory B.E.12s. A more powerful development of the B.E.2c, the B.E.12 was armed with a single forward-firing Vickers machine gun, synchronised to fire through the propeller arc.[44] Like all other aeroplanes of the time, the B.E.2c had no radio and no parachute; pilots had to be rugged individuals, especially at night-time. Hargrave's squadron was based at Woodham Mortimer in Essex[45], and also had flight stations at Rochford, Stow Maries and Goldhanger,[46] all north east of London. From those locations 37 Squadron aircraft operated inland and along the English Channel. Billy recalled:

'Night-flying … in small aircraft was a fearsome business … We took off between two rows of flares, and soared into the night sky, praying to goodness we would be able to find our aerodromes when the time came to return. Our knowledge of navigation was completely elementary. We had a lecture or two … and a rudimentary knowledge of the stars in their courses, but … whenever we flew by night, it was strictly by the seat of the pants. I would pick myself a few shadowy landmarks and try to orient myself by them. There was no … voice contact with the ground … and no control tower telling [us] what to do and when to do it. Consequently, it was always an awesome business to get back to the starting point and … to land.'[47]

Meeting Heroes

Billy flew patrols to and from 37 Squadron's various small fields. During such a flight in late January 1917 he had his first encounter with two nationally-known military air heroes, Captain Frederick Sowrey and Lieutenant Claude A. Ridley. Bishop knew about both men, possibly from reading accounts in *Flight* magazine and citations in *The London Gazette*, the latter being an official newspaper of record. In that way he would have learned about Sowrey's role in destroying the German airship L.32, for which he was presented with the Distinguished Service Order,[48] Britain's second highest bravery award. Likewise, Billy would have read about Ridley's exploits in evading capture behind German lines, which earned him the DSO[49] and, earlier, Ridley's part in downing the airship L.15, for which he was awarded the Military Cross.[50]

Clearly, Billy enjoyed meeting these highly honoured airmen – after all, the DSO was presented personally by King George V.[51] Telling Margaret about his chat with Sowrey and Ridley marks the first of his many mentions of high awards:

'Yesterday Pearson and I flew over to Goldhanger and saw Sowrey [then a member of 37 Squadron]. He is such a cheery person. One likes him more and more every time you see him. We [also] met Ridley there. He landed in Belgium some time ago and hid before the Huns came up. For six months he roamed about, eating roots and things [before] finally escaping to England after raiding some German HQ and getting a lot of valuable information. He was given the DSO, besides which he has the MC.'[52]

A single-seat Royal Aircraft Factory B.E.12 of the type Billy Bishop flew on
night-time missions with 37 (Home Defence) Squadron. (Colin A. Owers)

Any hopes that Billy Bishop had for becoming a 'Zeppelin hunter' ended on Thursday, 28 December 1916. Unbeknownst to British authorities, that day the German Naval Airship Division dispatched six dirigibles to 'attack southern England [and], if at all possible, London' but, due to high winds, they had to be recalled. On returning, one airship was irreparably damaged and two others caught fire at their base and were destroyed. There were no more German airship raids until the following spring. [53]

Billy could not have known about those developments, of course. And in his next letter, he noted that his career was still advancing:

'Yesterday [21 January, Major Hargrave] … came over for lunch and in the course of conversation he told me that I had been recommended for … flight commander. I am to go over and see him tomorrow … Then the colonel arrived and inspected us with all due pomp and ceremony, and he gave us the very welcome news that we are to get another type of machine. [They are] the fastest thing out, a very small [Sopwith] scout for day work and B.E.2es for night work. The [Sopwiths] will be an improvement on B.E.12s … [and] nicer to fly.'[54]

Cockpit view of a Sopwith Pup much admired by Billy Bishop because it was armed with a single belt-fed Vickers machine gun. The aeroplane seen here, A.6174, was the 54 Squadron presentation machine 'CANADA,' which was forced to land by German ace Ltn Werner Voss on 9 May 1917. (Dr. Volker Koos)

Mention of a possible advancement to flight commander was no doubt meant to impress Margaret – but it was wishful thinking for such a junior pilot with so few flight hours. Over five weeks later – and with no entry in his service record to account for the change – Billy was assigned to instruct student pilots at the Central Flying School. But he kept that dream promotion in mind when he wrote:

> 'I am still here … until I am posted. In the meantime I fly [Sopwith] "Pups" whenever I find one not being used … At other times I instruct on Avros, a machine I hate. Yesterday I had three forced landings on them, two of which I managed to get into the aerodrome, but the last I crashed on the side of a hill, [but] not very badly. Nobody was hurt and the machine is repairable. The engines are so unreliable … They are an obsolete type, thank God. Today I had better luck and managed to get several pupils ready for their first "solo".
>
> 'Last night we had a boy killed here and another in my squadron this morning. I saw them both, perfectly ghastly sights. The one today was in a Sopwith. He was diving it, and the wings fell off … The thing fell like a stone [for] 3,000 feet, the poor beggar struggling all the time, helpless …
>
> 'These things used to upset me horribly, but now I think I have become an absolute firmly-believing fatalist, and they don't worry my nerve in the least …'[55]

It was another stroke of good fortune when Billy Bishop was switched to the Sopwith Scout, a small, rotary-engine-powered single-seater affectionately known as the 'Pup'. Developed the previous year, the Sopwith Scout was armed with a single belt-fed Vickers .303-calibre machine gun that was synchronised to fire through the propeller arc. Its 250-round ammunition belt offered far better chances for combat success than the 97-round ammunition drums on the Mk. II Lewis machine guns[56] that Billy had operated up to this point.

There was a minor hazard attached to rotary engines used in the Sopwith Pup and other aeroplanes. They were lubricated with light-weight castor oil, which was mixed with fuel and air by the carburettor. Consequently, engine fumes laden with partially burnt castor oil blew back into cockpits, were ingested by pilots and often caused diarrhoea. This condition was best countered by generous swigs of 'blackberry brandy' locally distilled with boosted alcohol content. Steady consumption of this 'remedy' often promoted alcoholism among pilots of early rotary-engined aeroplanes.

In any event, Billy Bishop's training in Sopwith Scouts and his ever-rising number of flight hours qualified him for air combat duties in a more active area. With no explanation, suddenly he was transferred from 37 Squadron to a daytime fighter unit on the Western Front. Years later, he wrote:

> 'As to my assignment as a night-flying Zeppelin hunter, a job which obviously was not my forte, it consisted primarily of sitting on our isolated station, waiting for the telephone to ring to tell us that the Hun was about to visit London. I never liked the job and was extremely happy when I received word at the end of February 1917 that I had been released from the duty of saving Britain and was to be sent to France.'[57]

CHAPTER FIVE

First Triumphs

'I can't write today, except [to say] I love you, and all I do is for you,
and I am going to make good. I feel it.'
– William A. Bishop[1]

By year-end 1916 Billy Bishop must have realised the futility of daydreaming about being appointed a squadron flight commander. For one thing, he still had too little flying experience to hold that position; at this point he had flown as a pilot for a total of twenty-seven hours and thirty-five minutes. [2]

But believing in himself and once again applying the value of hard work, Billy continued to fly two-seat trainers and single-seat scouts (as fighter aeroplanes were then called) at every opportunity, even during bitterly cold weather. Consequently, by Saturday, 3 March 1917, he had logged another forty-eight hours in the air – for a total of over seventy-five hours' flight time.[3] Would that amount of time in the air be enough to be considered for advancement? True, he had more than doubled his hours at the controls, but only time would tell whether a squadron commander would feel Billy was ready for leadership of a flight.

Ever eager to show Margaret Burden he was progressing in his work and to tell her about the widening circle of prominent flyers he was meeting, Billy wrote:

'At last I am going … On Tuesday [6 March] I report to the War Office for orders and after that I expect to go to France on Wednesday. I am to go on "rotary scouts", which means Sopwith Triplanes, Sopwith Pups or Nieuports. All of these are wonderful machines and I am a lucky boy, indeed. I shall explain the work later; it is all fighting, nothing else.

'Last night I had dinner with [Albert] Ball, the man who has [received] three DSOs, two MCs[4] and a foreign order.[5] He was on Nieuports when he was out [at the Front].'[6]

One can only wonder what the two men discussed, as Billy Bishop did not mention more than that brief comment. If Albert Ball noted their meeting in his diary, that source was last seen 'in the 1930s … [and] along with other papers [has] disappeared and is not held in the Ball Papers in the Nottingham Archives', according to the latest Ball biography. [7]

Posted to 60 Squadron, RFC
On the eve of departing for the Western Front, Billy dashed off a note to Margaret, rein-

forcing the central role she had in his life:

'I think I cross tomorrow, back to … France. I have been on the rush here, saying goodbye to people and getting my final arrangements made.

'I can't write today, except [to say] I love you, and all I do is for you, and I am going to make good. I feel it.'[8]

With his personal and professional matters in order, Billy was ready for the challenges that lay ahead of him. His first days with his new squadron were a mixture of feelings:

'With a dozen other flying men I landed at Boulogne on 7 March 1917, for my second go at the war. At the Boulogne quay we separated … [and] meandered along over the slow French railroads for nearly two days before reaching our destinations.

'One other pilot [RMC classmate Ernest J.D. Townesend[9]] and I … had been ordered to join [60 Squadron, RFC] on the southern sector of the British line. The squadron … had a great reputation … and we were proud to become members of it. Captain Albert Ball, who was resting in England at the time, but who came back to France in the late spring … had brought down [twenty] Hun machines as a member of "our" squadron. That was an inspiration in itself.'[10]

January 1917 line-up of 60 Squadron C Flight Nieuport 17s at Filescamp Farm. Recognizable serial and side numbers are, from left: Lt E.J.L.W. Gilchrist's A.6646 (C5), Capt H. Meintjes' A.311 (C1), 2/Lt K.L. Caldwell's A.307 (C3) and 2/Lt W.M. Fry's A.274 (C2). (Greg VanWyngarden)

Organisationally, 60 Squadron was one of five units comprising the Royal Flying Corps' 13th Wing, which was under 3rd Brigade, RFC.[11] The squadron was assigned to Filescamp Farm, which one former inhabitant recalled as 'a fine old place, like a château'[12] outside the village of Izel-lès-Hameau, north west of Arras in the Artois area of northern France. The current frontline, eight miles east of Arras, was easily reached when 60 Squadron needed to respond to hostile air incursions in the area. The location was also home for 'a vast aerodrome in open countryside, with accommodations for three squadrons … [Living] quarters are most civilised … [with] a pleasant mess, [curved metal] Nissen huts for officers and [non-commissioned officers], a hard tennis court of sorts, and a badminton court in an empty hangar next door. And all this in a large orchard full of luscious fruit trees …'[13] Joining 60 Squadron's Nieuports at Filescamp Farm were 11 Squadron equipped with F.E.2b rear-engined two-seat scout and bomber aircraft, and 29 Squadron with Nieuport Scouts.[14]

At his new posting, Billy did not fly Sopwith Pups, with which he was familiar. But, as fighter pilots of all eras need to feel supremely confident that they fly the best aircraft available, Billy quickly embraced the Nieuport 17 Scouts assigned to 60 Squadron. Indeed, he rhapsodised about them, as when he recalled the sight of one at St. Omer the previous autumn:

'The first I saw was one of the original Nieuport … single-seaters. A little daisy of a ship … with all the daintiness of a Parisienne … [yet] she had an extremely lethal look about her, as if she were the mistress of some nabob … on her way to shoot her lover.' [15]

Billy began using frontline-area jargon – e.g., referring to Germans as 'Huns', without realising the phrase was inspired by Kaiser Wilhelm II himself in 1910.[16] Most of all, the new aeroplanes dominated Billy's thoughts, even when over-stating their value, as in the following letter to Margaret:

Lt Billy Bishop in flying gear and Major Jack Scott outside one of the wooden sheds at Filescamp Farm in June 1917. (Dan McCaffery)

'At present we have the only [aircraft] the Huns fear, although I think better machines will be out shortly. Anyway, for the first time in my history I am on really good machines. They are … made by the French, and beautifully finished, etc. That and the fact that we have a delightful crowd of pilots here make things quite just what I want.'[17]

Major Jack Scott
Billy arrived at 60 Squadron shortly after the arrival of the unit's new commanding officer, New Zealand-born Major Alan John Lance Scott – generally known as 'Jack'. The new

CO's colourful background was described by his friend Sir Frederick Smith, 1st Viscount Birkenhead and Lord Chancellor:

> '[While still in training, Scott's] machine collapsed when he was at 2,000 feet in the air. During the terrible fall that followed he was working and trying and testing and, when some sixty feet from the ground, he regained a degree of control which saved his life but left him permanently [crippled] …
>
> 'As soon as [Scott] became strong enough to walk unaided, he began again to strain every influence he possessed to obtain leave to go on active service in France. "To fight in an aeroplane," he said, "is the one thing a lame man could do as well as another…"
>
> 'He had accident after accident, and escape after escape, and those who knew him said that he [led] a charmed life. And he continued to fight in the air … habitually violating the rule which, in the later stages of the struggle, forbade the commanding officers of squadrons to engage personally in air combat. When positively forbidden to engage, he positively refused to obey, saying, "I will not send boys to fight unless I go with them. Lower my rank if you like, and then I can fight". He met with accident after accident, until hardly a part of his body was quite unscathed, but it seemed as if no risk, or combination of risks, could destroy so tenacious a life or daunt a spirit so buoyant.'[18]

It is easy to understand how Major Scott – fighting daily to walk with two canes, but driven by an indomitable will, and questioning authority freely – had an air about him that appealed to Billy Bishop. As an added bond, both men began training in Nieuport 17 Scouts at the same time. Billy later wrote:

> 'It rather pleased and in a sense comforted me to know that the new [squadron] commander was also [training on Nieuports] … He had been flying up to this time a two-seater [Sopwith] machine, which calls for entirely different tactics during a fight. Two-seater machines … have [rear-seat] guns that can be turned about in different positions. On the fighting scouts they … are rigidly fixed [forward]. This means it is necessary to aim the machine at anything you wish to fire at.' [19]

Flying Nieuports
From the outset, Lieutenant Bishop and Major Scott understood that the Nieuport 17 Scout had a markedly different wing design than the Sopwith single- and two-seat biplanes with which they were familiar. The Nieuport was a sesquiplane, with the top wing being 3 ft. 11½ inches wide and the bottom wing – which mainly helped to stabilize the machine in flight[20] – was 2 feet 4½ inches wide.[21] The few inches' variance made a great difference in the way the Nieuport handled and, surely, Billy's subsequent mastery of the sesquiplane's distinctive flight characteristics was an important factor in his air combat success with 60 Squadron. Among items Billy mentioned to Margaret was the operational reality of the new aircraft type:

'Just before I left Merry England, Lady St. Helier gave me a glorious flying coat with fur collar and fur lining. It cost £25. She is a perfect dear, if ever there was one.

'I have been flying the Nieuports. [Flew] one-and-a-half hours yesterday in them. They are very difficult to fly, but it is a great joy when you can fly them … Tomorrow or the first fine day I go on my first patrol on them. I am looking forward to it very much.

'Yesterday, two of our people were shot down. One landed safely [within] our lines, but the other, I am afraid, was killed. Poor beggar.'[22]

The 60 Squadron loss, Lieutenant Arthur D. Whitehead,[23] became the fifteenth victim of Leutnant Werner Voss, a rising star among German aces. The official German victory list for March[24] credits Voss with shooting down 'Nieuport A.279,' Whitehead's aeroplane. At the time, Voss flew with the élite unit Jagdstaffel 2, which had been founded by the legendary air combat tactician Oswald Boelcke; 60 Squadron faced some of the top German fighter units.

On Monday, 12 March 1917, 60 Squadron suffered a different form of loss when one of its most successful combat pilots, New Zealand native Captain Keith L. Caldwell, was posted back to England for ten-weeks' sick leave.[25] He had been leader of C Flight. As noted in a tribute from his native land: 'Keith Caldwell had … a reputation for being fearless and he inspired great confidence in others who flew with him. He had earned the nickname of "Grid" thanks to his habit of referring an aircraft as a "grid", which was an old [New Zealand] slang term for a bicycle.' [26]

Two days later, Billy Bishop mishandled a Nieuport while landing at Filescamp Farm, but suffered only slightly for his mistake. He wrote:

'Today [Brigadier-General John F.A. Higgins] was to come over, and I was selected to give an exhibition of flying for him. He didn't come, so up I went anyway and, coming down, what should I do but spin on one wing-tip when landing, and smash a perfectly good lower wing. I was glad the old boy wasn't there.'[27]

Billy's flight logbook noted only that the lower wing was 'strained'.[28] Apparently he experienced a ground loop, which occurs when aerodynamic forces cause one wing to rise and the other wingtip to touch the ground. It was a momentary scare and Billy had been more fortunate than other 60 Squadron members who had close calls when experiencing Nieuport 'lower wing twisting'[29] due to the sesquiplane design.

Anticipating another Allied advance on the Somme at about this time, German Quartermaster-General Erich Ludendorff ordered a methodically-staged major troop withdrawal to reinforced positions behind the so-called Siegfried Line (known as the Hindenburg Line by Allied forces). Beginning on the evening of Monday, 12 March 1917, Ludendorff 'arranged for the utter devastation of the whole area inside [the abandoned area] … Houses were demolished, trees cut down, and even wells contaminated, while the wreckage was littered with a multitude of explosive booby-traps,' according to British historian Basil Liddell Hart.[30]

At the end of the week, on Friday, 17 March, Billy made his first flight over the lines with 60 Squadron. The aeroplane he flew – Nieuport 17 A.274 – was more of an air combat veteran than Billy.[31] It had arrived brand new at the squadron four months earlier and had been flown by several pilots who achieved aerial victories in it.[32] Typically, the aeroplane was passed down to a new man, which proved to be a wise policy, as Billy 'crashed' on landing and 'damaged' it that day.[33] Prior to that event, the aeroplane gave Billy a good ride over the abandoned area, where British forces pursued withdrawing German troops. He wrote about the new wasteland and pointed out a squadron-mate's unusual air attack on German soldiers:

> 'You should see the [battlefield] here now. This advance is just in front of us, and it is the most extraordinary thing to see. We flew over yesterday[34] only 500 feet high and hardly a shot [was] fired at us. It is so hard to tell just where [German troops] are … [Lieutenant George] Lloyd flew over and threw some rotten turnips at some Huns he saw on a road.'[35]

As Billy Bishop gained experience by flying with veteran squadron pilots over the lines, he was assigned to one of three formations (called flights) and informed Margaret:

> 'I am now in C Flight and my machine,[36] which is newly painted in brown and green dabs, has the huge letters C6 on [the fuselage]. It is a glorious machine, having an exceptionally good engine, which is running beautifully at present. In other words it is a good "grid".'[37]

Major Jack Scott was also very enthusiastic about the Nieuport 17 and, in that mood, hailed it as:

> '[The] best fighting machine on either side. Strong in construction … it could turn inside any German aeroplane we encountered. It was not very fast, but, with an exceptionally good climb [rate] to 10,000 feet, it was no bad "grid" on which to go Hun-hunting …
>
> 'It was armed with a single Lewis [machine] gun carrying a double drum [each] with ninety [-seven] rounds[38] of .303 [-calibre] ammunition and two spare drums. The gun was mounted on the top [wing] and fired over the propeller at an angle slightly above the horizontal. The earlier [RFC] Nieuports were all treated with a bright silver-coloured "dope" – the substance used to tighten the fabric – and when properly turned out had a very smart appearance. Another characteristic of all [Nieuport] types was the V-shaped interplane struts, which, although the Germans also used them in their Albatros D.III [fighters] made the machines easy to recognise in the air.
>
> 'The silver Nieuport was a good machine to fight in, but a bad one either for running away or for catching a faint-hearted enemy, as its best air speed, even near the ground, rarely exceeded ninety-six or ninety-nine miles per hour.'[39]

The Nieuports' principal German opponent, the new Albatros D.III series, which appeared

Early Nieuport Scouts were armed only with an upper wing-mounted Lewis machine gun. It was operated by a flexible Bowden cable from the gun to the pilot. The gun fired over the propeller arc and had to be carefully aimed. (Dr. Volker Koos)

in early 1917, helped 'German pilots regain … air superiority over the Allies'.[40] It, too, was of a sesquiplane design, but was faster than the Nieuport 17[41], and had more firepower. Allied scouts equipped with a single Lewis or Vickers machine gun that fired short bursts of bullets now faced German fighter aeroplanes armed with a pair of Spandau 7.92mm machine guns, each one capable of 'firing at the rate of about 400 rounds a minute and fed with ammunition belts holding 500 rounds or more'.[42] Even the German bullets, equal to about .312 calibre, were slightly larger than the standard British .303 calibre round.

The advantages Billy Bishop brought into this mixture of aircraft capabilities and basic firepower were his experience and achievements as a marksman. Those long ago days of proficiently shooting elusive squirrels in his back yard in Owen Sound nurtured a skill that would save his life and help him to triumph in aerial combat. He knew to aim ahead of his target and, whether squirrel or enemy aeroplane, let it fly right into the bullets he had fired.

Bishop's First Aerial Victory
In the late afternoon of Sunday, 25 March 1917, C Flight went out on a defensive patrol, flying over the city of Arras, along the Scarpe river, and south to the village of St. Leger. Good weather that day allowed Royal Flying Corps bombing, reconnaissance and artillery observation aircraft to be out in force. With fifty-five German aircraft 'observed opposite the [British] First Army' sector,[43] there was plenty of work for the scout squadrons. And,

according to the initial report, 'two hostile machines were brought down near Mercatel, on our side of the lines, by Lieutenants [Alan] Binnie and [Frank] Bower, both of 60 Squadron'. [44]

Billy Bishop, flying in Nieuport 17 A.306, another older aeroplane,[45] also claimed a victory in that aerial combat. But he had been forced down just within British forward lines, where he was stranded for two days. Billy used his time prudently and found a pencil and paper to jot down details of his first aerial combat in a single-seat scout. Thus, his combat report was filed later than the others.

Albatros D.IIIs were armed with twin Spandau machine guns synchronized to fire through the propeller arc. Gun sights provided reasonable accuracy.
(Greg VanWyngarden)

After reading it, Major Scott penned in at the bottom of Billy's report: 'It seems that this HA [hostile aeroplane] was wrongly allotted to Lieutenant Bower.'[46] Billy's report was forwarded to 13th Wing headquarters, where, after reviewing all of the reports, 'the wing commander allowed or disallowed each claim made … '[47] In this case, Billy's claim was accepted over Bower's and he was credited with his first aerial victory.

While at the Front, Billy also wrote a longer account of his first air combat and later mailed it to his mother:

'I am writing this in a dug-out (evacuated by the Germans three days ago) 300 yards behind our new front line. Today, I have had the most exciting adventure of my life.

Four of us were on patrol and three Huns met us. We did battle, as they say. I opened fire on one [German] and another fired on me. I hit my man, I think, for he fell out of control. I dove after him from 8,000 to 600 feet [altitude], firing all the way. When he reached the … latter height, he regained control and crossed the line. The infantry claimed that he crashed there, but it isn't confirmed yet. If it is, it will count as one [aerial victory] for me, but if not, it won't. There was I, [at] 600 feet over No Man's Land. God only knows the number of machine guns which were firing on me. I glided down into a field, [and] made a perfect landing … I was not sure whether I was on the Hun's side of the line or on our side, so I jumped out of the machine and hid in a ditch. Then I saw English soldiers. In ten minutes the Huns were shelling my machine, but we moved it and it was untouched. I am spending the night here with the 106th Battery, RFA …'[48]

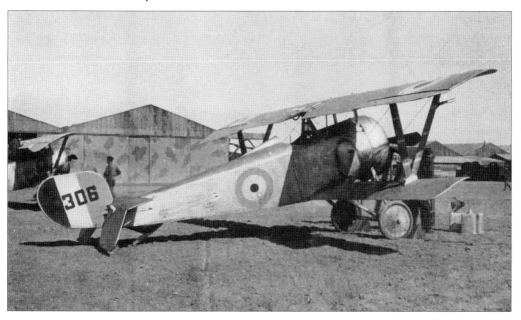

Billy Bishop was credited with his first aerial victory, on 25 March 1917, while flying Nieuport 17 A.306, seen here. (*Cross & Cockade International*)

Billy also wrote about this epic event to his father and to Margaret. Four days later, he concluded his recollection of events in another, longer letter to Margaret; portions of it are quoted below. As happened often, he was not modest in telling her about his achievements:

'At last my adventure is over and opposite my name at HQ is the figure 1, representing one German Albatros Scout. The "Archie [anti-aircraft] people" who saw my fight confirmed it and it goes to my credit … I am now the only person in 60 [Squadron] who has brought down a Hun without help from other machines. The general commanding the RFC [Major-General Hugh Trenchard, CB] sent my CO a telegram congratulating him and me. Then yesterday the [RFC] general second in command [Brigadier-General Higgins] and my colonel [Lieutenant-Colonel George F. Pretyman, commander of the 13th Wing] came over and congratulated me. It appears that the great thing I did was the death dive of 7,000 feet with my engine full on. It has never been done before in a Nieuport and they didn't think [the aeroplane] would stand the strain. I'm glad I didn't know that …

'All [the following] day the battle went on and, in spite of it all, the Hun evidently found time to search for my machine. I had to keep moving it. No sign of the tender [small lorry] coming to my relief … I tried to start the engine myself and succeeded, but alas, a bit of mud flew up and smashed my propeller. So I started to walk back [through] three miles of seething mud and met some "Archie people". They loaned me a Ford car and I left at 6:00 pm to try and get back [to the aerodrome], little knowing that it is only possible to get through on one road, all the rest being blown

Billy Bishop had many encounters with Albatros D.III aeroplanes, with hallmark V-struts. This particular aircraft is from Jasta 30, with which 60 Squadron fought on numerous occasions. (Greg VanWyngarden)

up. I returned at 6:00 [the following] morning … Major [Scott] gave me a great reception.

'I don't think I told you that in the (temporary) absence of Captain [Keith] Caldwell, I have been in command of C Flight for the last two weeks.

'P.S. My machine is full of bullet holes, I learn now.'[49]

No one questions that Billy Bishop was a daring and courageous pilot, but embellishments seen in this letter (and other writings) came back to harm his reputation decades later. To clarify a point, he was not 'the only person' in 60 Squadron to shoot down a German aeroplane 'without help from other machines'; the unit had an impressive record of aerial victories long before his arrival, as recorded in Major Scott's history of the unit. And, while Billy made skilful aerial manoeuvres in his Nieuport 17, that aeroplane's previously noted history of wing failures suggests that his claim of making a 'death dive of 7,000 feet with [the] engine full on' most likely would have had fatal consequences.

On the other hand, when Billy was temporarily put in charge of C Flight, he gained the leadership experience needed to fulfil his hope of becoming a flight commander. The appointment came through within a fortnight, as will be seen in the following chapter.

During air operations on Sunday, 25 March 1917, RFC pilots claimed a total of five aircraft as 'brought down' and 'driven down'.[50] In hopes of determining corresponding German losses, that day's entry in the weekly intelligence summary – *Nachrichtenblatt der Luftstreitkräfte* – was reviewed, but it reported only one casualty: fighter unit Jagdstaffel 6 pilot Leutnant Friedrich Mallinckrodt, who shot down a British aeroplane over Seraucourt, south west of St. Quentin, and also suffered an arm wound.[52] However, Mallinckrodt[51] was too far away from 60 Squadron's operational area and, as the German pilot returned to his airfield, he could not have been Billy Bishop's victim.

A more complete German casualty list[53] shows that a Gefreiter [Lance Corporal] Berkling of Jasta 22 was wounded that day, but offers no details. Finally, a listing of German aircraft captured by British forces includes two Albatros D.III aeroplanes initially claimed by Lieutenants Binnie and Bower of 60 Squadron and given the captured identification numbers G 15 and G 16.[54] The latter aeroplane was the subject of the victory claim credited to Billy Bishop by his wing commander, Lieutenant-Colonel Pretyman, but, while both German pilots were reportedly taken prisoner,[55] neither man is named in RFC records. Hence, it is not possible to provide a name for Billy's first confirmed downed opponent.

Bishop's Second Aerial Victory

The rest of the coming week produced times of sadness and triumph. On Wednesday, the 28th, the notorious Nieuport wing failure took its toll on 60 Squadron when twenty-four-year-old Lieutenant Challoner M.H.M. Caffyn was killed during a practice flight in Nieuport Scout A.6673; according to the casualty report: 'Both top and bottom [right wings] … were seen to collapse at about 2,500 ft. and the machine came down in a spinning nosedive at 10:20 am.'[56] Following that sad event, there was no more loose talk at Filescamp Farm about full-speed 'death dives' in Nieuport Scouts.

Over the next three days, Billy lost two comrades in battle while attaining another air combat success. He wrote to Margaret:

'Yesterday [30 March] … I was detailed to lead six machines on an offensive patrol [covering Arras, Vitry and Douai]. Everything went well, we flew very low, as clouds were below us and the ground [was] obscured. Suddenly two Huns popped out of the clouds. I signalled to my [men] … by wobbling the machine and dived at [the German aeroplanes]. They flew away like mad, but I followed and, over my shoulder, I saw the other five [Nieuports] following. Finally I got within firing range and opened fire. At that moment I heard the pop-pop-pop of a machine gun behind me and knew that another Hun was on my tail. I kept on after mine, thinking the remainder of my lot would drive him off. But bullets were piercing my machine within inches of me, and I did a three-quarter loop and evaded him, only to find myself alone.

'It appears [that] a dozen of the best Hun scouts had suddenly appeared and engaged all the rest. Then I saw them miles further [inside] Hunland and went over to help. Oh my God! It was awful. We steadily lost height and a terrific gale was blowing us further into Hunland. We were only 2,000 feet up, miles inland and fighting like fury. Garnett,[57] a dear old soul, was shot down. Bower,[58] a great pal of mine, we couldn't find or see anywhere. We learnt later [that] his machine was shot to bits and he … [was] shot through the stomach with a flaming bullet [incendiary – or tracer – ammunition]. He died at noon today [31 March]. These things we must harden our hearts to. The remaining four of us … fought our way all the way home. When we landed, colonel [Pretyman] came over and congratulated us on going so far and so low (and we certainly didn't … do it on purpose).

'This morning we went out again to escort some other machines. About ten Huns attacked us. I had two fights. [In] the second one I got on a Hun's tail, one of the fast scouts, and shot him down. It was just over the lines and the whole proceeding was confirmed by the "Archie people".[59] So this afternoon again general [Higgins] and colonel [Pretyman] came over to congratulate me. It is marvellous luck – two Huns in one week.'[60]

Billy was correct in his assessment that C Flight had fought with some 'of the best' German combat pilots during the 30 March encounter. *Nachrichtenblatt* and German 6th Army victory lists state that a Nieuport 17 – almost certainly Garnett's[61] – was brought down near Gavrelle, just north of Fampoux, as the fourth victory of Leutnant Kurt Wolff of Jasta 11.[62] The twenty-two-year-old German pilot was a protégé of that unit's leader, newly-promoted Oberleutnant [First-Lieutenant] Manfred Freiherr von Richthofen. Billy Bishop and his flight-mates may even have duelled with 'the Red Baron' himself, who was known to be actively in the air during that time period.

For the 31 March aerial combat, Billy was fortunate in having two witnesses to his victory: an anti-aircraft battery and a member of C Flight. The latter, Second-Lieutenant Lawrence H. Leckie, who was flying behind Billy, confirmed he 'saw the Albatros Scout go down in a spinning nosedive, seemingly out of control'[64] – but neither he nor Billy said they saw the German aeroplane hit the ground. That day's entry in the *Nachrichtenblatt* summary contained no Western Front casualties.[65] In its weekly summary of air operations, the German 6th Army, directly opposite British First and Third Armies, reported only that a Leutnant Botsch, an observer with two-seat unit Flieger-Abteilung (A) 255, had been badly wounded.[66] There was no mention of a single-seat fighter casualty that matched 60 Squadron's encounter with Albatros Scouts. On the basis of the anti-aircraft battery crew's and Leckie's reports, Wing Commander Pretyman credited Billy Bishop with his second aerial victory.

Adding to that honour, Billy's gained another distinction when his latest air combat triumph was also mentioned in the RFC Communiqué for 31 March:

'Major Scott, squadron commander … destroyed a hostile machine south east of Arras. Captain Black, also of 60 Squadron, assisted Major Scott. A second hostile aeroplane was destroyed north east of Arras by Lieutenant Bishop …'[67]

Following that official publication, officers at all levels in the Royal Flying Corps read about Billy Bishop's early air combat success.

There would be many more achievements to come.

CHAPTER SIX

Bloody April

'I have all the luck in this squadron. Poor old Smart, a pal of mine,
was killed today, and two others, as well. It is horrible.'
– William A. Bishop[1]

It was the best of times for the German Luftstreitkräfte, which claimed a total of almost 300 British aircraft shot down or forced to land by German airmen within thirty days.[2] It was the worst of times for Britain's air forces, which, in the same period, lost one third of their airmen then at the Western Front: 316 pilots and observers out of '912 aircrew in fifty squadrons'.[3] It was the month that became known in European military aviation history as 'Bloody April'.[4]

As part of the Allies' spring 1917 offensive, the British military establishment committed to an operational line that ran from eight miles south of Arras to seven miles north of the city. This part of the operation was carried out by fourteen divisions of the British First and Third Armies,[5] which initially fielded twenty-five squadrons, 'representing 365 … aeroplanes, of which a third were single-seat fighters. Opposed to these two British armies was the German 6th Army with an air strength of eighteen [two-seat] reconnaissance and artillery [-ranging] flights, five [single-seat] fighter flights and seven [two-seat] protection flights, comprising a total of 195 aeroplanes, nearly one half of which were equipped for fighting'.[6] While the aircraft numbers on both sides were nearly equal, at the same time German airmen enjoyed certain advantages, as noted in the official World War I British aviation historical account:

'On the five days from 4 to 8 April, seventy-five British aeroplanes fell in action with a loss in flying personnel of 105 (nineteen killed, thirteen wounded, and seventy-three missing). In addition, there was an abnormally high number of flying accidents … due in part to insufficiency of training … and in part to the strain imposed on pilots who had to meet in the air an enemy equipped, with few exceptions, with superior fighting aeroplanes.'[7]

Billy Bishop's first letter in April hinted at what was to come:

'Just a short note … I am still in command of C Flight and we are being worked to death. Yesterday morning I led the escort of six F.E.s [two-seat reconnaissance and bombing aircraft] and had rather an exciting time. All the other Nieuports dropped out on account of various engine troubles and I had to plod on all alone. Luckily, no

Huns were about and we got back safely.

'I then went off on my own, looking for a prize, but found none. At 8:15 [am] I returned only to find that I had to go out again at 9:00, and lead a defensive patrol. We chased various Huns, but did battle with none.

'Then today I went on an OP [offensive patrol] and managed to get back safely. We lost a chap named Williams.'[8,9]

Billy may have been looking for Margaret Burden's sympathy in claiming he was 'being worked to death', as on Monday, 2 April, he flew two sorties totalling three hours and twenty minutes' flight time and reported no contact with German aircraft.[10] The only other events noted in the 60 Squadron record book for the day were that Billy became slightly disoriented and had engine trouble, which required him to land at 16 Squadron's aerodrome at Norrent-Fontes,[11] some eighteen miles north of Filescamp Farm.

Perhaps recalling his January meeting with two Military Cross recipients, Captain Frederick Sowrey and Lieutenant Claude Ridley, at this time Billy began raising the possibility of his also earning that award. An example of his growing interest in recognition for performing a 'Big Job' – an extremely hazardous undertaking – is seen in this letter to Margaret:

'Yesterday [Wednesday, 4 April], the weather was bad and all jobs were called off. Today, the Big Job was ordered and off we went to do it, but no luck. The weather was horrible, thick mist and clouds, and, as the job was to shoot down [German tethered observation] balloons, we couldn't even find them, let alone bring them down. So again that [assignment] is postponed. If we get the balloon detailed to us and [come] back safely, we get an MC.

'Poor Townesend (one of my flight, he was at RMC with me, too, as well as an observer in 21 [Squadron]) has failed to return[12] [today]. I do hope he is OK. Hervey, another one of my flight, is lost, I'm afraid, and 21 Squadron lost either two or three machines. The [13th] wing lost five more, so it was rather a bad day.

'Darling, I have heard a very interesting rumour, and it is that I have been recommended for the Military Cross for shooting down those two machines [on 25 and 31 March]. But, of course, that doesn't say I will get it.'[13]

On the face of it, Billy's mention of being recommended for the MC sounds like another daydream. In fact, on 2 April his name and a summary of recent accomplishments were sent for 'favourable notice' to Lieutenant-Colonel George F. Pretyman, commander of the 13th Wing. The recommendation was submitted by 60 Squadron Commanding Officer Major Jack Scott,[14] who may have mentioned it to the hard-charging young Canadian.

A Missed Victory?

Eager to raise his victory score, the following day, 6 April, Billy was out by himself on his second flight of the day, at about 15,000 feet, when he spotted a lone Albatros Scout below him just east of Arras. He dived after it and later reported:

'I fired a burst of fifteen to twenty rounds at 150 yards' range, when the gun stopped. I dived again and opened fire at 100 yards' range. He dived steeply and flattened out 1,000 ft. lower. I opened fire again at fifty to seventy yards' range. He dived steeply, but seemed to have his machine under control. I followed him down to 11,000 ft. and he was still diving when I left him.'[15]

On 6 April 1917, Billy Bishop may have shot down an Albatros D.II, noteworthy by I-struts between the upper and lower wings. (Author's Collection)

Major Scott's only comment on Billy's combat report was 'this fight was not observed by A.A.'[16] and no credit was assigned. However, a German 6th Army air staff report for that day[17] noted that Vizefeldwebel [First-Sergeant] Ludwig Weber of Jagdstaffel 3 was wounded in an air fight. Another source[18] adds that Weber was flying in Albatros D.II 510/16 when he was hit north east of Chérisy and came down near Biache-Saint-Vaast, which is less than ten miles east of 60 Squadron's aerodrome. It is possible that Vzfw Weber was Billy's third (but uncredited) air combat success.

Meanwhile, Second-Lieutenant Hamilton E. Hervey, who was in the patrol attacked on 5 April, had his aircraft shot up in a fight two days later.[19] Indeed, that Saturday, 7 April 1917, was a particularly hard day for 60 Squadron. While Hervey again managed to struggle back to Filescamp Farm in his damaged aeroplane[20], other squadron-mates were not so fortunate that day, as Billy wrote about one of them:

'Today ... four of us went out to shoot down four balloons ... I saw my balloon under me when I was only 6,000 feet up, so I dived on it. At the same time a Hun dived on me and filled my machine with holes. I turned on him and, in a short scrap, shot him down[21]. In the meantime the Huns had pulled the balloon down to the ground, so down I went after it, to a height of fifty feet, and set it on fire. I came back all the way, ten miles, over the trenches at 200 feet. I think I am fairly certain of [receiving] a decoration for it. Tonight the General Commanding RFC [Major-General Hugh Trenchard] wired my CO: "Congratulate Lieutenant Bishop on his fine feat today" ...I have all the luck in this squadron. Poor old Smart, a pal of mine, was killed to-day, and two others, as well. It is horrible.'[22]

The Red Baron Strikes

Billy Bishop did seem to 'have all the luck' on 7 April. Another 60 Squad-ron formation out that day ran into trouble over Arras – it was attacked by a five-plane patrol from Jagdstaf-fel 11 led by newly-promoted Ritt-meister Manfred von Richthofen, known as the Red Baron. The Ger-man ace scored his thirty-seventh victory[23] when he shot down and killed Second-Lieutenant George O. Smart. Somewhat of an 'old-timer' at age thirty-one, Smart was 'original-ly an NCO [non-commissioned of-ficer] pilot who had lately been com-missioned for gallantry in the field.'[24]

Parsival-Sigsfeld 'Drachen' German tethered observation balloon, seen here with the observer's basket suspended below the hydrogen gas-filled 'envelope,' was a type often targeted by Allied fighter aircraft. (National Archive & Records Administration)

As part of the same action in which Richthofen brought down Smart, 2/Lt Charles S. Hall[22] was shot down and killed by Jasta 11 pi-lot Leutnant Karl-Emil Schäfer.[27] Fi-nally, while leading an early evening flight, Captain Maurice B. Knowles[28] was shot down by Leutnant der Reserve [Second-Lieutenant, Reserves] Wilhelm Frankl,[29] who led an Albatros patrol. 2/Lt 'Ham' Hervey, who was brought down and captured the following day, later wrote home and reported that Captain Knowles was alive and un-wounded.[30]

Amid all the bad news on 7 April, Billy Bishop reported that, at about 5 pm, he shot down a German observation balloon and an Albatros D.III south east of Arras. There was no witness to either attack and even Billy was uncertain of his success. His combat report recounts that the Albatros 'dived away steeply' after the attack and it was not seen to hit the ground. Yet, both claims were confirmed as aerial victories by 13th Wing headquarters. At that time, full credit for aerial victories – or 'kills' – was given for enemy aircraft seen to go down 'out of control'. The practice ceased over a year later (on 19 May 1918[31]) when it became clear that 'OOC' claims, as they were called, did not reflect accurate losses of enemy aircraft. Meanwhile, many British Empire airmen received credit for such claims.

As for Billy's two victories that day, it can be surmised that 13th Wing HQ staff felt that evidence of his success was established by his use of incendiary, or 'tracer', bullets in which brightly burning pyrotechnic charges made their trajectories visible to the human eye and also could have ignited the highly flammable hydrogen gas used to inflate German balloons.[32] In that case, 13th Wing – or even 3rd Brigade-level officers who reviewed Billy's report – may have envisioned the effects of 'tracers … seen going into the' Albatros and what happened after tracer 'bullets entered the balloon and black smoke was visible, coming out of it'.[33]

Again, his latest achievements were published in the RFC Communiqué[34] – ever so briefly, but in a publication that was read widely by Billy's contemporaries.

Die fünf erfolgreichsten Flieger der Jagdstaffel Richthofen.

Vizefeldwebel Festner Leutnant Schäfer
Leutnant Frhr. von Richthofen
Rittmeister Frhr. von Richthofen Leutnant Wolff

Rittmeister Manfred Freiherr von Richthofen (centre) and members of Jasta 11 who shot down several 60 Squadron aeroplanes. Seen here in a popular postcard view are, from left: Vzfw Sebastian Festner, Ltn Karl-Emil Schäfer, the Red Baron, Ltn Lothar Freiherr von Richthofen and Ltn Kurt Wolff. (Author's Collection)

On the German side, the *Nachrichtenblatt* did not list balloon casualties and its entry of 'one aeroplane' was the total Western Front air loss reported for 7 April.[35] Likewise, the 6th Army air staff (Kommandeur der Flieger) did not record balloon losses, as the various army corps commands had their own field balloon (Kommandeur der Luftschiffer) and anti-aircraft (Kommandeur der Flak) staffs to report losses and other incidents.

The 6th Army air staff provided further information about the one aircraft lost on 7 April: the two-seat Rumpler (works number) C.I 2600/16, crewed by Gefreiter Schoop (pilot) and Leutnant Hupe (observer) from Flieger-Abteilung (A) 233, failed to return from a patrol over the lines that day, but were not killed.[36] It is possible that Billy misidentified his opponent, a not uncommon occurrence – i.e., that he shot down a Rumpler and not the single-seat Albatros mentioned in his combat report. Otherwise, historians are unable to identify the German aeroplane that opposed him in this action.

Easter Losses

The weather was 'fine, but cloudy'[37] on Easter morning, 8 April 1917, when Major Jack Scott led five B Flight Nieuports (and included Billy Bishop) on an offensive patrol to the frontlines.[38] Scott and his men engaged nine German aircraft,[39] among which were Albatros D.IIIs from Jagdstaffel 11. Scott's patrol lost two pilots in the ensuing fight: Major J. Adelard A. Milot,[40] formerly of the 1st Central Ontario Regiment[41] and a newcomer to aerial combat,[42] and 'Ham' Hervey, who had been sent down again.[43] Milot was shot down[44] by Vizefeldwebel Sebastian Festner,[45] whose aeroplane – Albatros D.III '223/16'[46] [sic] – became disabled and was forced to land within German lines.[47] Billy reported that he pursued an Albatros Scout that 'flew away eastwards after I had fired forty rounds at him. Tracers hit his machine in [the] fuselage and [wings] …'[48] Such damage was consistent with Jasta 11 leader Manfred von Richthofen's after-action statement about the left wing of Festner's Albatros being 'torn to pieces and diminished by more than one third of its surface …'[49] Or Richthofen may have recalled his own experience in January, when a lower wing broke on his Albatros D.III,[50] and thought that Festner's aeroplane had the same weakness.

After the fight, Billy earned praise from his CO, who noted on the Canadian's combat report: 'It will be observed that this officer engaged five HA single-handed at one period during this patrol.'[51]

Billy Bishop was given a day's use of this Crossley car as a small 'reward' for his successes on 8 April 1917. (Stewart K. Taylor)

Also worthy of note is Billy's remaining calm and counting the number of bullets he fired. As noted above, after he fired forty rounds at the two-seater, he expended the rest of his ninety-seven-round drum at the Albatros Scout he sent down. [52]While his Lewis gun was a fully-automatic machine gun, Billy Bishop and many other flyers used automatic weapons artfully and counted their shots with trigger pulls. They knew when they had enough ammunition for a long engagement or whether it was time to change the drum, as Billy did while he continued to pursue the retreating Albatros.

Billy wrote to his mother about the post-combat rewards he received:

> 'I had to come home then, as my ammunition was used up. In the afternoon, (censored[53]) came over and congratulated me … and told me if everyone did as well as I have, we would win the war, so I know a decoration is on the way. The colonel [George Pretyman, commander of 13th Wing] told me to take a day off and my CO gave me [the use of] his touring car and I spent yesterday and today visiting other squadrons and seeing pals …'[54]

In a briefer message the same day to Margaret, however, he concluded by reinforcing his greatest source of inner strength: 'It must be your prayers, dearest. My life seems to be charmed. I have remained untouched [while] in the most awful circumstances.' [55]

The 13th Wing commander credited a destroyed two-seater to Major Scott, and a destroyed two-seater and two Albatros fighters sent down out of control to Billy; hence, one victory for Scott and three for Bishop.[56] The same information was reported in the RFC Communiqué.[57]

According to the *Nachrichtenblatt* daily listing, there were no Western Front German air casualties on 8 April.[58] Yet, the German 6th Army air staff, which did not record the damage to Vzfw Festner's aeroplane (even though Richthofen filed a report on it), reported that twenty-victory fighter ace Leutnant der Reserve Wilhelm Frankl[59] of Jagdstaffel 4 – a recipient of Prussia's highest bravery award, the Orden Pour le Mérite[60] – fell in aerial combat over Vitry that day.[61] But Frankl was not one of Bishop's victims.[62] Another German fighter pilot killed on 8 April and not mentioned at the time was Ltn.d.Res Roland Nauck of Jasta 6, who was shot down by a French pilot.[63] Thus, while Scott's and Bishop's victory credits remained on record, due to the RFC enemy air casualty recording system then in effect, some of their opponents must have either slipped away or died of their wounds a day or so after the combats that took place between Douai and Flesquières. In the latter event, it is not possible to link their losses to any Allied pilots.

The Bigger Picture

Victory counts became important in the news and a propaganda contest waged between the Allies and the Central Powers, as each side sought to influence world opinion in its favour. An example of such 'image shaping' – and an explication of the British victory claims system – was seen in an early April 1917 *Times* article headlined 'The Struggle for Air Supremacy', which stated in part:

> 'Only since the beginning of the Battle of the Somme have the monthly losses of

APRIL 12, 1917.

FLIGHT

AERIAL SUPREMACY

DAWN?

337

K 2

Although German aerial supremacy was acknowledged during 'Bloody April,' British resolve ultimately to prevail was symbolized by this editorial cartoon in the 12 April 1917 issue of *Flight* magazine. (Courtesy of *Flight International*)

aeroplanes on the Western Front exceeded those which were officially recorded in March [1917] … Last month the losses numbered 262, made up as follows: British (acknowledged by general headquarters in France), 58; French (on the assumption that the German reports are trustworthy), 71; German (based on the British and French daily communiqués), 133.

'British airmen accounted for 84 machines and these were officially classified as follows: Destroyed, 14; driven down, damaged, 34, and out of control, 11; brought down, 22; fell in our lines, 3. Of the 58 British machines, eight were brought down in air fights or by anti-aircraft guns, and 50 were returned as "missing" …

'German main headquarters, for the first time, acknowledged [air] losses in its daily reports. But the admissions were obviously only intended to magnify their successes, and cannot be taken seriously …'[64]

The Red Baron Again

That battle of words continued for the remainder of World War I. Meanwhile, the latest round of 60 Squadron casualties must have put intense pressure on Billy, as evidenced in what he wrote to Margaret:

'We are having the most awful time. Yesterday, [14 April, Alan] Binnie, a friend of mine, and three others were shot down[65], and today four [members] of my flight went down in a scrap. I'll pay a few [Germans] off for this, I swear I will. The [men lost] were such good people and one was at RMC with me, he always flew on my left, and one was such a nice kid, just out [from training], and really a very promising pilot.'[66]

In the letter above, Billy seemed to be so distraught that the four losses from another flight became magnified to include the same number of losses that day from his own C Flight, including an unidentified Royal Military College alumnus. To clarify a point: Major Scott later wrote that A Flight – not C Flight – suffered four casualties that day.[67]

German records show that Jasta 11, led by Rittmeister von Richthofen, ripped through A Flight on 14 April. As most Western Front air combats took place over German lines, on-the-ground witnesses and attendant 'souveniring' of downed Allied aircraft contributed to the accuracy of Luftstreitkräfte air combat claims. Hence, it is nearly certain that Manfred von Richthofen shot down 60 Squadron's Lieutenant W.O. Russell for his forty-fourth victory, his younger brother Lothar downed Lieutenant Binnie for his sixth, Vizefeldwebel Sebastian Festner shot down Second-Lieutenant L.C. Chapman for his eleventh, and Leutnant Kurt Wolff brought down Second-Lieutenant J.H. Cock for his fourteenth victory. [68]

'Low clouds and rain all day'[69] curtailed flying on Sunday, 15 April. The official Royal Air Force history noted that, despite similar weather on 16 April, 60 Squadron incurred further high losses:

'The offensive formation of 60 Squadron … consisting of six Nieuports, had met with severe fighting on its outward journey. As the formation crossed the lines near Monchy, the [flight] leader saw a corps aeroplane to the north [being] attacked by four German fighters and went to help … The German pilots turned to meet the Nieuports and shot four of them down with a loss of one aeroplane to themselves.'[70]

Billy Bishop, who had flown his regular patrols and volunteered for additional flights, was not scheduled to go out with C Flight on that disastrous 16 April patrol. Major Scott's squadron history records that the only survivor of the patrol was Lieutenant Graham Young.[71] Commenting on his squadron's high casualty rate, Scott later wrote that:

'[In] three days, ten out of eighteen pilots were lost, and had to be replaced from England by officers who had never flown this particular type of machine … Our new machines were collected from Paris and the chance of a trip to fly one back was eagerly looked forward to by every pilot. Some of these new machines were not well built, and began – to add to our troubles – to break up in the air … The reason for these accidents was that badly seasoned wood was … used by the French manufacturers, who also allowed a lot of little screws to be inserted in the main spars, thus weakening them considerably. [RFC] HQ were informed and the matter was put right.' [72]

Nieuport 23s Arrive

The new aircraft, designated Nieuport Type 23, were intended to be a structurally-improved version of the Nieuport 17 with which Billy Bishop attained his first seven victories and possible success in the uncredited fight on 6 April 1917. Once the issue of seasoned wood was resolved, the '23' performed better than the '17'. As an extensive volume on French aircraft stated: 'While some [Type 23] aircraft retained the standard 110-hp Le Rhône 9Ja engine, many Nieuport 23s were fitted with a 120-hp Le Rhône 9Jb.' [73] A noted World War I British aviation history expert, the late Mike O'Connor, added:

'Due to a different synchronisation system, the French had been obliged to mount the [belt-fed Vickers machine gun] slightly offset to the right. As the RFC … had removed the Vickers from their Nieuports and replaced it with the over-wing Lewis [machine gun], there was no real way of distinguishing [the Type 23] from the Type 17 …' [74]

For the next few days the weather worsened. It was characterised as 'Rain all day, and very little work was possible.'[75] Billy wrote to Margaret:

In his Nieuport 23, Billy Bishop demonstrated how he pulled his Lewis machine gun down along the Foster mounting rail to fire upwards as he flew beneath German aircraft. (Greg VanWyngarden)

'Thank the Lord for another "dud" day. I feel absolutely played out from flying too much, and this spell of dud weather has been a godsend … I have a beautiful new machine with a glorious new 120hp engine. It … is painted silver and [is] very pretty, not a spot of dirt on it. I have spent most of the day fussing around it. Tomorrow, if the weather is fine, it must carry me through a nasty experience. I have been detailed to do in another balloon. I hope I succeed, but I wish it didn't have to be done, [as] it is too nerve-wracking …

'Ball [who has received] the DSO (three times), MC (twice) and several other things, is coming over to see me, I believe tonight. He is a little fire-eater and absolutely one of the best [fighter pilots] in the world.'[76]

Again, no further information has come to light about Billy's meeting with Albert Ball, a thirty-one-victory ace who was heading back to the Front for a new assignment – this time with 56 Squadron, a unit that attained legendary status. Surely trying to forget 60

Nieuport 17 A.200 of 60 Squadron fitted with a *cône de pénétration* in an effort to streamline the aeroplane. At one point Albert Ball flew this aeroplane while with the unit. (*Cross & Cockade International*)

Squadron's aerial blood baths on 14 and 16 April, Billy mentioned to his mother only his own recent work and success:

'I had an exciting scrap with a Hun two-seater yesterday [20 April], all alone, the two of us above a sheet of white fleecy clouds.[77] I sighted him first and crept up behind and underneath him. I then pulled my gun down so as to fire vertically upwards, and got about twenty feet or more under him without being seen, then I [opened fire]. Oh, there was consternation in the camp. The old Hun [pilot] did the most extraordinary turns and [the observer] opened up on me with two machine guns. I climbed and dived at him, but opened fire too soon. I dived again and missed again. Apparently the Hun observer was firing at a terrific rate, so I turned and dived in close to about fifty feet, firing as I came. The old Hun must have got awful "wind up" [a terrible fright], because he didn't even hit my machine. Then as I passed [over him] I saw him smoke and a moment later fall in a flaming mass.[78] It was a glorious sight and I came home in a jubilant mood ... After seeing one's pals [go down] in flames, this was a great satisfaction. That [one] makes my eighth [victory] ... I am getting known.

'[Later] the mechanics presented me with a scarlet "spinner" ... a round thing that fits on to the nose of the machine in front and revolves with [the propeller]. Nobody uses them unless they have [shot down] six or eight Huns, or are at least an "Ace" ... a man with five Huns to his credit, so I am very proud of mine.'[79]

The 'spinner' (actually, a French-designed *cône de pénétration*) had nothing to do with pilots' scores; it was an attempt to streamline Nieuport aeroplanes. British historian J.M. Bruce noted: 'The RFC seemed to be quick to discard this refinement from its early Nieuports ...'[80] Hence, there are no known photographs of Billy Bishop using the device on any Nieuport he flew.

Perhaps to highlight Billy's courage, Major Scott wrote at the bottom of the combat report: 'Leutenant Bishop went out by himself on this occasion.'[81] Billy's roving commission status was also indicated after other such 'lone wolf' patrols.

As 60 Squadron had only one non-fatal injury – a crash by Lieutenant F.L. Atkinson[82] – the day was considered to be rather good. Billy's victory over the two-seater was reported in the RFC Communiqué,[83] but victim identifications are untraceable due to the 'blended' German casualty figures that follow. The *Nachrichtenblatt* summary for 20 April reported 'one combat flyer severely wounded'[84] with no further details. The generally more candid 6th Army air staff summary for the week listed, with no personal identification, only numerical losses in two categories: 'Shot down in aerial combat: four fighter pilots [and] two

Billy Bishop's eighth aerial victory was most likely an Aviatik C.I, one of several prominent two-seaters fitted with a 'chimney' exhaust pipe. It was easily confused with similarly equipped German aeroplanes. (Greg VanWyngarden)

artillery-ranging crews/Not returned: three [two-seat] reconnaissance aeroplanes.'[85] In any case, Billy was credited with his eighth aerial victory, which very likely was an Aviatik C-type.

Victories 9, 10 and 11

In the last full week of April, Billy Bishop was so tired and yet so excited by the flurry of air combat activity that it must have been difficult for him to keep it all straight in his mind. Consequently, his letter to Margaret was somewhat jumbled:

'Forgive me for not writing you for three days, but they have been one awful rush. One day I did seven hours over the lines. I don't know if I told you about my ninth and tenth Hun[s] … It was very interesting, short and sweet. [On 22 April] four Huns attacked … Major [Scott],[86] and I went to his assistance, fired at one and he went down. Then I got another fat one in … my sights, so I simply had to shoot him and down he went. Then the day before – oh, I must tell you about the rest of that day first of all.

'In the afternoon I was alone and had no less than four fights, during which I had no luck at all. In one case I had a Hun cold, but my gun jammed. Then the day before yesterday [23 April], I had three fights. I made one two-seater land[87] and then I fired at him on the ground. In the other scrap, I surprised the Hun and sent him down to earth, where I saw him crash [half a mile north of Lorches, west of Denain].'[88]

Billy Bishop's 22 April action against German aeroplanes attacking Major Scott was reported in the RFC Communiqué[89] and he was credited with his ninth victory. This triumph was also within the week of 20 to 26 April, when, as mentioned above, the 6th Army air staff withheld information on their own casualties. Consequently, identification of the German pilot or his unit cannot be made with certainty.

Billy's tenth and eleventh victories – a two-seater and an Albatros Scout on 23 April – were officially credited to his growing victory score, as reported in the RFC Communiqué[90] and, in 1931, mentioned in the official RAF history:

'As a contrast to the mass fighting, Captain Albert Ball of 56 Squadron, and Captain W.A. Bishop of 60 Squadron, flew alone on roving commissions and had successful encounters …

'Captain Bishop, in a Nieuport, forced down a two-seater near Vitry and kept up his attack after the enemy aeroplane had landed. He climbed again and, at 6,000 feet, found another Nieuport under attack by three Albatros fighters. He took one of the enemy pilots by surprise, put in a burst [of machine-gun fire] at close range, and watched the Albatros spin down and crash.'[91]

Despite 6th Army air staff's obscuration of losses that week, a lower level of command reported a casualty that closely matched the circumstances of Billy's tenth victory. The war diary of the two-seater unit Flieger-Abteilung (A) 211 recorded that 'the crew of Ltn.d.Res Möbius and Ltn.d.Res Goldammer … were over enemy territory during artillery-ranging

Although an older fighter aeroplane, the Halberstadt D.II had its virtues. As British ace J.T.B. McCudden wrote: 'I have never … seen a machine, under control, dive so steeply and for so long.' (Greg VanWyngarden)

when they were shot down by a Sopwith. Ltn Möbius, even though he was lightly wounded, brought [his] burning aeroplane down near Évin-Malmaison, within his own territory, where it burned completely and exploded.'[92] Sopwith Pups and Nieuport Scouts were frequently mistaken for each other. Further, the two-seater's crash site was about eight miles north of Vitry-en-Artois, where Billy began his attack; that reasonable distance makes it likely that such an air combat could have occurred. Möbius and Goldammer lived to fight another day, but their aeroplane was destroyed.

Victories 12, 13 and 14
Billy Bishop's eleventh victory was attained during the fourth of six patrols[93] he flew on 23 April. He also went up on each of the next four days, during which time 60 Squadron sustained three casualties: Second-Lieutenants R.B. Clarke[94] on the 24th, N.P. Henderson[95] on the 26th and F. Stedman[96] the following day. On the 27th, however, Billy scored again and, as usual, he shared with Margaret his thoughts about that early morning patrol:

> 'At nights sometimes I can't sleep from the excitement or from the incessant noise of the guns, and I lie there and think of you. I sometimes wonder if you will approve of the bloodthirsty strain that has appeared in me these last few weeks. I simply can't help it. I detest the Huns, [who] … have done in so many of my best friends. They are cowards, too. It is impossible to make them stand up and fight, unless they are three to one, at least.
>
> 'This morning I shot down another balloon in flames and I think I killed the two [observers] in the basket. It was great fun.
>
> 'Yesterday [26 April] General Trenchard had lunch here. He was awfully nice and

said some things I will rather treasure.

'I spent yesterday afternoon flying about, seeing people. I went over to see old Jack Leach from Toronto, and [Albert] Ball. Ball got his 34th Hun yesterday…'[97]

Major Scott must have thought that Billy's flight on Friday, 27 April was particularly audacious, as he added this notation to the combat report: 'Lieutenant Bishop went over the lines in the clouds to surprise this balloon.'[98] Billy's second balloon victory (and twelfth, overall), was reported in the RFC Communiqué.[99] However, relevant German Feld-Luftschiffer [field balloon] archival material, which might have identified names of balloon crew casualties and their units, has not been found.

Billy Bishop flew two combat patrols the following day, 28 April, both without success. Sunday, the 29th, however, was a big day for him. He was notified of his appointment to flight commander, effective 8 April, and 'while so employed', he held the rank of temporary captain.[100] Late that morning, he also scored his thirteenth victory, which he described in a letter to Margaret:

'At last I have got my captaincy … thank God for small mercies.

'Yesterday I had three merry aerial combats and sent one merry Hun [down] in flames to his merry grave. This morning I had my record trip. I went out leading my flight, and saw a big Hun under me. I dived at him and failed to hit him. Then I attacked two Huns from underneath, but my gun jammed, and I had to come back to the aerodrome. I went out again, alone, and had seven more fights. In the course of which I forced two Huns to land and made another one crash. It was exciting, I can tell you, better than rabbit shooting. At one time I was in the middle of eight dirty Huns.

'Then, this afternoon, the CO and I went out and got mixed up with four really good Huns. We chased them away, but – oh heavens – they did shoot well. Seven bullets went through my machine [to] within six inches of me, and one within an inch. But, still, a miss is as good as a mile, isn't it?'[101]

Almost certainly, the crew of Billy's thirteenth victory were Leutnants Bruno Kittel (pilot) and Hermann Waldschmidt (observer) in a Bavarian Flieger-Abteilung 48 two-seater. The 6th Army air staff reported their deaths 'in aerial combat over Baralle' on 29 April[102] and a report from the air group staff Gruppenführer der Flieger 4 confirmed that the same crew went down at 10:55 am[103] (German Time, an hour ahead of British Time). According to Billy's combat report,[104] the German aeroplane 'burst into flames' at 11:55 am (British Time), east of Épinoy, less than five miles west of Baralle.

But Billy, who was escorting a photo-reconnaissance flight from 11 Squadron, broke away[105] and claimed a single-seat fighter in that fight: 'I dived at him from the sun side, opening fire at 150 yards. I fired in bursts of threes and after about twelve shots he went down in a spin … At about 11,000 feet he burst into flames.'[106] To count this Fl.-Abt 48b aeroplane as Billy's 13th air combat triumph requires accepting that the Canadian erred in his combat report. In this author's view, the time and location matches allow for a margin of error in mis-identifying a two-seat reconnaissance aeroplane as a single-seater during

Billy Bishop flew directly beneath his two-seater targets to keep from being hit. He avoided the scenario seen here, where the Albatros C.VII observer had a clear shot at attackers. (Greg VanWyngarden)

the swirl of aerial combat 450 feet away from the target and in an aerial arena two miles above the ground. Further, it is likely that Kittel and Waldschmidt flew in a widely-used two-seat Albatros C.VII, which bears a strong familial resemblance to its smaller single-seat counterpart, as the accompanying in-air photograph shows.

The Bloody End

Billy's fourteenth victory is easier to determine, as he claimed a 'two-seater' escorted by 'five Halberstadt Scouts'[107] south of Lens. German 6th Army air staff reported the loss of Ltn.d.Res August Rodenbeck, an observer from Fl.-Abt (A) 233, in a fight over Oppy, less than five miles south of Lens.[108] There is no record of what happened to the pilot or the aircraft; certainly, the observer's death thwarted the purpose of Rodenbeck's patrol and in that sense was a victory for the RFC pilot who killed him.

Clearly, Billy Bishop was bent on emulating Albert Ball's air war triumphs and enjoying the rewards that came with them. And it must have been gratifying that the same RFC Communiqué that reported Ball's combats of 29 April also noted Billy's success that day[109] and his fourteenth victory the following day; the latter report read:

'Captain Bishop, 60 Squadron, had eight combats during a patrol of two hours, and in six of these he engaged two or more enemy machines, and succeeded in bringing one down out of control and two in badly-damaged condition.'[110]

It was Billy's first two-time mention in the same Communiqué and a personally triumphal way to end 'Bloody April'. Despite 60 Squadron's high loss rate, Billy's good luck held – he survived and was credited with prevailing over another twelve opponents that month.

He returned to the skies of northern France the next month, eager to achieve more.

CHAPTER SEVEN

Transformations

'You mustn't worry about me. I know the fighting game well and am
successful because I fight with my head all together.'
– William A. Bishop[1]

Fine flying weather in the closing days of April 1917[2] ushered in changes in warfare over
the Western Front. On Tuesday, 1 May,[3] Luftstreitkräfte command staff members were so
confident of their aerial dominance that their most successful fighter pilot, Rittmeister
Manfred Freiherr von Richthofen, was able to return to Germany to rest and to be honoured by Kaiser Wilhelm II. In the fifty-two-victory ace's absence, his younger brother,
Lothar,[4] commanded Jagdstaffel 11 and maintained the family reputation.

Despite German optimism, Royal Air Force historian H.A. Jones observed that the
senior Richthofen brother's departure:

'... coincided with a slackening of the German [air] effort. The fighting formations
which he led, and others on the Arras Front which were closely associated with
him, had had long experience on … [the Albatros fighter] aeroplane which was still
supreme, and their practice had had opportunity to flower, during the Arras battle
… It was, perhaps, asking too much of human nature that the same pilots should
go on with their fighting spirit unimpaired. Many of them must have been tired in
body and mind.' [5]

As for British airmen, Jones pointed out:

'The pilots and observers of the Royal Flying Corps had … more cause to be tired,
for they had fought no less strenuously and had suffered severe casualties. But …
they had struggled on, throughout April … They had stood up to the [Germans] …
no matter what the odds. They were, therefore, immediately ready to profit from any
reaction, no matter how slight, in the fighting spirit of the German pilots. They had,
also, old scores to pay off …'[6]

15th and 16th Victories
Having endured 'Bloody April' and added to his personal aerial victory score, Billy Bishop
seemed to be in fine spirits and ready for the battles to come. On Wednesday, 2 May, in the
middle of a hectic day, he wrote to Margaret Burden:

'I have done four hours [of] flying already today and am now standing by for another show. This morning eleven of us went out, and I managed to get separated in a scrap which took place. During the return trip I was fighting all the time and, to my intense joy, [shot] two big fat Huns down…

'In two weeks I should be going to England on leave … It will be wonderful to have that feeling that there is really a good chance of living for a few days.'[7]

Expanding on Billy's letter, his first victories for the month were a pair of two-seaters operating near a railway switch line that was part of a German defensive system west of Cambrai. In his combat report Billy stated that at about 10:10 am:

'I saw five HA [hostile aeroplanes] at about 6,000 feet doing artillery observation [work]. I manoeuvred to catch one party of three when [it was] just west of the Dro-

Billy Bishop (standing) outside a temporary wooden building at Filescamp Farm. Seated from left are: Capt W.E. Molesworth, Lt G. Young and Capt K.L. Caldwell. (Dan McCaffery)

court-Quéant [railway switch] line, as that was the nearest they were coming to our [battle] lines. I attacked the rear one and, after [I fired] one burst of fifteen rounds, he fell out of control and crashed … just east of the Drocourt-Quéant line. While I was watching him another two-seater came up under me and opened fire. I [then] attacked him, firing about forty rounds. He fell out of control and I followed him [for] 1,500 feet, finishing my drum. He was in a spinning nosedive and my shots could be seen entering all around the pilot's and observer's seats …'[8]

The German 6th Army air staff produced an exceptionally detailed listing of its air losses for the month of May, making it possible to suggest two reconnaissance aircraft that Billy Bishop may well have shot down. One was DFW C.V 5866/16 from Flieger-Abteilung 26, which was recorded as having 'not returned from a flight over the lines' on 2 May.[9] The German two-seater reportedly came down within British lines near Bullecourt, less than two miles from Quéant. British troops seized the wreckage, which was later assigned the captured identification number G 31. The aeroplane was reported to have been brought down by ground machine-gun fire;[10] more likely, Billy sent it down and ground gunners

More DFW C.Vs were built by Deutsche Flugzeugwerke and its licensees than any other German two-seater in the war. Rugged and well-armed, it was a formidable opponent in combat. (Dr. Volker Koos)

also fired at it. The pilot, Gefreiter [Lance-Corporal] Karl Prill, was taken prisoner and the observer, Leutnant der Reserve Paul Reichel, was dead.[11] Further, that day's RFC Communiqué added that Billy 'destroyed one of his opponents, while a second was driven down completely out of control and a third was forced to land in a field'.[12] The third aircraft may have been the Fl.-Abt 26 DFW C.V, thereby strengthening Billy's claim to sending it down. The other possible Bishop victim that day was DFW C.V 5178/16 from the two-seat protection unit Schutzstaffel 7. It was listed as having been 'shot down near Gavrelle',[13] about nine miles north where the other two-seater went down, but within German lines. The pilot, Vizefeldwebel [First-Sergeant] Seifert was 'severely wounded' and the aerial gunner, Unteroffizier [Corporal] Wilhelm Niess, was killed. [14]

17th, 18th and 19th Victories

The flurry of combat activities in the first week of May must have made it difficult for Billy to sort out his various air fights. He wrote similar letters to his sister Louise and to Margaret on Saturday, 5 May; the one to Louise contained more information – evidencing his excitement – and is quoted here:

'I have been awfully lucky lately, having got several Huns this week, four by myself, and one with [Lieutenant William] Fry yesterday [4 May]. It was rather interesting. On Wednesday [2 May], I fell into a trap they laid for me by doing what we call cunning battle. I ... shot down two out of five of them ...

'The day before [1 May] I had a scrap with and [shot] one down, and the day before that [30 April], I caught one lonely soul ... over Hunland and so sent him forthwith spinning earthward in flames ...[On another matter] I have been granted permission to paint the nose of my machine royal blue. It is rather pretty, as the rest of the machine is silver – and it is such a pretty little machine anyway.'[15]

Nine-victory ace and early Pour le Mérite recipient Ltn Gustav Leffers of Jasta 1 was among German pilots who flew captured Allied aircraft in combat. He attained his seventh victory in this Nieuport 16 Scout. (Greg VanWyngarden)

Billy Bishop did not need special permission to have the engine cowl of his Nieuport 23 painted blue. Rather, in the normal scheme of things, it was decorated in the colour then assigned to aeroplanes flown by 60 Squadron's C Flight.[16] Billy's successes on 30 April and 2 May are discussed above. He was too far away to engage any of the five hostile aircraft he saw on 1 May, as noted in his squadron flight log. [17]

On the early evening of 3 May, an unusual event occurred when five German fighters attacked Billy's patrol along the main road between Arras and Cambrai. The German pilots steered a downward course with the sun at their backs, a favoured position to keep from being spotted until they were close to their adversaries. Billy reported: 'This patrol … was led by a silver [-coloured] Nieuport Scout, apparently Type 17, with black crosses on tail and wings.'[18] Distinguishing various aircraft types in the air was often difficult and, most likely in this case, a German pilot flying a captured aeroplane confused Billy and his comrades. The RFC pilots flew identical-looking aircraft and, in the swirl of aerial combat, when opponents are often seen in silhouette, only the German patrol leader knew which Nieuport was not a target for his men. But his comrades might also have mistaken him for a British Nieuport. Hence, he abruptly broke off the encounter and led his men away.

On the afternoon of 4 May, Billy led a hostile aeroplane patrol toward Douai, looking to attack German aircraft in the area. Just after 1:30 pm, he and Lieutenant Willie Fry dived on a pair of two-seat biplanes, thought to be AEG C.V reconnaissance aircraft,[19] and then concentrated on one of them. Billy reported:

'I fired twenty rounds … and turned off, [with] Lt Fry diving on it and firing. I dived again as [Fry] stopped firing and fired about forty rounds, in the course of which the observer stopped firing. The machine did two turns of a spin and then nosedived to earth, where we saw him crash. I fired a short burst at long range at the second [aeroplane], which flew away and did not return.'[20]

AEG C.IV variations had a long wartime service life as two-seat reconnaissance and bombing aeroplanes, as well as for low-altitude close air support missions.
(Greg VanWyngarden)

Fry added: 'I dived with Captain Bishop and fired a long burst at close range at the same time as him. The HA spun and crashed west of Brebières.'[21] The RFC Communiqué reported simply that both pilots 'dived at one of two German aeroplanes and destroyed it'.[22] Some listings recorded this downing as a full victory each for Billy Bishop and Willie Fry,[23] but, as was clarified later in the month, each pilot received a one-half victory credit to his score for his role in bringing down this German aeroplane.

That recognition was based on the two eye-witness accounts of the two-seater's destruction; however, no comparable aircraft loss was recorded by the German 6th Army air staff. The closest such incident that day was at Flesquières, some twelve miles south-south east of Brebières, where a two-seater from the nearby German 2nd Army Sector went down. Both crewmen – Ltns.d.Res Kurt Leidreiter, pilot, and Kurt Böttcher, observer, of Fl.-Abt. (A) 210 – were killed.[24] Leidreiter and Böttcher may have been Bishop's and Fry's victims, as their crash site was geographically close enough to be considered.

In an odd and unexplained occurrence, the weekly *Nachrichtenblatt* air intelligence summary published no activity accounts from 4 to 8 May.[25] That information deficiency adversely affects attempts to match possible German casualties for that five-day period – aside from those noted in the various army air staff reports.

Billy Bishop flew two patrols on Saturday, 5 May, but could not get close enough to any German aircraft that he spotted. He did not fly the following day, but on the following Monday, in 'fine, but cloudy' weather,[26] Billy flew three times. He went up at 7:20 am for a forty-minute look-around, but saw nothing and returned to his aerodrome. Some two hours later he was flying alone north west of Douai when he spotted a lone Albatros fighter, probably out 'hunting', as he was. Billy executed a classic hawk-like attack, as noted in his combat report:

'I dived from [out of] the sun at one EA going north and, with the speed from my dive, I overtook him. Flying underneath, I pulled my gun down and opened fire from fifteen yards' range, firing twenty rounds. All of which entered his fuselage. He fell in a spin and smoke was coming from the machine.'[27]

Nieuport 23 B.1597 of 60 Squadron was declared 'lost in action' on 6 May 1917. It is seen here in German captivity. The pilot, Lt G.D. Hunter, was unwounded and taken prisoner. (Greg VanWyngarden)

At 2:00 pm, Billy led C Flight in escorting F.E.2b two-seat fighter-bombers from 11 Squadron. A fight started about an hour later, south of Brebières, and Billy reported:

'While escorting F.E.s, one HA attacked one F.E. and another was flying in towards it. I dived and fired at the last one from long range and it flew away. I then attacked the HA fighting with the F.E. [2]. I fired ten rounds and he turned on me, [whereupon] I dived and held my tracers in front of him. He ran into them and then flew for about 300 yards, seemingly only partly under control.'[28]

Major Scott added to Billy's combat report: 'An observer in 11 Squadron saw a [machine] land under control.'[29] That comment seemed to indicate the German aeroplane, identified as an Albatros D.III fighter, had been forced out of the fight, but was still flyable. The RFC Communiqué reported that Billy 'drove down two German machines out of control'.[30] Consequently, he received credit for two 'OOC' victories, which was appropriate under the RFC criteria then in effect.[31] German 6th Army air staff listed only losing one two-seater that day[32] and no fighter aircraft – but the total lack of *Nachrichtenblatt* activity reports (noted above) left no challenge to Billy's 7 May claims, which in any event, were accepted by 13th Wing, RFC.

Albert Ball Killed

Also on 7 May 1917, Britain's then highest-scoring fighter ace, Captain Albert Ball, died during an encounter with Albatros D.IIIs from Jasta 11. That day's RFC casualty listing cited a message dropped by a German aircraft:

'RFC Captain Ball was brought down in a fight in the air on the 7th of May, 1917, by a pilot who was of the same order [of magnitude] as himself. He was buried at Annoeullin.'[33]

Ball, who was found dead in the wreckage of his S.E.5 biplane, had fought with Jasta 11's acting commanding officer, Leutnant Lothar von Richthofen. It was later learned, however, that the lack of wounds on Ball's body indicated that he died in the crash of his aeroplane and was not killed by the German ace's bullets.[34] It is a fine point, but the Luftstreitkräfte sought propaganda value by insinuating that Ball had fallen under the younger Richthofen's guns. That story made a favourable propaganda link to Rittmeister Manfred von Richthofen, who six months earlier was hailed in Germany for shooting down Major Lanoe G. Hawker, the first airman to receive Britain's highest bravery award, the Victoria Cross.[35] Thus, it was favourably received in the German press that both Richthofen brothers had vanquished significant British flying heroes. Ball had not yet received the VC, but later a posthumous award was made. [36]

News about Albert Ball's status was slow in making its way throughout the RFC. Two days after the ace's last flight the RFC War Diary reported only that Ball 'failed to return from … [a] patrol and no details as to what happened are obtainable'.[37]

Billy on Leave

By the time the ranking RFC ace's death was confirmed, Billy Bishop – to whom Ball had become an idol, as well as chief competitor – was aboard a Channel steamer, bound for England to enjoy some well-deserved rest. Once in London, he went to 52 Portland Place, where Lady St. Helier was always glad to see him. After mixing with the latest round of guests, Billy wrote to Margaret:

'I have just this moment arrived in London. Special leave of fourteen days came through very suddenly and off I came, leaving Arras at noon and arriving here to-night. I am trying to screw up the courage to go into the next room. There was a dinner party here tonight. Princess Marie Louise [of Schleswig-Holstein] is here and about four [couples of] Lord and Lady Somebody.'[38]

Two days later, Billy told Margaret about being joined as a guest at 52 Portland Place by her older brother, Henry, who had just transferred from a Canadian ground unit to the RFC.[39] Hank Burden, as he was known, became a fighter pilot and by war's end had sixteen confirmed aerial victories to his credit.[40] Billy also wrote about having lunch with Sir Frederick Smith, the attorney-general, and dinner with Canadian-born newspaper magnate Lord Beaverbrook (Sir Max Aitken) – all of which he put within the context of his aerial achievements:

'[It] helps having more Huns to your credit than any other Britisher. (I forgot to tell you that now [that Albert] Ball is dead, I head the list of RFC pilots, having fourteen Huns crashed and two balloons – confirmed – sent down in flames.) Did I tell you that I am getting the DSO to wear beside the other [medal, i.e., MC]?'[41]

What seems to be a passing reference to Albert Ball's death belied a deeper respect that Billy had for the ace and one-time member of 60 Squadron. Some months later he wrote a stirring tribute to Ball. In mid-May 1917, however, Billy was focused on his ambition to become 'the' high-scoring British Empire fighter pilot.

Billy must have been told by Major Jack Scott that he had been proposed for the Distinguished Service Order a week earlier and assumed it would come through as a matter of course. Existing documentation proves that Scott knew when Billy's DSO was approved, as the major received this message from 13th Wing: 'Under authority granted by H.M. the King, CinC. awards DSO to Capt W.A. Bishop, MC … General Higgins adds his congratulations.'[42]

Henry John Burden, older brother of Billy Bishop's [then] fiancée Margaret, painted 'Maybe' on the S.E.5a he flew with 56 Squadron. By war's end, he had fifteen confirmed aerial victories and had been awarded the DSO and DFC. (DHH/DND photo RE-19742-1)

It is likely that Billy was similarly informed about the Military Cross. Thus in his deepest thoughts, which he could always express to Margaret, Billy let his love-struck dreams take flight in a letter sent before he returned to the battle front:

'At last my DSO has come or, rather, a letter from the CO, saying I have it. It is rather nice to see Capt. W.A. Bishop, DSO, MC, isn't it? Imagine them giving it to me. Some people have the luck, don't they, and I am the one, I should say. Chiefly lucky in having you, beloved.'[43]

Five days later, Billy wrote to her again, reinforcing his feelings: 'I am leaving in ten minutes … but I must scribble this note to say goodbye to you, beloved, as I feel I am going farther [away] when I go to France.'[44]

Victory No. 14½

After he returned to Filescamp Farm aerodrome in France, Billy raised an interesting historical point about a change in awarding shared aerial victories. Previously, as one history of British World War I air victories pointed out: '… in the vast majority of cases, shared victories involving two or more [British] pilots were credited to each pilot as a whole individual victory …'[45] Accordingly, when Billy and Major Scott combined to bring down a German aeroplane on 8 April, each pilot was awarded a full credit. By that reasoning the claim for one aircraft was inflated to show two victories – until the RFC began awarding a half-victory credit to each participant in a shared victory claim. Such became the case when Billy and Lieutenant Fry claimed a role in shooting down the same aeroplane on 4 May, as Billy mentioned to his parents:

'Well, I am back at it again and really very glad to be back … My total [score of] Huns by the official books is now 14½, which means that I shared one of them with Fry, a pilot here. I got my [latest] one this morning. It was really quite easy as he didn't see me at all. I crept up under him and fired from fifty feet range. Poor devil, he never knew what hit him, but went down in a glorious spin …

'Dad, you mustn't worry about me. I know the fighting game well and am successful because I fight with my head all together …'[46]

To amplify the circumstances of Billy's latest victory: Once again he was flying alone, on Saturday, 26 May, when he spotted a German single-seat fighter at about 9,000 feet over Lens. Billy dived on it, firing his Lewis machine gun and then pulled up into a climb, to again use the speed of a dive to pounce on his opponent. But in the few moments of Billy's climb to higher altitude, the German slipped away.

Billy then rose higher, to over 11,000 feet, while heading east. Just over ten minutes later he saw a six-plane Albatros fighter formation west of Douai, a known centre of German fighter aircraft. Next, he wrote:

'I attacked … the highest and rear [-most] machine of [the] formation …I fired twenty-five rounds from underneath at fifty yards' range with my gun down. The tracers went in his machine under the pilot's seat and the HA fell completely out of control in a spin.'[47]

Billy was credited with another 'OOC' victory, which was noted in the RFC Communiqué.[48] The weekly *Nachrichtenblatt* summary reported for 26 May: 'Three [German] aeroplanes shot down, [and] one has not returned. Additionally, three officers are dead, [and] three officers, three Vizefeldwebels, [and] three aerial machine gunners were wounded.' [49] The 6th Army air staff recorded only one loss that day, a Fl-Abt (A) 258 two-seater that 'crashed without being caused by the enemy',[50] and very likely was an accident. No single-seat aircraft losses were reported.

For all of Billy Bishop's talk about his aspirations – including medals not yet awarded – he was the hardest working pilot in 60 Squadron. The 13th Wing summary of the unit's work as of 26 May 1917[51] (below) shows that he flew more patrols and was credited with more aerial victories than any other pilot then assigned to the unit.

Rank & Name	Date posted to squadron	No. of flights	Machines brought down	Balloons brought down
Capt. Bishop, DSO, MC	7/3/17	53	14½	2
Capt. Caldwell	22/5/17	4	Nil	Nil
Capt. Molesworth	22/5/17	10	1½	2
Lieut. Patterson, MC	1/4/17	5	1	Nil
Lieut. Horn	14/4/17	8	Nil	Nil
Lieut. Rutherford	17/4/17	6	Nil	Nil
Lieut. Fry	22/4/17	21	2½	Nil
Lieut. Sillars	29/4/17	6	Nil	Nil
Lieut. D. Lloyd	29/4/17	6	Nil	Nil
2/Lt. Penny	8/4/17	6	Nil	1
2/Lt. Young	8/4/17	5	Nil	Nil
2/Lt. G. Lloyd	12/4/17	7	Nil	1
2/Lt. Pope	17/4/17	4	Nil	Nil
2/Lt. Henderson	17/4/17	2	Nil	Nil
2/Lt. Gunner	17/4/17	6	Nil	Nil
2/Lt. Jenkins	29/4/17	6	1	Nil
2/Lt. Parkes	7/5/17	2	Nil	Nil
2/Lt. Harris	9/5/17	Nil	Nil	Nil
2/Lt. Phelan	19/5/17	Nil	Nil	Nil
2/Lt. Adam	26/5/17	Nil	Nil	Nil

In addition to his heavy work schedule, Billy and his comrades broadened their mission. He explained to Margaret:

'Excitement is at its height here. We have been given a new job. [Now] we are responsible for keeping all the Hun artillery-ranging machines from carrying on with their work. It is exciting because the moment we appear, they go miles away and very low. You have to chase them right [down] to the ground and then, of course, there is the awful trip home [at] a few hundred feet up. We are on the rush all day. It is awfully annoying, [as] one never knows from one hour to the next when you will be going up.

'Yesterday [Sunday, 27 May], I got another Hun to my great joy. I had five fights in two hours, two with the same fellow[s]. The second time, I shot him down and he crashed into a village.' [52]

On that occasion, Billy led C Flight on three patrols. During the first one, at 8:25 am, he and his men attacked six German fighters east of Monchy. Billy had to leave his men, however, when his Lewis machine gun jammed. He landed at 12 Squadron's aerodrome at Wagnonlieu,[53] west of Arras, to seek help. After his machine gun was repaired, he returned to Filescamp Farm in time to re-fuel and lead another patrol against German reconnaissance aircraft. Over Lens at about 9:20 Billy saw a two-seater, manoeuvred into a 'kill' position behind it and fired three bursts. He was interrupted when two German fighters flew over and chased him off. Some twenty minutes later, however, he spotted the same reconnaissance aeroplane farther east, over Dourges, and attacked again. This time, Billy 'opened fire at fifty yards' range … [and the German aeroplane] immediately went into a spin and crashed' below.[54]

The day's *Nachrichtenblatt* account was too vague to be useful in comparing Billy's victory claim with German losses: 'Two aeroplanes [lost] in aerial combat, two through [an in-air] collision [and] two have not yet returned.'[55] The German 6th Army air staff daily report, however, identified a pair of two-seaters downed over German lines;[56] one, an aeroplane from Fl.-Abt (A) 256, could have been Billy Bishop's opponent. It went down over Brebières, about seven miles south of Dourges; both crewmen, Uffz Fritz Johänniges and Oberleutnant [First-Lieutenant] Gerd Jungschulz von Roebern, perished.

It became increasingly cloudy during the last week in May and Billy's gun jammed again while leading C Flight against a German patrol on the morning of the 30th.[57] Luckily for him, the German aircraft flew off. Billy was even more fortunate during a lone patrol on Thursday, 31 May, when he flew north west of Cambrai. He reported:

'I dived from the sun at the back of one of two [Albatros Scouts], firing about ten rounds from fifteen yards' range. He turned and manoeuvred with me for a few seconds. I finally succeeded in getting another burst of fifteen rounds in and he went down out of control. I watched him and he crashed [about a mile west of the southern edge of Bourlon Wood] … The other HA dived away.'[58]

Attempts to determine the identity of Billy's latest victim were obscured by vague German reports. The day's *Nachrichtenblatt* account noted Western Front casualties as: 'One officer, one Vizefeldwebel, one Gefreiter [are] dead; one Unteroffizier [and] one Gefreiter [were] injured.'[59] German 6th Army air staff reported the non-combat-related fatal crash of a Schutzstaffel 21 two-seater north of Douai,[60] some twenty-seven miles north of where Billy's victim crashed. The neighbouring 4th Army air staff reported that Jasta 10's Uffz Christoph Hertel was making a turn on 31 May, apparently unrelated to combat, and crashed; the pilot was injured.[61] In the absence of more information, it is not possible to determine which German airman was sent down by Billy Bishop.

Military Cross Awarded

Billy's fame was truly growing. His 31 May victory was reported in the RFC Communiqué[62] and in that day's issue of *Flight* magazine[63] he was included among recent Military Cross recipients, in his case for shooting down an Albatros Scout and an observation balloon on 7 April.

But even that recognition was not enough for Billy. He continued to push himself physically and be his own worst critic at any missed opportunity to be the best in all that he did. Again, he confided to Margaret his deepest thoughts and now boundless ambitions – quite a departure from his listless days before the war:

> 'There has been little excitement here lately. I have had a few scraps, with no results. I do get so mad with myself when I let wonderful opportunities slip by. I have now 15½ Huns to my credit and I must get some more, and quickly, too. I think I am holding the top [-scoring position] now, having the most machines to my credit.
>
> 'Yesterday [30 May], I had to go to No. 2 Aircraft Depot [at Candas,[64] south west of Doullens] to test a new type of machine, the Sopwith Camel, which has just come out. It is really a wonderful machine, with two [machine] guns, very fast, but not quite so [manoeuvrable] as a Nieuport. I flew it awfully badly … I make no pretence of being a pretty pilot … I was lucky to get the thing on the ground again …
>
> 'I have a great plan in my mind. A real hair-raising stunt, which I am going to do one of these days. It should help to [earn] another decoration. It will be done long before you get this [letter].'[65]

Due to wartime censorship, Billy could not tell her that Major Scott had approved his assignment for the most daring – and later most controversial – mission of his military flying career.

CHAPTER EIGHT

Attack in the Darkness

'A fine performance. Heartiest congratulations. D.H.'
– Field Marshal Sir Douglas Haig, BEF Commander-in-Chief[1]

The failed Allied spring 1917 offensive in the Aisne sector was marked by French troop mutinies, and Général Robert Nivelle's dismissal and replacement as commander-in-chief of the French armies by Maréchal [Field Marshal] Philippe Pétain. The aftermath of those traumas was put in a broader perspective by British aviation historian H.A. Jones: 'While the confidence of the French troops was being restored, the British [armies] in Flanders had to shoulder the burden of the western offensive.' [2]

To that end, dramatic plans to shake German confidence were advocated by Field Marshal Sir Douglas Haig, Commander-in-Chief of the British Expeditionary Force (BEF). One such plan was the Thursday, 7 June attack on a German high point in Flanders, preceded by detonating 600 tons of explosives in nineteen mines planted under Messines Ridge in Belgium.[3]

RFC on the Offensive
In the weeks prior to that event, British air units were urged to attack German ground positions whenever opportune. As Major-General Hugh Trenchard, General Officer Commanding, Royal Flying Corps, wrote to the RFC's 9th Wing commander:

'My advice to the pilot is, although I would leave it for him to decide, that he should cross the line … very low and then shoot at everything he can, re-crossing the lines at high altitude. This is in order to harass the enemy as much as possible and to spoil the morale of his troops …' [4]

Such spontaneous attacks against German ground targets became broadly sanctioned 'roving commissions' of the type which Major Jack Scott had encouraged Billy Bishop to carry out. In typically bold fashion, Billy took General Trenchard's urging a step further. While at home later in 1917, Billy wrote in his first memoir:

'My record of machines brought down was now in the vicinity of twenty, and I saw I had a rare chance of getting a lot [more victories] before going on my next leave – at the end of my second three months at the Front.

'With this object in mind I … came to the conclusion that if [I] could get to a [German] aerodrome when there were some machines on the ground and none in

the air, it would be an easy matter to shoot them down the moment they would attempt to come up. It would be necessary for them to take off straight into the wind,
if there was a strong wind at all, so I could not be surprised that way, and I would
be able to hit them if I came [in] low enough, before they … [had] a chance to ma-
noeuvre or turn out of my way.'[5]

Next, Billy reviewed the plan with Major Scott,[6] after which he needed only to select a
day. In 'fine' weather[7] on Friday, 1 June, Billy flew four patrols.[8] During the early morning
patrol, he and his C Flight deputy commander, Lieutenant William Fry, made a short, inconclusive attack on an Albatros two-seater over Pelves,[9] about seven miles east of Arras.
There were no contacts with German aircraft during the other flights, but Billy gained a
general sense of the weather.

He decided to carry out the special patrol the next morning. While General Trenchard
urged daring action, participation in such a raid was entirely voluntary. In that spirit, Billy
asked two trusted squadron-mates to help with the work – and earn some of the glory.
The first was Lieutenant Willie Fry, with whom he had shared a victory almost a month
earlier. Most likely, the second was Captain 'Grid' Caldwell, commander of B Flight. While
Billy formed the final elements of the special patrol in his mind on the evening of 1 June,
the pilots of 60 Squadron were enjoying themselves and releasing tensions with a raucous
party in the mess. In his 1974 memoir, Fry wrote:

'Bishop approached me … and said something about shooting up an enemy
aerodrome the next morning and [asked] would I care to go with him. I did not take
much notice, was non-committal and soon afterwards went to bed.

'Early the following morning, before [day-] light he came into my room and
asked if I were going with him. I had a headache from the night's party and an-
swered that I was not for it, turned over and went to sleep again …'[10]

2 June 1917
The weather for Saturday, 2 June, was reported as 'Fine, but cloudy in the afternoon'.[11]
While the special patrol was still relatively fresh in his mind, Billy later wrote:

'At 3 o'clock [a.m.] I was called and got up. It was pitch-black [outside]. I dressed
and went in to tell two of my friends[12] that I was off. They were not entirely in favour of the expedition and said so again. Notwithstanding this, I went on to [my]
aerodrome and got away [alone] just as the first streaks of dawn were showing in
the upper sky.

'I flew straight across the lines towards the aerodrome I had planned to attack,
and coming down low, decided to carry out my plan … But on reaching the place, I
saw there was nothing on the ground. Everyone must have been either dead asleep
or else the station was absolutely deserted. Greatly disappointed, I decided to try
the same stunt some other day on another aerodrome, which I would have to select.

'In the meantime, for something to do, I flew along low over the country, in the
hope of coming on some camp or group of troops … I felt that the danger was nil, as

most of the [gun] crews … would still be asleep, and I might as well give any Huns I could find a good fright. I was in rather a bad temper at having my carefully laid plan fall through so quickly … I was just thinking of turning and going home … when ahead and slightly to one side of me, I saw the sheds of another aerodrome. I at once decided that here was my chance, although it was not a very favourable one, as the aerodrome was pretty far back from the [front] lines … Furthermore, I was not even certain where I was, and that was my greatest worry, as I was a bit afraid that if I had any bad fights I might have trouble in finding my way back …'[13]

This low aerial view of a German airfield, taken in sunlight, is similar to what Billy Bishop encountered, in mist and partial moonlight, in the early hours of 2 June 1917. Aeroplanes housed in wooden hangars along a tree-lined road posed obstacles to aerial marauders, as described in Billy's combat report. (Dr. Volker Koos)

The Attack

Billy described his attack on the German airfield in a combat report, written right after he returned from the patrol:

'I fired on seven machines on the aerodrome, some of which had their engines running. One of them took off and I fired fifteen rounds at him from close range sixty feet up and he crashed. A second one [was] taking off, I … fired thirty rounds at 150 yards' range, [and] he crashed into a tree. Two more were taking off together. I climbed and engaged one at 1,000 feet, finishing my drum, and he crashed 300 yards from the aerodrome. I changed drums and climbed east. A fourth HA came after me and I fired one whole drum into him. He flew away and I then flew 1,000 feet under four scouts at 5,000 feet for one mile and turned west, climbing. The aerodrome was armed with one or more machine guns. Machines on the ground were six scouts (Albatros type I or II) and one two-seater.'[14]

The RFC Reaction

Major Scott's addendum to Billy's combat report alluded to the tactics General Trenchard communicated to RFC units:

'Captain Bishop had been encouraged to catch the HA referred to in VII Corps Daily Intelligence Summary No.151. His method was not quite what I intended. He was several times at a height of fifty feet over this enemy aerodrome at least seventeen miles east of the lines. His machine is full of holes caused by machine-gun fire from the ground.' [15]

Being able to read the VII Corps Daily Intelligence Summary No.151 might have shed light on Billy's special patrol. However, as pointed out by the late Philip Markham (whose Bishop research is discussed below), a copy of that document 'has not been located in [Royal] Air Force or army records at the [UK National Archive], but the gist of its content is given by Maurice Baring [author of *Flying Corps Headquarters*], who says: "A certain corps complained of some [German] machines flying low over its lines."'[16]

Authorisation for the attack was never in doubt. But, in a breach of military protocol, someone – most likely Major Scott – immediately forwarded a copy of Billy's combat report directly to General Trenchard. The RFC commander responded the same day in a note to Billy: 'Congratulations on your splendid and gallant action.'[17]

Meanwhile, back at Filescamp Farm, Willie Fry was among the first to hear about Billy Bishop's early morning attack. Fry recalled:

'[An] hour or so after dawn, Bishop came into my room in an excited state and told me how he had shot up a German aerodrome and also destroyed several aircraft which had come up to attack him. He said he had managed to [re-]cross the line further south in the French sector, despite being followed and attacked all the way [back], had landed in a field … [within] French lines to find out where he was, and having got his bearings from some French workers … flew back home.

'[Bishop] arrived back without his machine gun, having undone the screw-up release on the securing collar and thrown the gun overboard after he let it [drop] down … to put in a fresh ammunition drum while being attacked on the way home. At that point he had found himself unable to get the new drum on or [put] the gun back into its firing position.'[18]

After breakfast, Fry was invited along as Major Scott took Billy to the nearby 3rd Army Advance Headquarters. Fry explained:

'Our CO, Major Scott, had access to [Lieutenant-General Edmund] Allenby, commanding 3rd Army, through his friend [Captain] Lord Dalmeny, who was Allenby's military secretary. Major Scott telephoned [Dalmeny] about Bishop's exploit and was invited to take him over to see the army commander who wanted to hear his story at first hand. For some reason … I was taken too and after Bishop told his story to … [Allenby] we had luncheon in one of the headquarters messes.'[19]

On the evening of 3 June, Billy wrote a brief account of his special patrol to Margaret Burden. He offered no additional details, but his comments on the recognition he already received – and might yet receive – portended things to come:

'I received wires of congratulation from everybody, and [had] to go and see the army commander [Allenby] himself. Now I learn that I have been recommended for the VC [Victoria Cross], which I won't get, I'm sure, but I'll probably get a Bar [in lieu of a subsequent award] to something.'[20]

Also that day, Major Scott wrote to his wing commander, Lieutenant-Colonel George F. Pretyman, and offered additional information about Billy's special patrol:

'I wish to make a special report on an extremely brilliant individual attack on a German aerodrome near Cambrai, planned and executed by Capt. W.A. Bishop, DSO, MC on 2 June 1917.
    'He left the ground [at 3:57 am] … and flew intending to attack the aerodrome at Neuville [-Saint-Rémy], but on arriving there found the hangars closed and no signs of any activity. He then flew south and east of Cambrai until he arrived at an aerodrome where seven machines were on the ground …
    'As a preliminary manoeuvre before any of the machines [noted] above had left the ground, he engaged the mechanics who were starting the engines and at least one of these was observed to fall.'[21]

It is noteworthy that, after Billy Bishop's name, Scott used the initials of the Distinguished Service Order, which the young Canadian had not yet been awarded. Also, Scott identified the pilot's primary objective as a German airfield at Neuville-Saint-Rémy, just north west of Cambrai, on the city's edge. After returning to Filescamp Farm, Billy wrote a reconnaissance report in which he identified Anneux aerodrome, about five and a half miles south west of Cambrai, as his first objective.[22] Then, consistent with his combat report,[23] he listed his eventual target as either 'Esnes or Awoingt' airfields, less than ten miles south east of Cambrai. As stated above, Billy 'was not even certain where [he] was'.[24] That comment is not surprising, as he began his attack in darkness at 4:23 am over an area that was farther south and east than he had flown at this point; in fact, those locations were in the German 2nd Army sector, and Billy's previous aerial combats had taken place farther north, over the 6th Army sector. Why Billy selected an objective outside of his usual operational area is only one of the questions raised about this special patrol.
    On 4 June, Colonel Pretyman endorsed Major Scott's letter of the previous day and added: 'With reference to the attached report from the commanding officer [of] 60 Squad-

ron, I beg to bring to your notice the very gallant exploit of Captain William Avery Bishop, DSO, MC, and submit that it is worthy of some further recognition.'[25] Pretyman sent the combined correspondence to Brigadier-General John F.A. Higgins, commander of the RFC's 3rd Brigade.

Willie Fry, then on his second tour of duty with 60 Squadron, was not aware of Major Scott's Bishop-related correspondence since the 2 June event, but he must have sensed the purpose of the recent visit to General Allenby. In his memoir, Fry described Scott as a:

'… man with a host of friends, many in high places. [Scott] was obviously ambitious and determined that the squadron should be the best in France. He was the first commanding officer I had served under who was what today would be described as public-relations-minded … All the others in my previous short experience had the old Regular Army outlook and shunned publicity of any sort. [Scott] was determined that his squadron's and his pilots' deeds should be known by all … and he was generous in recommending for honours pilots who did well.'[26]

However, Major Scott's external communications ability had not yet been able to advance beyond 'the old regular army outlook'. An example is the diffuse official information about 2 June RFC activities provided to such national news media as *Flight* magazine:

'Activity in the air continued … [On 2 June] four German aeroplanes were brought down in air fighting, and five others were driven down out of control. Another German machine was driven down by our anti-aircraft guns. Four of our aeroplanes are missing.' [27]

The German Response

The weekly *Nachrichtenblatt* intelligence summary was at odds with British air combat claims. It reported no early morning attack on a German airfield on 2 June; rather, the publication related only the day's Western Front casualties: 'One officer, dead; four officers, three Vizefeldwebels [and] one low-ranking enlisted man, wounded.' [28]

It should be mentioned, however, that at the same time as Billy's 'lone wolf' aerial assault in the vicinity of Cambrai, a flight of two-seat bombers from 5 Squadron, Royal Naval Air Service, carried out an early morning attack on the Bruges Docks, on the Bruges-Ostend ship canal to the North Sea. During that action, RNAS airmen shot down one German fighter and chased off another, while 'all [British] pilots and machines returned safely'.[29] That raid was reported in *The Times* [30] and *Flight* magazine[31], to cite two examples of broad publicity given to the naval airmen's bold attack.

Within German-held territory, as in the case of Billy Bishop's exploit, there was no public mention of the RNAS raid. Further, the naval air attack was not referenced, either in the *Nachrichtenblatt* or in the weekly summary of the German 4th Army air staff, whose aircraft protected the Flanders coast; in fact, the latter publication also listed no casualties at all for 2 June.[32] Likewise, the German 2nd Army air staff, responsible for the area around Cambrai, reported no casualties for that day. [33]

Returning to Bishop's special patrol: The German 6th Army air staff, in the region nor-

During the 2 June attack, Billy Bishop may have encountered a sleek Albatros C.VII two-seater and mistaken it for an Albatros D.II scout. (Arthur Rahn album via National Museum of the USAF)

mally opposed by 60 Squadron, reported an intriguing casualty for 2 June: 'An aeroplane from Flieger-Abteilung 26 crashed for unknown reasons. The crew of Vzfw Delesse and Ltn Heinz [were] severely injured.'[34] Fl.-Abt 26's airfield was outside the town of Émerchicourt, less than ten miles north of Cambrai, and this cryptic notice of the crash invites conjecture.

We cannot know what Billy Bishop perceived during that flight. But, contrary to his recollection that 'the first streaks of dawn were showing in the upper sky,' he took off into early morning darkness. According to the US Naval Observatory's Astronomical Applications Department, sunrise on 2 June 1917 occurred at 6:03 am (local time in northern France and Belgium) and was preceded by some eighty-nine percent illumination from the moon.[35] Therefore, two hours earlier, the Canadian pilot would have flown and fought under whatever partial moonlight shone through any localised clouding or mist.

It can be conjectured that, instead of heading south east from Neuville-Saint-Rémy, Billy inadvertently swung north over unfamiliar German 2nd Army territory to Émerchicourt, in the eastern area of the 6th Army. He would have had little help in maintaining his bearing from a standard issue aeroplane compass according to 1917 published complaints about RFC and RNAS equipment: 'It appears that the twisting and turning of an aeroplane are so sharp and sudden that no existing compass was trustworthy in an aeroplane.'[36]

Likewise, Billy could have encountered aircraft taking off from Émerchicourt. In the moonlight and the mist, he might have mistaken the straight inter-plane struts and point-

Albatros D.II aerial view shows a familial resemblance to an Albatros C.VII, both with sleek fuselage and tail designs, as well as distinctive I-interplane struts. (Greg VanWyngarden)

ed nose of a Fl.-Abt 26 Albatros C.VII with the familial design characteristics of the smaller Albatros D.I or D.II, an older type, then no longer in frontline squadron use. The accompanying in-air views of the two Albatros types illustrate the point.

Other Questions

In recent times, other questions about Billy Bishop's 2 June 1917 special patrol have been raised. A 1995 detailed and illustrated report about that flight appeared in the World War I aviation history journal *Over the Front*.[37] Prepared by the late Wing Commander Philip Markham, RCAF (Ret.), a 'distinguished Canadian engineer and historian … [his article] proved that the mission duration of one hour, forty-three minutes was certainly within the capabilities of the [Nieuport Scout] aircraft, given the flight profile reported, which included altitudes ranging from fifty feet to 7,000 feet'.[38] Markham's article made a case that Billy could not have attacked a German airfield south of Cambrai; it even considered Jagdstaffel 5's facilities at Boistrancourt (Estourmel), near the south-east edge of the Nieuport's possible operating range. But that article focused only on Billy's admittedly imprecise identification of potential German airfield sites within the German 2nd Army area.

While Markham mentioned the Fl.-Abt 26 casualties noted above, he did not consider whether that aircrew might have been among Bishop's reported adversaries and Émerchicourt airfield a possible raid site. This author believes that both are worth considering – while also noting that no evidence of other German casualties on the early morning of 2 June 1917 has come to light. The identities of German airmen and aircraft counted among Billy's other confirmed victories that day – Nos. 23½ and 24½, as they were numbered after his shared victory with Fry – remain unresolved.

Battle damage to Billy's aeroplane during that mission has also invited inquiry. In a 1934 *Popular Flying* magazine article, former Sergeant-Major Alfred A. Nicod, who maintained that aeroplane and knew it well, recalled:

'[His] machine was badly damaged by anti-aircraft guns and machine-gun fire. There were a dozen bullet holes in the radius of a few inches just behind his head as he sat in the cockpit. A miraculous escape …'[39]

To which Willie Fry's 1974 account added:

'I remember clearly seeing a group of about five bullet holes in the rear half of [Bishop's] tail-plane, the elevator, within a circle of not more than six inches diameter at the most. Whatever [German] machine was on his tail must have been very close indeed to achieve this group …'[40]

Detailed view of a Lewis machine gun on a Foster mounting rail, used when pilots changed ammunition drums, and a flexible Bowden cable that enabled pilots to fire the gun.
(Author's Collection)

The Missing Lewis Gun

Fry's version of Billy's post-attack comments has led to questions about the damage. Fry recounted Billy as saying he became disoriented, landed his aeroplane en route back to Filescamp Farm aerodrome to get his bearings and threw away his Lewis light machine gun after being unable to re-arm it with a fresh ninety-seven-bullet[41] ammunition drum.[42]

Arthur Bishop's 1965 biography corroborated only the latter point, about the Lewis gun, noting that while returning home, his father's 'gun was smoking from the stress of firing a whole drum of ammunition without interruption. When it had cooled after a few miles, Bishop disconnected it from its mount and hurled it overboard. It was now dead weight and he would need all the speed he could muster.'[43] But not much weight, as the gun and an empty ammunition drum weighed only nineteen pounds.[44]

In 2002, these accounts led Billy Bishop detractor Brereton Greenhous to conclude in his book:

'[If] Fry's recollections were correct, Bishop did … land somewhere behind the French lines. And it would seem likely that he then turned off his engine, detached his Lewis gun from its mountings, fired a short burst into one of the less vital parts of [Nieuport Scout] B.1566 from his hand-held [machine] gun and then (with no time to spare, since he wanted his engine warm for easier starting) failed to remount the gun, chucked it aside and took off again, all within six or seven minutes …'[45]

The question about 'self-inflicted' damage to Nieuport Scout B.1566 was addressed by Billy Bishop biographer and former fighter pilot Lieutenant-Colonel David L. Bashow, OMM, CD, RCAF (Ret.):

'If [Bishop] landed, and even that is questionable, he probably needed the momentary comfort of being earthbound to regain his composure. He could well have been suffering from what today would be referred to as Post-Traumatic Stress Disorder, something unrecognised in 1917. He also may have needed to ask for directions, as he was rather unsure of his exact location by this time. With respect to shooting up his own aircraft to enhance his credibility, this is quite simply a ludicrous supposition. In June 1917, Nieuport [Scouts] were falling out of the sky with alarming regularity due to structural failures of the lower wings that were not yet totally understood. In fact, there had been five such accidents on Bishop's squadron alone, several of which had proven fatal. Any contention that a pilot would intentionally weaken an airframe with known structural defects defies logic.

'Additionally, the Nieuport [Scout] had neither wheel brakes nor a parking brake, and combined with the high and unpredictable idling speed of the 120-horsepower Le Rhône rotary engine, this would have required the pilot to shut down the aircraft in order to disembark and shoot it up. As well, the Nieuport [Scout] did not have a self-starting capability, which meant that Bishop would … probably have had to invite a witness or witnesses to fraud, since someone would have had to swing the propeller through for the engine start. The battle damage is readily explained by small-arms fire encountered at … [the German] airfield, and flak over the lines, which Bishop claimed he experienced on his return flight. The location of the damage on the aircraft is well documented. Most of it was in the trailing bays of the lower wings and the elevators, and is thus inconsistent with the "self-damage" theory, which would have resulted in lateral damage to the aircraft, such as in the fuselage and the rudder. However, the wing, elevator and fuselage damage is not inconsistent with what could be expected from ground fire …

'Then there is the matter of the missing Lewis gun… [which] was never observed by others, nor did Billy Bishop ever mention it himself. Also, there is no record of a missing Lewis gun from 60 Squadron in the weekly routine machine-gun accountability report from RFC headquarters France to higher headquarters. Furthermore, the only place the landing behind Allied lines has been mentioned is in Fry's … [book]. There, Fry claimed Bishop told him he had become lost and landed in the French sector to ask directions of farmhands. Billy Bishop never said anything about an interim landing, nor did his son Arthur.'[46]

The Path to Glory

The RFC Communiqué,[47] usually made up of terse one- or two-line vignettes, published ten lines about Billy Bishop's 2 June exploit. Likewise, that day's RFC War Diary[48] entry had a lengthy text. Both official accounts were based on Billy's combat report and Major Scott's proposal for recognition of 60 Squadron's current leading air combat ace. The story was refined as it made its way up the chain of command, with important sponsors tending to its progress along the way. For example, having received no response to Colonel Pretyman's recommendation of 4 June, his successor in command of 13th Wing, Major Arthur V. Bettington, sent another missive to RFC 3rd Brigade headquarters on 1 July: 'With reference to … [correspondence] dated the 3rd June 1917, recommending Captain W.A. Bishop, DSO, MC, 60 Squadron, for further decoration, since that date this officer has been conspicuously gallant as a leader and daring in action.' Bettington added Billy's five latest aerial victories to the tally of his achievements.[49]

As Billy mentioned in his next letter to Margaret, acclaim for his special patrol continued to grow:

'There is no other news of any sort with one exception. I have received congratulations from [Field Marshal] Sir Douglas Haig. He wrote on the bottom of my [combat] report: "A fine performance. Heartiest congratulations. D.H." That was rather nice, wasn't it?' [50]

But in a rambling letter two days later, a grim side of flying and the frailty of Nieuport Scouts shook Billy to the core:

'No excitement since Thursday [7 June] except that I had four fights yesterday and managed to get one beautiful red Hun.

'On Thursday night we had an awful accident here … A chap named Harris[51] went up to fly … [and, in] diving at the aerodrome, one of his wings gradually folded up and of course he came down. The other wing went in the same way and he came crashing down at our feet. What an awful sight … he was killed instantaneously.

'We are praying for bad weather, but it never seems to come … I am so tired of this war, all I want is you and our home.'[52]

Victory No. 25½

Billy Bishop's aerial victory of 8 June showed how his ambition and work ethic overcame his temporary despair. In his book, he wrote specifically about that particular 'lone wolf' patrol, thinking more about the opportunity for additional aerial victories than the danger of flying alone and being attacked by a German fighter aircraft formation:

'[It] was again my day off, so I had deserted my own part of the lines and flown way up north, where the Battle of Messines was raging … I had heard that there were more German machines up in that direction. It was a good tip …' [53]

His mention of shooting down a 'red Hun' seems to imply an encounter with red-coloured aeroplanes of Manfred von Richthofen's Jagdstaffel 11, but the Messines area was not the Red Baron's hunting ground.[54] According to Billy's combat report, just after noon during continuing 'fine' weather,[55] he was flying at 11,500 feet a few miles north of Lille when:

> 'I attacked the two top machines in a larger formation of six [Albatros] Scouts. I got on the tail of one and fired the remainder of my drum, about forty-five rounds, at him. He fell out of control. I watched him and he kept spinning all the way down and seemed to go straight into the ground.' [56]

The *Nachrichtenblatt* report for 8 June reported that 'one aeroplane [fell] in aerial combat',[57] with no further details. That day's 6th Army air staff account, however, noted that twenty-one-year-old Vzfw Franz Bucher of Jasta 30 was shot down in aerial combat over Wytschaete bend[58] at the confluence of Messines and Ploegsteert Forest. The crash site is about eleven miles north west of Lille. The date and place match so closely that this Albatros D.III was surely the aeroplane mentioned in Billy's Combat Report No. 475 of 8 June 1917. The combat was reported in the day's RFC Communiqué[59] and eventually confirmed as his victory No. 25½ (as seen in the author's tally in this book's Appendix).

Further, Billy's adversary would have borne standard Albatros colours of the time, mauve and green wings and a mottled fuselage. From a distance under the bright noontime sun, the mauve most likely reflected as red. See the photograph (overleaf) of a dark-coloured Albatros D.III in typical markings of the time.

Victoria Crosses Awarded

In London the following day Buckingham Palace announced that King George V approved awarding the Victoria Cross to 'twenty-nine officers, non-commissioned officers and [lower ranking enlisted] men for acts of 'conspicuous bravery and devotion to duty', according to that day's issue of *The Times*.[60] Two pilots were among that group to receive 'the supreme British award, taking absolute precedence over all other [British] awards and decorations':[61] Lieutenant (temporary Captain) Albert Ball, DSO, MC and Lieutenant Frank Hubert McNamara. Ball's award was posthumous, presented for air combat actions from 25 April to 6 May 1917,[62] and McNamara's was presented for his deeds on 20 March 1917 when he landed his aeroplane amidst a bombing raid and braved 'hostile cavalry' to rescue a squadron-mate and then fly him to safety.[63] Of the eleven aviation recipients of the VC at that time, Australian-born McNamara was the first to hail from an overseas British Commonwealth nation.[64]

At that point in the war, it was rare for individual British Empire aviators to gain public recognition, but, as the Victoria Cross was and remains truly a democratic award, bestowed upon all ranks, some publicity was allowed. Consequently, the full citations for Ball's and McNamara's awards were published in *Flight* magazine.[65]

Brief Respite

Meanwhile, Billy Bishop hoped for more air combats – to enhance his chances of earning the VC – but he may have been disappointed by the summary of 60 Squadron's work issued on 9 June. It showed he was still the most ambitious pilot in the unit, with sixty-seven

A darkly-coloured Albatros D.III gaining altitude over the French countryside. (Bayerisches Hauptstaatsarchiv Militärarchiv München/Staudinger photo 017754)

combat flights logged in, but, due to 13th Wing's slow aerial victory confirmation process, on 9 June Billy was listed with twenty-and-a-half victories.[66] Further, his hopes of adding to his victory score were dashed by a 'dry spell' for over two weeks. On 10, 11, 12 and 13 June, Billy and his C Flight comrades either did not see or could not fly close enough to engage any German aeroplanes.[67]

During this relatively quiet period, Billy was given time off to relax. On Friday, 22 June, the day after Billy returned to 60 Squadron, his former deputy flight leader, Willie Fry, was posted back to England. Fry, too, needed a rest, as he noted 'the pressure and pace were so great that the nerves of a number of pilots were a little stretched and nearly everyone was liable to flare up at slight provocation'.[68]

In his 1974 memoir, Willie Fry alluded to a personal issue he had with Billy Bishop. Major Scott asked Fry whether he wanted home leave, as his 'relations with [the] flight commander and consequently with the CO and some of the other pilots [had] deteriorated during the month'.[69]

Fry's later account, which appeared in the *Cross & Cockade International* journal in 2001, added to what he had written in his memoir: 'Whether I should have been prepared to apologise to Bishop if Major Scott tackled me, I still do not know, as in my mind I felt sure that Bishop's story [about the 2 June attack] was untrue, but there is no way of know-

Billy Bishop standing by Nieuport 23 B.1566 at Filescamp Farm aerodrome after it was completely refurbished following damage received during the 2 June attack on a German airfield. (Greg VanWyngarden)

ing what I should have done if pressed.'[70]

Fry may have been an early sceptic, but he was not the last person to question the veracity of Billy Bishop's account of that mission. Philip Markham's 1995 article (noted above) raised concerns about Billy's subsequently being awarded the Victoria Cross based only on his own narrative of the 2 June attack. Markham also learned that paperwork associated with the award was 'destroyed sometime since the end of World War II'.[71] He concluded that 'no record of the correspondence concerning Bishop's VC was found. It is now considered very doubtful that it ever will.' [72]

Meanwhile, Billy Bishop learned that, as of 18 June, he was 'appointed a Companion of the Distinguished Service Order,' [73] the British Empire's second highest award for valour. Billy's was the only DSO awarded that day and cited him for actions on 2 May. The DSO warrant also noted: 'His courage and determination have set a fine example to others.'[74] His spirits, buoyed by slightly disingenuous self-esteem and devotion to Margaret, rose to a new level when he wrote to her:

'My four days' rest is at an end and I am back at work … My machine has been taken down and gone over, new [wings] and everything put on it. It is gorgeous now, all shining silver colour with a deep sky-blue nose. Oh, it's wonderful. It's a hundred times the best in the squadron, and I am so fond of it I call it "Pepita".

    '[Now] I must get busy and get some more Huns, though, or my reputation will fade away. Darling, you are the inspiration of it all. Everything I try to win is just to make you proud of me. I'd gladly die to make you that, sweetheart.'[75]

CHAPTER NINE

Growing Success

'[I] stalked them from the east. There were two and I took the rear one.
It was gorgeous. He didn't see me coming at all and I had him cold.
After about twenty rounds he went down.'
– William A. Bishop[1]

Initially, German reports seemed to ignore British accounts of successful air operations in the morning darkness on 2 June 1917. That appearance of denial has led some researchers to presume that Billy Bishop's 'lone wolf' attack did not occur. Yet, before the month was out, the German army air branch's intelligence summary related the first of several references to Billy's special patrol – and none denied that it took place.

In its 28 June issue, the *Nachrichtenblatt der Luftstreitkräfte*, produced by the office of the commanding general of the German air force and classified as 'Geheim' [secret], carried a review of British news accounts of air operations before and after the 7 June assault on Messines. Of particular interest is the following portion of that examination:

'A report in the *Daily Express* shows that there are great variations in attacks on airfields. That is claimed by no less an authority than Member of Parliament and flight expert [William] Joynson-Hicks, who was then chairman of a parliamentary fact-finding committee for aviation in France, and … [who] claims to have overheard: early one morning, a young RFC officer flew over the German lines, observed on an airfield that the aeroplanes were being brought out for the morning flight, dived down to fifty feet above the ground and encountered a German [aeroplane] just taking off. Approaching quite close to him, the Englishman [sic] opened fire and the German crashed into the ground. Just at that moment another German aeroplane rose up, the Englishman gave him about fifty rounds in the back, [and] the German fell and crashed into a tree. A third aeroplane tried to escape, [but] the Englishman caught up with it at 1,000 metres' altitude and also sent this one down to the ground. During the entire time of the fight, the Englishman was under heavy anti-aircraft fire; his aeroplane was riddled with holes.'[2]

The article's description tracks with Billy Bishop's combat report, quoted in the preceding chapter.[3]

Mysteries of Flight
Understandably, in his letters to Margaret Burden, Billy Bishop portrayed himself as a top

combat pilot. But by the time he wrote his first memoir, later in 1917, he was self-assured enough to admit that he had faced some very capable German adversaries. On Sunday morning, 24 June, Billy and three other C Flight comrades – Lieutenants William Rutherford, Frank Soden and Graham Young[4] – encountered 'a German pilot of exceptional quality'[5] about whom Billy wrote:

> '[The Albatros D.III pilot] managed to get in the middle of us, and it was all we could do to keep from colliding as we attacked him. Finally, to add to our disgust, he broke off the combat of his own sweet will just at the moment he felt he had had enough and dived away.'[6]

Colliding aeroplanes were a grim reality to 60 Squadron's pilots and the memory was fresh. On Thursday, 16 June, their comrade Lieutenant David Rhys Cadwgan Lloyd's Nieuport[7] reportedly struck a German Albatros piloted by Vizefeldwebel Robert Riessinger of Jagdstaffel 12; both men were killed.[8] By an odd coincidence, *The Times* published an article about Riessinger's death and, in it, paid anonymous homage to twenty-year-old Lieutenant Lloyd's selfless heroism:

> 'A telegram to the *Frankfurter Zeitung* reports the death of … German airman Robert Riessinger in aerial combat. Riessinger succeeded in setting his opponent's aeroplane on fire, and the English pilot, with certain death before his eyes, rammed Riessinger's machine. Both aeroplanes fell to the earth. The Englishman's identity is not disclosed.'[9]

Suffice to say, Billy's next letter to Margaret did not mention the masterful Albatros D.III pilot or Lieutenant D.R.C. Lloyd's fatal collision. Instead, Billy wrote about his later patrol on 24 June 1917:

> 'I went out by myself. Had three fights and got … one down in flames, adding another Hun to my list, which is now at twenty-two. I am awfully pleased. I flew miles into Hunland … There were two and I took the rear one. It was gorgeous. He didn't see me coming at all and I had him cold. After about twenty rounds he went down.'[10]

Captain 'Grid' Caldwell, appointed to lead 60 Squadron temporarily while Major Jack Scott was on leave, added to the bottom of the combat report: 'Captain Bishop was out alone'[11] when this victory occurred. Caldwell thereby notified the 13th Wing commander there was no independent verification of Billy's latest air combat triumph. Nonetheless, the fight was reported in the day's RFC Communiqué,[12] after Billy received credit for aerial victory No. 26½.

From the German side, the *Nachrichtenblatt* for 28 June reported: 'Two aeroplanes [were lost] in aerial combat behind enemy lines … as well as one Flugmeister [naval petty officer] dead, four officers wounded.'[13] More information about one of those German air casualties appeared in a German 4th Army air staff summary about the loss of 'Leutnant der Reserve Erich Reiher, Jagdstaffel 6, down in flames [west] of Ypres'.[14] That casualty's events seem to match what Billy told Margaret (above) that he had flown 'miles into Hunland' and might have gone farther north east than Beaumont. But a reliable source notes that Reiher's Albatros D.III 'was downed by [anti-aircraft] fire of the [British] 12th Balloon Section … [and was assigned the captured identification number] G 49'.[15] Lacking more information about the other German air casualty – particularly its fiery end – it is not possible to match Billy's victory with a known German loss.

Three More Aerial Victories

That combat began a three-day winning streak for Billy. The following day he wrote:

'Yesterday [25 June] we had a big fight, four Nieuports … [against] twelve Huns, and I got one of them, and Rutherford got another. This morning [26 June], I got two more. Three scouts were protecting a two-seater and … [I] dived from the east at them, slipping under the back one, and opening fire up at him. Into flames he went, and down … One of the other scouts … came back at me. I engaged him in mortal combat, and after a few manoeuvres down he went out of control.

'That makes twenty-five in all for me, so the number is growing fast. I received a wire from General [J.F.A.] Higgins, congratulating me on a "fine performance".[16]

Billy Bishop's parting sight of the two-seater he pursued on 26 June may have looked like this view of an LVG C.II flying off. (Greg VanWyngarden)

The 25 June fight began east of Arras. Billy led Lieutenants Rutherford, Soden and Young against four Albatros Scouts.[17] Billy and Rutherford were each credited with an out of control (OOC) victory in the day's RFC Communiqué.[18] The comparable *Nachrichtenblatt* entry, however, recorded 'one aeroplane [lost] in aerial combat on the other side of the lines',[19] offering too little information to determine whether it might have been one of the two RFC pilots' opponents. And, as often happened with OOC claims, one or both Albatros pilots could have regained control of the aircraft and landed safely. Neither 4th nor 6th Army air staffs reported a single-seater loss that day.

Billy Bishop's double victory the next day, Tuesday, 26 June, occurred while he was alone north east of Lens. In his combat report, he wrote that 'after twenty-five rounds' were directed at him, the first Albatros went down in flames; Billy said he fired the remainder of his ninety-seven-bullet drum at the second Albatros as it 'went down completely out of control'.[20] Then Billy said he climbed away, put a fresh ammunition drum into his Lewis machine gun and tried – unsuccessfully – to attack the remaining Albatros and the two-seater it protected.

Upon his return, Billy dictated his combat report to Lieutenant H.W. Guy, 60 Squadron's recording officer. Before forwarding the report to 13th Wing's commander, Major Arthur V. Bettington, Lieutenant Guy noted at the bottom: 'Captain Bishop was by himself.'[21] The RFC Communiqué entry reported two victories for Billy.

The *Nachrichtenblatt* Western Front report for 26 June noted: 'One aeroplane [was lost] in aerial combat. Additionally, two officers [were] wounded.'[23] No single-seater losses were reported by German 4th or 6th Army air staffs. Thus, lack of further information makes it impossible to match Billy's victories with German losses.

Apparently unconcerned about administrative matters between the squadron and wing commands, Billy was content with his run of good luck. On 27 June, he and Lieutenants Rutherford and Soden attempted an early morning attack on three German two-seaters – to no avail.[24] A late morning patrol made with Captain Caldwell also did not result in victory.[25] Billy did not lose hope; rather, he remained eager about the time ahead:

'Another Hun today [28 June]. This is certainly my lucky week. That makes twenty-six in all … Major Scott is away on leave. When he comes back next week I am going to apply for a special machine. I think … General [Higgins] will give me one if Scott will forward the application. It will mean dozens more Huns for me, I'm sure. On an S.E.5 or a SPAD with a 200-hp engine one could shoot down every Hun in the sky …

'In my scrap this morning the poor old Hun's two left-hand [wings] came off at 11,000 feet. I must have hit a wire or something important. I tried to surprise him, but he saw me a moment too soon, and turned and fought.'[26]

That air battle began when Billy was flying alone south of La Bassée canal, about eighteen miles north east of his aerodrome. He saw four Albatros D.III fighters and attacked from above. The smoke trails from his incendiary bullets scattered the German patrol, which allowed Billy to concentrate on one aeroplane, about which he reported: 'I fired at him from 100 yards' range and my tracer [rounds] seemed to hit around his engine.'[27] The last he saw of it, the Albatros was falling vertically while Billy climbed away and headed for his aerodrome.

'Grid' Caldwell, still leading the squadron in Major Scott's absence, noted on Billy's report: 'Captain Bishop was again by himself.'[28] Billy's victory was reported in the RFC Communiqué.[19] German 6th Army air staff reported no losses at all for that day and the *Nachrichtenblatt* recorded only that 'one aeroplane for unknown reasons [was] shot down in flames; one officer has fallen in aerial combat'[30] on 28 June. No other details were given and neither air staff of the German 4th and 6th Armies acknowledged such an exceptionally violent event for that day. More details about the *Nachrichtenblatt* account of a destroyed German aircraft would be needed to clarify this victory.

Tallying the Score

Tallying aerial victory scores was and remains subject to interpretation; it should be noted that Billy's air triumph on 28 June was preliminarily listed as No. 25½[31] in the 13th Wing's summary of 60 Squadron's work as of 30 June. That count lagged behind the wing's finally confirmed number. Hence, when revised reports were released later, the 28 June victory was listed as No. 30½ (see Appendix in the back of this book). The tallies can be confusing, but the summary clearly shows Billy as the most productive member of the unit; he logged in eighty combat flights, more than twice that of the pilot with the next highest number of flights, Captain 'Grid' Caldwell with thirty-five.[32]

Meanwhile, even Billy's recent triumphs could not ward off mood swings that troubled him. They are evident in this letter to Margaret:

'[Major Jack Scott] comes back from leave in two days and … then I will have a better idea of when I will be back [home]. In any case, I don't suppose my nerves will last me more than three months more out here. They are getting shaky now. I find myself shuddering at [taking] chances I didn't think of six weeks ago.'[33]

The next day, Billy was in a more positive frame of mind when he wrote:

'The colonel came over for tea and … told me he would forward my application for an S.E.5 immediately [after] the major sends it on … I want to get one immediately. It will make a difference of many Huns to me and I want to get more than forty-three, which Guynemer (the leading Frenchman) has. It would be nice to lead for the Allies and I could do it if I get [that aeroplane].'[34]

Echoes of the June Attack

While Billy Bishop was looking forward to his next aerial triumphs, the staff of the Luftstreitkräfte commanding general (abbreviated Kogenluft) showed a lingering interest in British press reports about successful RFC air raids earlier in the month. A week after its first reference to Billy's 2 June attack, the *Nachrichtenblatt* published a correction to its earlier information without editorial comment:

'The British officer, who shot down three aeroplanes, as described in the previous [*Nachrichtenblatt*] issue had, according to the *Morning Post*, during this attack … brought another aeroplane crashing down in the attack, so that, collectively, he shot down four German aeroplanes over a German airfield thirty kilometres behind the frontlines.'[35]

Also at this time, Billy himself attracted the attention of the Kogenluft staff. In early August the *Nachrichtenblatt* reported a prisoner of war's comment: 'Since [Captain Albert] Ball's death, Captain Bishop, [credited] with twenty-nine aeroplanes shot down, is said to be the best British fighter pilot.'[36] A month later, German air intelligence officers determined:

'Captain Bishop (60 Squadron) flies S.E.5 [aircraft]. Based on a newspaper report, after shooting down twenty-one aeroplanes and two captive balloons, [Bishop] has recently received the Victoria Cross.'[37]

Moving briefly to November, Kogenluft staff finally connected Billy's 2 June 1917 attack with his subsequently receiving the VC. But confusion arose when the *Nachrichtenblatt* reported on a French aviation journal's account of the attack that appeared with the wrong date. The Kogenluft publication stood by its original loss statement and – only then – challenged the number of aeroplanes Billy was credited with shooting down during the 2 June attack:

Featured on the front cover of France's pioneer aviation journal, Billy Bishop was shown at his battle station; a Bowden cable is within his grasp. (Author's Collection)

'Captain [W.A.] Bishop, according to [the] *Guerre Aérienne* [issue] of 4 October 1917, has achieved over forty aerial victories and thereby is the best British combat pilot. It is apparent from *Guerre Aérienne* that Bishop is the British flyer who, on 7 [sic] June, from twenty to 1,000 metres' altitude over a German airfield, is said to have shot down four German aeroplanes (see *Nachrichtenblatt Nr. 18*). This achievement was at the time extolled in many British newspapers. Bishop received the Victoria Cross for it. In fact, only two German aeroplanes were shot down on that day on the entire British Front. As Bishop fought the battle alone, details about the four alleged victories can come only from himself.'[38]

Obviously, *Nachrichtenblatt* editors failed to re-read their earlier issue,[39] which listed 2 June German casualties 'on the entire British Front' as: 'One officer, dead; four officers, three Vizefeldwebels [and] one low-ranking enlisted man, wounded' – and made no mention of lost aeroplanes. Likewise, it did not clarify why 'an aeroplane from Flieger-Abteilung

26 crashed for unknown reasons', as reported that day by 6th Army air staff.[40] Such contradictions call into question the completeness, and validity, of *Nachrichtenblatt* casualty information.

Arrival of New Aeroplanes

Meanwhile, Billy Bishop's wish for a Royal Aircraft Factory-built S.E.5 was soon realised. Major Scott later wrote that 60 Squadron was already in line to receive 'the newest type of scouts, as the Nieuports were by then rather out of date'.[41] The first S.E.5s were assigned to 56 Squadron, with which Billy's idol Albert Ball had led the unit's first combat patrol in that aeroplane in April.[42] Billy Bishop and 'Grid' Caldwell quickly flew to 56 Squadron's aerodrome to be trained on the new type.[43] Billy shared more good news with Margaret, even if with some embellishment:

> 'The most exciting [thing] that has happened is that our first (censored) has arrived for us to learn to fly on. And learn to fly on it we are now trying to do. The next one, when it arrives, will, I expect go to me, as the CO has applied for a special one for me to use. And I hope it comes soon. By Jove, there will be a huge difference in fighting out of a thing like that … and I'll be glad to be able to catch Huns, instead of just seeing them disappear.'[44]

Line-up of early S.E.5s at Central Flying School at Upavon. The third aeroplane from left, B.18, was a two-set training version of the type. (Author's Collection)

Indeed, Billy experienced 'disappearing' opponents on the morning of Saturday, 7 July. He and Lieutenants Spencer Horn and Frank Soden were flying east of Arras, where they spotted several German aircraft. Each time Billy's patrol went after them, the German aircraft slipped away.[45]

It was a different story three days later. Accompanied by Major Scott, Billy led C Flight on an evening patrol over Arras. He wrote to Margaret:

> 'We've had some glorious fights, on the night before last [10 July] in which I got my (censored) Hun and the CO was slightly wounded in the arm while bravely saving

me from a horrid Hun man. [The German] was diving on me and the CO dived on him and I went on and brought down another.

'Then this morning [12 July] I led the patrol into another scrap and in the middle of it we were joined by [Flight Sub-Lieutenant Robert A.] Little, the RNAS pilot who is next to me in numbers [of aerial victories]. He has (censored)[46] now counting one he got this morning, and I also crashed one, making my total (censored)[47]. It is growing, isn't it?'[48]

Indeed, Australian-born ace Robert Little had also taken part in the 10 July air battle west of Douai. According to the day's RFC Communiqué, Bishop and Little each achieved an OOC victory.[49] Neither the *Nachrichtenblatt* nor the German 6th Army air staff reported losses for 10 July. Hence, there were no reported German casualties that might correspond with the two British Empire pilots' victories.

While reading Billy's letter of two days later, a 60 Squadron officer assigned to censor outgoing mail blanked out the wing's sequential number of Billy's victory of 12 July, which was also his total victory count at that point. The endnotes offer pertinent numbers from a credible source.

Chivalry Abused

In his history of 60 Squadron, Major Jack Scott wrote that, on 22 July, he 'was promoted [to] wing commander and sent to the [11th] … wing of the 2nd Brigade in the Ypres Sector. W.J.C.K. Cochran-Patrick … who had been doing brilliantly in 23 Squadron on SPADs, succeeded to the command of 60 [Squadron].'[50] While Scott was being treated for his wounds and until Captain Cochran-Patrick arrived, 'Grid' Caldwell was in charge of 60 Squadron. In his letters Billy made no mention of Scott's absence or of his victory on 12 July, when he led an early afternoon patrol between Arras and Douai. According to Billy's combat report, from 10,000 feet altitude, he led a dive on four Albatroses, which:

'… were later joined by two more. I fired two drums in eight or ten bursts. One EA [enemy aeroplane] went into a spin and crashed near Vitry. At the end of the fight only three EA flew away. I saw Flight Lieutenant Little cause an EA to go into an uncontrollable spin.'[51]

The 15 July issue of RFC Communiqués, produced by Major-General Hugh Trenchard's staff at advanced headquarters in France, placed that battle within a larger perspective:

'On the 12th, more fighting took place in the air than on any day since the commencement of the war. The activity was chiefly pronounced on the front of the [British] Fifth Army, but our artillery [-spotting] machines were less interfered with than they have been for the last week …'[52]

This Communiqué recounted several air fights, including Billy's latest encounter, which included an incident of successful German trickery:

'Flight Lieutenant Little, Naval Squadron No. 8, and Captain Bishop, 60 Squadron, observed a formation of Nieuports engaging Albatros Scouts, [and] joined in the fight ... Bishop shot down one of the enemy machines, which crashed near Vitry-en-Artois, and ... Little drove one down, and the enemy pilot waved a white handkerchief, so ... Little temporarily ceased firing. The German pilot, however, flew east and ... Little pursued him, but [the German] escaped. Shortly after this ... Little engaged a second machine, which he drove down out of control.'[53]

Little and 60 Squadron's Lieutenant A.W.M. Mowle both confirmed seeing Billy's adversary 'crash' or 'spin into' the ground.[54] The *Nachrichtenblatt* offered only vague comments,[55] which were surpassed in detail by the German 6th Army air staff's accounting of three two-seaters and a fighter aircraft lost. In the latter instance it reported: 'Leutnant [Günther] Pastor, Jagdstaffel 29 [was] severely wounded in aerial combat.'[56] It would be easy to conclude Ltn Pastor as a Bishop victory, but the German unit's history[57] notes the Jasta 29 pilot went down at 8:04 pm (vs. Billy's claim of six-and-a-half-hours earlier) about ten miles north west of where Billy's adversary crashed. Hence – lacking further evidence of what Little and Mowle saw – this author classifies Bishop's 12 July victory as witnessed, but with no matching German loss found.

More Hard Work

Friday the 13th of July lived up to its ominous reputation with a bad scare over Croisilles,[58] south east of Arras, described below. It also led to a five-day luckless spell for Billy, who wrote:

'We have been working awfully hard, but not much excitement. Yesterday [13 July], we climbed up to 18,500 feet and there we found a beastly Hun. We had a short scrap, but our little machines in that thin air were useless, and he escaped. My head and lungs were bursting. I'll never fight that high up again.'[59]

The day after that futile encounter, 13th Wing staff issued a mid-month summary of 60 Squadron's work to date. In it Billy continued to lead in the number of flights, with eighty-seven as opposed to 'Grid' Caldwell's total of forty-eight flights. According to the wing, Billy's victory of 12 July was listed as No. 27½ on the official score[60] – but it was later adjusted to 33½. His own tally (noted below) was lower than the wing's count.

Rain, heavy winds and low clouds on 14, 15 and 16 July did not offer suitable flying weather[61] for the nimble, but fragile Nieuports. But Billy came roaring back on the 17th, about which he wrote:

'Tonight I got two more Huns, one in flames and the other burst into flames when it fell and crashed, so I'm much pleased. That makes thirty [victories] for me. Seventeen more and I will be up to Guynemer, the Frenchman, and then I'll lead the Allies [in scoring].'

Billy Bishop's latest double victory began during an early evening patrol south west of

In certain lighting conditions, this darkly-coloured DFW C.V could be hard to see against a dusky rural landscape. (Dr. Volker Koos)

Cambrai. Most likely, his opponents were Albatros D.IIIs.[63] The RFC Communiqué reported:

'Captain W.A. Bishop … attacked two EA near Havrincourt Wood … After firing three bursts into one of the enemy machines, it burst into flames and fell … Shortly after this he dived on another German machine, which fell out of control after two bursts and was seen to break [up] in the air and then to crash [at Marquion].'[64]

Billy's second opponent in this fight was an Albatros Scout attacking Bristol F.2B two-seat fighter bombers from 11 Squadron, which confirmed the Albatros 'crashed and burst into flames'.[65] Trying to identify the pilot and/or unit in such a witnessed crash, however, is another matter. The *Nachrichtenblatt*'s Western Front casualties[66] were vague and appeared to be under-reported, when compared with the German 4th Army air staff report for 17 July, which listed several single-seat fighter casualties: a Jasta 4 air combat fatal casualty, a Jasta 10 forced landing and a Jasta 11 pilot lightly wounded.[67] However, those incidents took place in Flanders, farther north east of the area patrolled by 60 Squadron; their mention is to clarify why this author considers both of Bishop's 17 July claims as witnessed and entirely possible, but no matching losses have been found.

Those encounters were followed by two days of bad weather, during which Billy did not fly. 'To tell the truth, I am rather glad of the rest', he wrote, 'it is hard work on a good day [in] this hot weather, with the days so long.'[68] At midday on Friday, 20 July, he scored his last victory in Nieuport 23 B.1566, which had served him so well since April. He flew by himself on a mid-day 'hunt' near Havrincourt Wood, where he tried to 'surprise three EA, but failed, and … fired forty rounds' at one of them, while the other two climbed away.[69] Before the other pair could return and dive on him, Billy broke off the fight and flew away. After fifteen minutes, he wrote later:

'I surprised the rear one of two EA, firing fifteen rounds diagonally, up from thirty yards' range. He side-slipped, turned on his back and went down completely out of control. I dived on the second EA, but was unable to catch him … The first EA … [was] still out of control when it went through the clouds at 4,000 feet.'[70]

A German two-seater, possibly an Albatros, downed within a shell-pocked battlefield, demonstrates the difficulty of precise aircraft identification. (Author's Collection)

Billy's 20 July target could have been a single-seat or two-seat aeroplane, as neither his combat report nor the day's Communiqué[71] identified the type of German aircraft he encountered. The *Nachrichtenblatt* recorded that day's loss of 'one aeroplane, after aerial combat, [which] landed on the other side of the lines, [and] one aeroplane crashed not due to enemy action',[72] while 6th Army air staff reported three two-seaters down, but only one from air combat.[73] In the absence of further details from both sides, it is not possible to match that victory to a German loss.

CHAPTER TEN

A Hero at Last

'My total is now thirty-six, making me second to Guynemer, the
Frenchman, and third to Richthofen, the German, and second in
record to any Englishman, Ball having had forty-three ...'
– William A. Bishop[1]

After attaining his thirty-sixth victory on 20 July, Billy Bishop did not score again for over
a week. He continued to fly several times a day, except during foul weather on 25 and 26
July. He also transitioned from his light and almost delicate Nieuport to the S.E.5, a heavier, rugged workhorse of an aeroplane.

Of note during what Billy regarded as an unproductive time was the clarification about
air fighting made after the 21 July patrol by the new 60 Squadron commander, Captain William J.C.K. Cochran-Patrick, DSO, MC and Bar. Billy had led Lieutenants Horn, Mowle,
Rutherford and Soden into an inconclusive early evening attack against unspecified EAs
just past Quéant, after which Cochran-Patrick, a twenty-one-victory ace,[2] added to Billy's
combat report: 'The fighting was very close and somewhat of a mêlée, consequently aiming
was almost impossible and the result of attacks on individual EA could not be watched.'[3]

Morning and evening patrols on Sunday, the 22nd, were also frustrating. Later Billy
wrote to Margaret Burden: 'Tonight we did our first job on S.E.5s and my gun was the only
one that fired, and it shot holes in my propeller. It will take days to get a new one.'[4]

The propeller mishap was caused by a malfunctioning 'Constantinesco hydraulic synchronising ... [mechanism, which] gave a good deal of trouble before it became understood', according to British aircraft expert J.M. Bruce. 'Frequently ... an S.E.5 pilot might
find that he had shot his own [propeller] off.' [5]

Undaunted, at noon the following day, Billy took off alone in Nieuport 23 B.1566 and
attacked three EA near Comines; at the end, he 'escaped by diving into the clouds'.[6] That
evening, he flew in his new S.E.5 A.8936, to Fampoux, some sixteen miles east of his
aerodrome, where he went after a pair of unidentified German aeroplanes, and noted: 'I
fired forty rounds at 300 yards' [distance] at one of two EA, who immediately re-crossed
the lines, diving away. Owing to orders, I was unable to follow.'[7]

S.E.5s in Combat
Billy's S.E.5 was one of fifty aeroplanes from the first production batch[8] and the type still
had some flaws. At this time, a unit history noted, 60 Squadron S.E.5 'pilots had been temporarily forbidden to cross the [front] line due to engine unreliability, three failures having
occurred within a week'.[9] Hence, Billy acknowledged he had been careful to avoid straying

over German-held territory, risking engine failure and possible capture.

Late on the afternoon of Tuesday, 24 July, Billy made his last combat flight in his Nieuport and reported seeing three EAs that were 'out of range'.[10] After his return to Filescamp Farm aerodrome, B.1566 was sent to 1 Aircraft Depot at St. Omer and thence to other locations. By November 1918, it ended up as a training aeroplane in Egypt.[11] At that point, it was surplus equipment – with no mention made of its part in the 2 June 1917 attack, for which Billy Bishop was later awarded the Victoria Cross. In wartime, only currently useful equipment is important. Hence, it was of little consequence that, if Nieuport 23 B.1566 somehow endured, it would have become a significant historical artefact. It did not survive.

Billy often became frustrated when he did not perform up to his own expectations – especially now that he flew a newer, more powerful aeroplane. He wrote to Margaret:

'A whole week has gone by and I haven't got a Hun … I had one flight and missed a lovely chance of getting a Hun this side of the lines. He was way above and I climbed furiously, but was unable to get up to him …

'But, sweetheart, just wait … in a month from now I hope to be famous throughout the whole army.'[12]

This aeroplane in 60 Squadron's markings is thought to be S.E.5 A.8936, with which Billy Bishop was credited with scoring his thirty-seventh to forty-seventh aerial victories.
(Greg VanWyngarden)

Billy's joy in his current status – with something bigger yet to come – led him to more rhapsodising about his S.E.5, which was being decorated like a knight's steed:

'This morning I searched the whole sky for Huns and couldn't find one … I do want some good scraps in … S.E.5s. They are … just the fastest things possible. I am painting mine [with] a long blue nose and blue undercarriage, a diagonal stripe on the [fuselage] and a red Indian crawling along it. Then [on] the fin I'll have [it] chequered with blue and white. I think it will look rather pretty, and on it I'll put "Pepita" in white [letters] …'[13]

Writing to his mother the following day, Billy continued to rave about the S.E.5 – with its belt-fed 'Vickers machine gun mounted on top of the fuselage … synchronised … to fire forward through the [propeller arc and with] … one [drum-fed] Lewis machine gun … above the upper centre-section'[14] of the top wing. He felt the new aeroplane would advance his flying career:

'At last I am working in my S.E.5. It is wonderful. I have had four fights in it and got two Huns, one last night [28 July] and one this morning … [No] words of mine can ever express the wonderful exhilaration of being in a machine like the S.E.5 after the Nieuport, to have the advantage over the Huns that they used to have over us …

'[I have] never enjoyed myself more since I've been here … My total is now thirty-six, making me second to Guynemer, the Frenchman, and third to Richthofen, the German, and second in record to any Englishman, [Albert] Ball having had forty-three. Believe me, the days of risk I feel have passed. In a few weeks I'll have a new[er] S.E.5 with a 200-hp engine, instead of the 150-hp [engine now installed], and it will be still more wonderful.'[15]

But Billy's triumph on the evening of Saturday, 28 July, also demonstrated his impatience to attain success. He was on a flight south of Lille with Captain Caldwell and Second-Lieutenant William H. Gunner, when, he recalled:

'Seeing three EA flying north west, I left the patrol to catch them. I attacked them from the rear, firing on one from 200 yards' range. After [I fired] twenty rounds from each gun, he burst into flames …'[16]

Billy's rash departure from his comrades did not help them or him. Indeed, he got so far ahead of them that no one witnessed his first victory in an S.E.5. The *Nachrichtenblatt* summary for 28 July offers several casualties – 'six aeroplanes [lost], of which four were in aerial combat [and] two are missing'[17] – but provides no details to suggest a match for Billy's claim. The victory was, however, recorded in the daily Communiqué.[18]

'A Tremendously Brave Act'

The following morning, 'Grid' Caldwell gave Billy Bishop a lesson in the value of staying with one's comrades. Billy, 'Grid' and Bill Gunner attacked four Albatros D.V fighters[19] west of Douai. After three more German fighters joined the fray,[20] the S.E.5 pilots were outgunned and in a fight for survival. Gunner's engine had problems typical of early S.E.5s and an all-black Albatros zeroed in on his obviously-stricken aeroplane. Billy and 'Grid' tried to draw the German away from their comrade – but in vain. When Caldwell's guns jammed, he left the fight. But, seeing Billy all alone, 'Grid' returned. Billy recalled:

'[Caldwell came] eight miles across the lines after both his guns had choked, and he was entirely useless as a fighting unit, just to try to bluff away seven of the enemy who were attacking me … [It] was a tremendously brave act on his part, as he ran great risks of being killed, while [being] absolutely helpless to defend himself in any way.'[21]

The bluff worked. Caldwell and Bishop escaped from the swarm led by Jagdstaffel 12's commander, Oberleutnant [First-Lieutenant] Adolf Ritter [Knight] von Tutschek. [22]But, twenty-six-year-old Bill Gunner fell over Hénin-Liétard and was credited as Tutschek's twenty-first aerial victory.[23] British casualty records are so much more complete and accurate than comparable German records that historians have easily confirmed Tutschek's role in Gunner's death.[24]

Billy Bishop was also credited with an aerial victory in that fight: '[The] EA rolled on its back and fell completely out of control. I was only able to watch it [fall for] 1,000 feet, when it was still out of control.'[25] It was noted in the Communiqué.[26] There was no Jasta 12 casualty that day[27] and, hence, no matching German loss from that fight.

Numbers Again
That week, 13th Wing released its summary of 60 Squadron's most recent performance. As of 28 June, Captain Billy Bishop still logged in the most flights: ninety-six compared with the next three most active flyers, Captain Caldwell's fifty-five, Lieutenant William Jenkins' forty-six and Captain William Molesworth's thirty-four flights. Moreover, Billy continued to have the highest battle score, with thirty-five confirmed victories.[28]

It is noteworthy that, although Billy had not shared air combat triumphs since the wing's 26 May summary, his victory score was 'rounded' upward for this tally by someone at Wing HQ. In contrast, Molesworth, with one additional victory since May, had his amount of 1½ confirmed victories routinely advanced to 2½ in the end-July figures. Existing records offer no explanation for this disparity, which only helped fuel sentiments that Billy Bishop received special treatment.

The Guns of August
Rumours were circulating that Billy was slated to receive the Victoria Cross and much of what he did was being scrutinised. After Margaret wrote that she had read about such speculation in a Canadian newspaper, Billy (who probably knew he had been recommended for the highest British Empire honour by Brigadier General John F.A. Higgins in June[29]) struggled to maintain a modest bearing, and wrote:

'I have just [received] your letter about my VC. How awfully awkward, such a thing getting into the papers when it isn't so. There is no [official] news of it. They keep such things in "abeyance" [for] a long time, but everyone tells me it is sure to come. However, the main thing is, I have been recommended, only I do wish just for you I had it. But I hope that [honour] and other things will come along quickly.'[30]

Heavy rain and low clouds from the end of July through the first week in August 1917 led to postponement of the ill-starred British offensive called the Third Battle of Ypres.[31] The same bad weather also curtailed 60 Squadron's flight operations; thus, when a change to mist and low clouds heralded the onset of better conditions, Billy leaped at the opportunity to go 'hunting' again. He seemed to be in high spirits when he wrote to Margaret about the first successful air combats in August:

'I've … had two fights this week, and both have been successful: The first one [on 5 August] I was leading Molesworth and Horn and we saw eight Huns. I dived on them, firing on the leader. He turned and went under me, bursting into flames as he did so. I've never seen such a sight, just a huge mass of flames, no smoke at all. Moley and Horn had to leave owing to gun jams, and I had a horrible fight with six of the remainder. Moley and Horn got the seventh. After a bit, I got another, leaving five. Then both [of my] guns jammed and I had a horrible time for fifteen minutes, diving away whenever their backs were turned, and turning to bluff whenever they fired at me.

'The flight yesterday [6 August] was amusing. I was fighting with three [Albatroses] under the clouds and suddenly suspected a trap, so I zoomed up through the clouds just in time to see three more dive through … I dived after them and opened fire on one and he went straight down into the earth, making … [my] thirty-ninth. Hurrah!'[32]

Albatros D.III in the markings of Jasta 12, with which Billy Bishop fought
on 5 August 1917. (Dr. Volker Koos)

While Billy's combat report for 5 August lists only his two claims in that fight,[33] the day's Communiqué also credits Captain Molesworth and 'Lieutenant Hall' with a victory apiece.[34] The latter name was erroneous, as Charles S. Hall had been killed on 7 April (see Chapter Six). In fact, Molesworth and Lieutenant Spencer Horn filed a joint report; both said they 'followed the patrol leader' in the dive and, while they also fired on the first Albatros, their statements confirmed Billy as the victor in the fight.[35] Billy's victim was almost certainly Jasta 12's only loss that day, Leutnant Burkhard Lehmann, who was killed in a combat over Hendecourt- lès-Cagnicourt, where Billy's victim crashed.[36]

Some German aeroplanes – such as this DFW C.V – had light colours applied to their under surfaces as a form of aerial camouflage. It was not effective. (Dr. Volker Koos)

That day's *Nachrichtenblatt* entry listed 'three aeroplanes [shot down] in aerial combat on the other side of the lines'[37] and German 6th Army air staff reported the loss of a two-seater in addition to Ltn Lehmann's aeroplane.[38] Lack of details in the former source makes it impossible to suggest a link with Billy's second victory or the two credited to Molesworth and Horn on 5 August.

There was more to Billy's successful encounter on 6 August than was indicated in his letter above. He was on a 'lone wolf' patrol that afternoon,[39] when, as the day's RFC Communiqué summarised: 'Captain Bishop was joined by Captain [Carleton M.] Clement and Lieutenant [Ralph B.] Carter in a Bristol … [F.2B] of 22 Squadron,[40] and the two machines then attacked the EAs and dispersed them.'[41]

German 6th Army air staff reported no single-seater losses on 6 August and the *Nachrichtenblatt* listed only 'one aeroplane burned during an emergency landing, the crewmen were injured'. The latter account would not have referred to an Albatros fighter; hence, this author considers Billy's victory to have been witnessed, but with no matching German loss found.

Billy was successful again three days later, this time against a German reconnaissance aircraft. His combat report states that he failed to hit an Albatros Scout south west of Douai and then headed farther south, where he:

'... saw a two-seater this side of the [front] line. I climbed up to him and when [I was] a mile from him, he put his nose down and re-crossed the line. I followed and [overtook] him. The observer was firing all the time and I kept under his tail-plane, waiting for his [machine] gun to jam or run out of ammunition. Finally I got within seventy-five yards of him and opened fire. He fell completely out of control and ... spun and crashed into a field north of Écourt-St. Quentin. The fight had taken us from 14,000 to 6,000 feet. The pilot seemed afraid to put his nose down to [attain] more than 130 mph.' [42]

Aerial victory No. 42 was added to Billy's score and the incident was recorded in the day's Communiqué.[43] But, without a witness, finding a corresponding German casualty is difficult. The *Nachrichtenblatt*'s Western Front summary listed 'one aeroplane [shot down] by anti-aircraft fire',[44] to which German 6th Army air staff added that an observer in Bavarian Flieger-Abteilung (A) 288 was 'wounded by AA fire';[45] very likely, both accounts describe the same incident, but do not relate to the destruction mentioned in Billy's report. Hence, no matching German loss for this claim has been found.

The Highest Honour
The following day, Friday, 10 August 1917, Billy Bishop received news that truly changed his life. He would never again be in the shadow of any family member or military man. He was about to become a hero at last and he eagerly wrote to Margaret:

'This afternoon a message came for me to ring up General Trenchard, which I did, and he said he wanted to be the first to congratulate me on my getting the VC. So it is added to my collection of ribbons. The three [VC, DSO and MC] look very swanky, really, and I try not to push my chest out, not any more than I can help.

'Tomorrow night the squadron is giving me a big dinner. Old Jack Scott, my ... Colonel [G.F. Pretyman] and a lot of other people will be here, so I imagine it will develop into the biggest of ... [drinking bouts], but then the occasion I truly feel warrants it.'[46]

And what a celebration it was – recounted in a letter home by Billy's friend Captain William Molesworth, who by then commanded A Flight:

'[Our] "stunt merchant", [as he called Billy] has been awarded the VC for that [German] aerodrome show I told you about. We celebrated it last night with one of the finest "busts" I have ever had. There were speeches and lots of good "bubbly" ...

'After dinner we had a torchlight procession to the various squadrons stationed on the aerodrome ... led by our Very-light [illumination flare] experts... We charged into one mess and proceeded to throw everyone and everything … out the window. We then went over to [another] squadron. The wretched lads were all in bed, but we soon had them out, and bombarded their mess with Very lights, the great stunt being to shoot one in through one window and out the other. I can't imagine why the blessed place didn't go up in flames. After annoying these people for a bit, we retired to our own mess, where we danced and sang till the early hours of the morning.'[47]

The grand celebration was as much an opportunity to release tensions of life at the Front as to hail the announcement of Bishop's Victoria Cross. The morning after, however, was another work day and Canada's air hero logged in two sorties: one in the morning, shortened due to bad weather, and an early evening outing in which 'no EA [were] seen'.[48]

In London on Monday, 13 August, *The Times* published a one-column-width, thirty-four-line article about Billy Bishop. In keeping with the government's policy of minimal individual publicity for British Empire heroes, the item simply quoted the official Victoria Cross warrant text from the *The London Gazette*. But *The Times*' headline said it all: 'An Airman V.C. – Single-handed Attack on an Aerodrome.'[49] Three days later, *Flight* magazine published a similarly modest piece under the headline 'A Canadian V.C.,'[50] highlighting that the highest honour for valour was bestowed upon men from around the British Empire. Other news media followed suit.

There were also other interesting and exciting matters, as Billy wrote:

'I've had a busy few days of it lately. Congratulations have been pouring in, of course, and I had to go and see General Trenchard yesterday [13 August] and I learnt some news which I suppose is good, but I don't want to hear it. He is recommending me [to become] chief fighting instructor at one of the … big schools they are building in England. I hate the thought of it … it will mean leaving all my friends here. It will also mean that my chance of a trip to Canada will be a wash-out.

'I had a great scrap last night with three Huns. I had just climbed through some clouds and three of the blighters dived on me. I went head-on for the first one, firing both guns. He lost his nerve and swerved and I filled him with lead. He fell in flames. I then fought the other two and sent one of them down in flames, while the other escaped.

'I go on leave Sunday [19 August] and I expect I will get all my medals then.'[51]

Billy's latest double victory – two Albatros fighters – was reported in the day's RFC Communiqué, this time with a celebratory leading sentence: 'When flying above the clouds, Capt. Bishop – who has just been awarded the VC (in addition to the DSO and MC, which had previously been conferred upon him) – saw three EA diving at him from above ...'[52]

Newly promoted Major William J.C.K. Cochran-Patrick noted at the bottom of Billy's combat report: 'Captain Bishop was out alone' on the patrol. Both German aeroplanes were accepted by 13th Wing HQ as destroyed and set on fire 'south of Douai,'[53] and credited as Billy's forty-third and forty-fourth aerial victories. The *Nachrichternblatt*'s Western

Front entry for 13 August mentioned the loss of 'one aeroplane in aerial combat [and] one aeroplane has not returned',[54] with no further details that might have confirmed or denied Billy's claim.

Air staff reports for the German 1st, 2nd and 17th Armies for this time have not been found to determine whether any of their single-seaters were lost. Of German records for 13 August, the 4th Army air staff reported three two-seaters (from two different units) with crewmen who suffered non-fatal wounds,[55] and its 6th Army counterpart listed yet another two-seater crew wounded by ground-based machine-gun fire.[56] It is unlikely that any of the two-seaters were Billy's adversaries, but the *Nachrichtenblatt*'s vague report and the lack of other German documentation makes it impossible to suggest a link – or the lack thereof.

During an early morning patrol on the 14th, Billy reported sighting three EA, which were too 'far out of range'[57] to pursue. But at 8:20 the following evening he reported:

'I chased three EA, diving at the rear and highest one, opening fire at 100 yards. He did not see me and after thirty rounds from each gun he side-slipped, turned over and fell completely out of control. I watched him for about 8,000 feet and he was still out of control. I was unable to see more owing to bad light.'[58]

Billy's inability to identify his target as a single-seat or two-seat aeroplane is an obstacle to finding a matching loss. The account of his combat in the RFC Communiqué[59] was equally vague and the *Nachrichtenblatt* reported only the non-specific loss of: 'One aeroplane in aerial combat, one aeroplane missing, as well as one officer dead, one Unteroffizier [Corporal] wounded.'[60]

German 6th Army air staff reported: 'One aeroplane of Flieger-Abteilung 5, after aerial combat near Pont-à-Vendin (this side of the lines), crashed in flames; the crew of Ltn.d.Res [Wilhelm] Liebert and Ltn.d.Res [Wilhelm] Merschmann [are] dead.'[61] The German aeroplane went down within five miles of the crash site of Billy's target; hence the German reconnaissance aeroplane could have been Billy Bishop's forty-fifth victory.

One More Pair

Billy's last combat flight of 1917 was another 'lone wolf' evening patrol on Thursday, 16 August. He reported that, within six minutes and about three miles apart, he shot down two German aeroplanes north east of Lens. While at 14,000 feet, he stated: 'I saw a two-seater approaching the lines slightly above me. I put my nose up and fired a short burst. He immediately turned and I closed in underneath [while] firing. He did a turn and a spin and two [wings] fell off, a moment later the [wings] on the other side fell off.'[62] After going a thousand feet lower, he wrote: 'I chased two scouts which were approaching and turned away, firing at the rear one at long range. He went down into a spin after eighty rounds and I watched him crash half a mile north of Carvin. The other EA escaped.'[63]

The 13th Wing HQ credited the pair as Billy's forty-sixth and forty-seventh victories, which assured they were noted in the RFC Communiqué.[64] Once again, no potential matches were offered in the *Nachrichtenblatt* daily loss report, which recorded only: 'One [unidentified] aeroplane in aerial combat, one G-Type bombing aeroplane not returned, as well as two pilots perished, [and] three observers wounded.'[65] As previously noted, air staff reports for the German 1st, 2nd and 17th Armies in 1917 have not been found. Of the archival sources available, German 6th Army air staff reported no casualties for 16 August, while the 4th Army air staff listed three fighter aircraft casualties, all of which were in Flanders,[66] some thirty-five miles north east of where Billy stated the fights took place and not a reasonable distance to 'stray'. Without clarification of the aircrew casualties noted in the *Nachrichtenblatt* – especially some mention of a two-seater that lost its wings – it is not possible to link Billy's victories to German losses.

Billy himself seemed to be unconcerned about the administrative side of his work. As his son Arthur, who heard many of his father's stories over the years, wrote:

'That night Bishop was not noticeably melancholy at the hilarious farewell party in 60 Squadron's mess. But for the first time he felt no regret at being done with killing – for weeks, or months, or for the rest of his life.'[67]

Bishop may have sensed that he was being pulled out of harm's way by a government that needed a living hero to inspire other young men. But he was leaving at the top of his form: credited with forty-seven confirmed aerial victories[68] – three more than Albert Ball attained[69] – and with the same high awards accorded to Ball.

Back to England

Billy Bishop could not have dreamed of the splendour that awaited him in England. Initially, he was put up in a cottage in Pangbourne, Berkshire, west of London. The following morning he wrote to Margaret:

'[I] have just come down here for the weekend. [This is] the most perfect place you could imagine, on the Thames with the river running by … the front of the house. I arrived in town last night [17 August] at 8:00 to find a banquet waiting for me and a dance after that. What time do you think I went to bed? A quarter to 6. I was dead tired and I couldn't even dance …'[70]

While Billy was enjoying his new life, other events were going on behind the scenes. Lady St. Helier, in touch with the War Office, shared with Billy's mother the details of the forthcoming medals presentation ceremony at Buckingham Palace:

'Billy is going to the investiture on Wednesday [29 August]. While he feels rather nervous about it, being his first time, I am so glad he has not been here before, because Princess Marie Louise [a granddaughter of Queen Victoria] told me last week that the King said the one thing he wanted was to give the VC, DSO and MC at the same time, preferably to a colonial officer and … Billy is the first [such] person who has won them all and the King is very pleased, as he has heard so much about him from the princess. [Billy] is very well, although he looks a little older perhaps, and one could never believe all he has gone through.'[71]

After the investiture, Billy dashed off a short letter to Margaret, going on about his bright future and then cutting through the pomp and ceremony that went with being awarded his medals from King George V:

'I am having the most awful rush. I have been transferred from the establishment in France to England and made a major to be dated last Tuesday [28 August[72]]. Then … I am to command a fighting school in Scotland …

'I received my medals from the King yesterday. Oh darling, it was too awful for words. For fifteen minutes the old boy talked to me in front of a huge crowd. I nearly died.' [73]

King George V (left) in conversation with Major William A. Bishop, VC, DSO, MC, and an unidentified Scottish colonel at Windsor Park. (DHH/DND photo RE 22072-2)

A Hero's Life

Before the VC investiture Billy complained to Margaret: 'I am, of course, having a wonderful time and being rushed off my feet, but one gets fed up with the artificial life here …'[74] After the ceremony and attendant publicity, however, he felt the full force of his new station in life. According to Arthur Bishop, his father learned that:

'[Now] he was a major celebrity and eminent Londoners were pulling strings to get invitations to Portland Place. "Granny" St. Helier hugely enjoyed the embarrassment of her protégé for a week (shrewdly divining that he too was finding the discomfiture not entirely unbearable), then packed him off with another of her "lodgers" on a tour of country houses owned by her friends.'[75]

Thus, it was not until mid-September that Billy wrote to Margaret:

'[Much] has happened since I … [last] wrote to you. First, I am having a bust done of [myself] by Claire Sheridan[76] for the Canadian government … secondly, I am to

131

have my portrait [done] next week by some big artist … also for the Canadian government.

'Thirdly, I've been to see General Turner, who says he may get me back to Canada for a month.

'Fourthly, I've been given a Bar to my DSO, I know not what for.

'Fifthly … Sir Max Aitken [Lord Beaverbrook, Canadian-born business and newspaper tycoon] may publish a book on my [air] combats, out of which I would receive royalties, which might mean much money, thousands of dollars, even pounds.

'And, lastly, you are the best and dearest woman in the world. My one desire is to get back to you.'[77]

The general who Billy mentioned so casually was a great Canadian military figure, the Boer War hero Lieutenant-General Sir Richard Turner, VC, KCB, KCMG, DSO, who then commanded Canadian forces in Britain. After learning that the flying school in Scotland was behind in its construction schedule, Billy wanted to return to aerial combat in France but was told by Lord Hugh Cecil in the War Office: 'That doesn't seem to be on the cards. In fact, there isn't a job for you just now.'[78] He confided his disappointment to Lady St. Helier, who quickly sent a note to her friend 'Dick Turner', whose office arranged home leave for Billy. Two good causes were served by that action: Billy and his reputation were saved for other purposes, and Margaret Burden's family could begin planning a wedding to bring the new national air fighting hero into the family.

Billy Bishop was aptly heralded as the 'Canadian airman who has thrilled the Dominion' on the eve of his triumphal return home.
(DHH/DND)

But Billy would not soon wear the Bar to the Distinguished Service Order. Surely, he knew that it was in the offing, as the recommendation had been signed on 27 August 1917[79] by Brigadier-General John F.A. Higgins, commander of the RFC's 3rd Brigade – but processing such a high honour took time.

Now, Billy's German adversaries understood his propaganda and morale value. As part of its regular review of Allied nations' news media, easily obtained by diplomats in neutral nations, the *Nachrichtenblatt* reported in September:

'According to information in the *Canadian Gazette* [issue] of 23 August 1917, there are 1,227 Canadians in the British air services. Of that number, 867 are in the RFC and 360 in the RNAS. The Canadians consider themselves to be the best flyers in the RFC. Also the currently best known British pilot, Captain W.A. Bishop, is Canadian.'[80]

While Billy Bishop was enjoying glory on both sides of the battle lines, another major competitor was not so fortunate. The highest-scoring French fighter pilot at that time, Capitaine Georges Guynemer – who, at age twenty-two, the same age as Billy – was shot down and killed on 11 September. He had fifty-three confirmed victories to his credit[81] and crashed within German lines.

But, while German heroes' exploits were lionised in the German press, for much of World War I military figures fighting for Britain's king and country served with little public recognition, as rationalised at the time by the journal *Flying*:

'The Royal Flying Corps is coldly impersonal in its official reports. It is in this aspect splendidly unique. It alone among the belligerents steadily refuses the limelight of publicity so far as its personnel is concerned. In its bulletins aeroplanes, but not men, are mentioned. The names of its flying officers and observers are recorded only in the Roll of Honour or in the list of awards. "Baron von Richthofen," says the German bulletin, "yesterday secured his sixtieth victim". Doubtless the Germans have some good reason for booming their Richthofens at the expense of their [lesser] comrades. It is their considered policy, and it has its advantages as well as its drawbacks. On the whole, our policy is peculiarly British, and it is based upon British traditions.

'It springs partly from the regimental spirit, partly from the public-school spirit, and partly from the sporting spirit which is found in the British wherever they are … The men who have built up the traditions of the Royal Flying Corps have made this spirit their foundation. They have put the efficiency of the service as a whole above the glory of its units or of the individuals … [in] those units. They have filled the service with an esprit de corps which is not surpassed by that of any of the older [branches] …' [82]

The effect on military and civilian morale by withholding publicity about heroic flyers would be debated in parliament in the months to come. Eventually, the heroism of more British Empire sailors, soldiers and airmen would emerge from under a cloak of overly modest anonymity. Perhaps the British government, populace and aviation establishment grew weary of having their noses rubbed in German propaganda. An autumn 1917 example was *Flight* magazine's article about the appearance of *The Red Battle Flyer*, the English translation of Manfred von Richthofen's memoir, in which the war's highest-scoring fighter ace wrote with his usual supreme confidence:

'My brother [Lothar]'s twenty-second adversary was the famous Captain Ball [VC], by far the best English flying man. The equally well known Major Hawker [VC] I had already taken to my bosom some months earlier. It gave me special joy that it should be my brother's luck to down the second of England's champions.'[83]

A positive example of publicising heroes was seen in a moment of acclaim Billy Bishop received while travelling back to his home in September 1917. Arthur Bishop described the scene:

> 'In the confines of a Canada-bound ship Bishop learned for the first time what winning of the … [British Empire's] premier award for valour entailed. On the first day out he strolled into a salon where a boxing tournament was being held. The two men in the ring stopped pummelling each other. The spectators stood up and cheered. Bishop reddened, turned on his heels and left.'

There would be more such recognition to come – for many years. Billy became accustomed to it.

CHAPTER ELEVEN

Winged Victory

'The true soldier fights not because he hates what is in front of him,
but because he loves what is behind him.'
– G.K. Chesterton[1]

Billy Bishop, the twenty-three-year-old fearless air combatant, finally faced something that overwhelmed him. When he got off the train in Montreal on Thursday, 17 September 1917, he was greeted by a sea of thousands of faces of people who were thrilled to see him back in his native land. And at the front of this jubilant mob stood the two women Billy loved most, his mother and Margaret Burden. As the trio were guided through the human mass – military and civilian dignitaries, newspaper reporters and photographers, and Canadians from all stations in life – to the official reception platform, Billy had a claustrophobic moment, described by his son Arthur:

'[Billy] leaned over to Margaret and said, "For heaven's sake let's get away from here". His mother was beaming with pride and enjoying herself hugely. Margaret patted his hand and said soothingly: "Cheer up. You'll have to get used to it – there's more to come."'[2]

Billy could not yet grasp that his homecoming was significant far beyond adoring crowds. The medals and recognition he strived for had become symbolically larger than marks of personal achievement and his determination to prove himself worthy of Margaret. Those facets of his young life became magnified to serve a national purpose within the perspective offered by Bishop biographer Dan McCaffery:

'By [autumn] 1917 … casualties were … reaching catastrophic proportions. The Canadian Corps, which had won spectacular victories in 1916 and 1917, was now badly depleted and there were not enough volunteers coming forward to fill the holes created by German machine guns. The situation was so serious that the [Canadian] House of Commons passed a conscription act in April of 1917. Unfortunately, conscription created bitter divisions in the country, splitting the population along [ethnic] lines. In Québec, French Canadians viewed the war as simply another of Europe's endless conflicts and bitterly opposed the draft. English Canada had a different opinion: it was willing to see the war through to the end, no matter how many Canadian boys had to be slaughtered in the process. Yet even in English Canada, enthusiasm for conscription was not universal. Many farmers, who needed help in the fields, were opposed to the drafting of their sons, and there were angry demonstrations against conscription in Toronto and Calgary.' [3]

Knight of the Clouds

On his travels from Montreal to Toronto and then to his home in Owen Sound, Billy Bishop was seen as a symbol of Canadian patriotism. A seasoned *Toronto Globe* writer summed it up:

> '[Although] I have seen many receptions of this kind, I admit that this was the first one that gave me a real thrill and I cheered for all I was worth. Come to think of it this was the first time I had ever seen a young hero – and heroes should always be young … This knight of the clouds was fresh from his triumphs, and his cheeks are still bronzed from voyaging through "lucent solitudes". No wonder we cheered, and just because he looked so modest we cheered all the more.'[4]

Billy was home, but not forgotten by his adversaries. When the *Nachrichtenblatt* weekly intelligence summary learned that Billy had left France, it quickly reported: 'Captain Bishop, who is said to have achieved over forty [aerial] victories, is, according to a [prisoner's] statement, presently in England.'[5] Billy's air combat successes had made him enough of a 'bogeyman' that the Luftstreitkräfte had a lingering interest in tracking his movements.

And he was considered significant among the Allied powers. In France, aviation journalism pioneer Jacques Mortane featured Billy on the front cover of his weekly magazine *La Guerre Aérienne Illustrée* and wrote a full-page article titled 'L'autre As des As: Bishop' [The Other Ace of Aces: Bishop].[6] Mention of an 'other' top ace alluded to Lieutenant René Fonck, who – the *Nachrichtenblatt* reported[7] – was hailed in French newspapers as 'Guynemer's avenger' for allegedly shooting down Leutnant Kurt Wissemann, the German pilot credited with killing top ace Capitaine Georges Guynemer. The German report begrudgingly recognized France's skill in publicising its airmen as martyrs and as heroes.

Meanwhile, Billy enjoyed a triumphant return to his alma mater, the Royal Military College in Kingston, Ontario. In Toronto, 'he was saluted by his old regiment, the Mississauga Horse'.[8] As proof of the positive power of his new status, after he made a speech for the Red Cross war fund in Toronto, 'the society's objective of $500,000 was surpassed by one-third of a million dollars'.[9] To top off Billy's good fortune, at the end of September, word came that the Bar to his Distinguished Service Order had been approved[10] and would be presented in the new year.

Aside from the good-will Billy's visit brought to Canada, a key purpose of his home leave was for him to marry Margaret. The wedding took place on Wednesday, 17 October 1917, in the Timothy Eaton Memorial Church in Toronto; the church is named for Margaret's grandfather, the founder of the Eaton's department store chain. Like so many other recent milestones in Billy's life, his wedding was reported in such international media as *Flight* magazine: 'Major W.A. Bishop, VC, DSO, MC, of the Royal Flying Corps, was married … at Toronto, Canada to Miss Margaret Eaton Burden, daughter of Mr. C.E. Burden and niece of Sir John Eaton.'[11]

In the newspaper photo caption of Billy's and Margaret's wedding, he was described as 'Canada's premier flier, winner of the Victoria Cross, DSO and other honors, with the record of 110 air battles and 47 airplanes destroyed'. (DHH/DND)

The honeymooners left the limelight in Canada and headed south for the Catskill Mountains in the US state of New York. They retreated to Yama Farms, an exclusive resort of international renown that assured privacy and relaxation to leaders in science, industry, the arts and even attracted nobility. It was one of the few places where Billy did not need the Victoria Cross or a discreet word to open doors for him and his new bride. It was their last respite before Billy's new RFC duties began.

After returning to Canada, however, Billy was assigned to the British War Mission in Washington, DC, to assist Lieutenant-Colonel Lionel Wilmot Brabazon Rees, VC, MC, in his work with Americans developing the US Army Air Service.[12] Rees, the seventh aviation recipient of the Victoria Cross, received that honour, as did Billy Bishop, for making a single-handed attack against overwhelming German opposition. Rees had gone after eight German bombers and shot down two, even while wounded and under continual fire from the other adversaries, which he scattered.[13] The pair of VC recipients were soon joined by noted RFC tactician Major Richard Graham Blomfield, former CO of 56 Squadron. But the fledgling USAS was too focused on the lagging production of its own aircraft to use effectively such high-value tactical assistance. Consequently, the trio of experts' duties 'while interesting, were not too onerous or time consuming.'[14]

During this time Billy wrote *Winged Warfare*, a book about his experiences inspired by his letters to Margaret. He also authored 'Tales of the British Air Service', an homage to Albert Ball, for the US-based *National Geographic* magazine. [15]

New Year, New Opportunities

In December 1917, Billy was again honoured with a high distinction. Listed as being 'Mentioned in Despatches',[16] his name appeared in an official report submitted by a superior officer to the Imperial High Command, describing his gallant, meritorious action in the face of the enemy.[17] Billy was also ordered back to England in January. That was good news made even better when Margaret was allowed to travel with him, as she 'qualified for overseas service as a … [member of a] voluntary aid detachment'.[18] The bad news came after their ship docked in England and they were informed that the aerial gunnery school project, plagued by high costs and other factors, had been cancelled.

But, in that dark moment, once again the Bishop luck emerged. A quick visit to Lord Hugh Cecil at the War Office assured Billy that he would have a posting more to his liking than running a school. As Arthur Bishop described it:

'[The] dire need for additional air power meant that Bishop was … assigned forthwith to form a fighter squadron of his own. Lord Hugh Cecil conveyed the good news and added … "Of course, you'll have to learn how to fly all over again … You haven't been in a 'plane for more than six months, and don't think we've been standing still in that time. The 'planes are more highly powered, get more altitude, [and] are more manoeuvrable …"' [19]

Billy was retrained at the Gosport Flying School, led by Major Robert R. Smith-Barry, who had commanded 60 Squadron before Billy's time there. After two weeks at the school, he was assigned to 'Hounslow aerodrome, just outside London, to take up his post as commanding officer of the newly-formed 85 Squadron'. [20]

Next, Billy and Margaret were invited to Buckingham Palace, where he received the Bar to his DSO. They also enjoyed some royal humour, when King George V told the flyer: 'If you win any more honours we will have to place them before your name, instead of after it – we will have to call you "Arch" Bishop.'[21]

Flight magazine reported that Billy's second DSO honoured his 'consistent dash and great fearlessness [which] have set a magnificent example to the pilots of his squadron … [He displayed] a fighting spirit and determination to get to close quarters with his opponents which have earned the admiration of all in contact with him.' [22]

85 Squadron

As CO of 85 Squadron, Billy Bishop was given considerable latitude in selecting pilots. First, he gathered former 60 Squadron pilots. His son Arthur wrote:

'Bishop ran down [Spencer] Horn in Scotland … and he did not need much persua-

The three American 'musketeers' of 85 Squadron, RAF, from left: First-Lieutenants John McGavock Grider, Elliott White Springs and Lawrence K. Callahan. They were immortalized in the World War I classic book *War Birds - The Diary of an Unknown Aviator*, inspired by Grider's diary, but written by Springs. With typical panache, Springs wore a specially tailored US Air Service uniform adorned with RAF wings; his compatriots wore USAS wings. (Courtesy The Springs Close Family Archives, Fort Mill, SC)

sion to join … as a flight commander of 85 Squadron … "Lobo" Benbow …wore a monocle in his eye and a Military Cross on his breast … Next came [Charles Beverley Robinson] MacDonald … who had been a battalion sergeant-major in Bishop's class at Royal Military College, and [yet another] fellow Canadian, Roy Hall.'[23]

Billy also sought recommendations. Thus, Horn proposed three Americans from the 'Oxford Group' of 204 cadets trained by the RFC but with no US squadrons in Europe to use them.[24] Retelling his father's account, Arthur described the Americans: 'Larry Callahan, a tall youth from Louisville, Kentucky, and two Princeton [University] graduates, Mac Grider and Elliott White Springs … the son of a millionaire textile manufacturer …'[25] They were earnest pilots and life-of-the-party types who brought a glow to the squadron officers' mess.

Billy and Margaret rented a house not far from Hounslow aerodrome. It quickly became an informal squadron headquarters and also the site of legendary revelry, which finally prompted Margaret to ask: 'Don't they ever sleep?'[26]

Billy's squadron was originally assigned to fly Sopwith 5F.1 Dolphin biplane fighters fitted with 200-hp Hispano-Suiza engines, which had development problems.[27] Billy appealed for and received new S.E.5a aircraft, equipped with Wolseley Viper 200-hp engines.[28]

The training and the parties continued in April, through the amalgamation of the Royal Flying Corps and the Royal Naval Air Service into the Royal Air Force on the 1st[29] and the death over British lines of the fabled and feared Manfred von Richthofen on the 21st.[30]

This S.E.5a of 85 Squadron is believed to have been flown by Elliott White Springs, who was credited with four aerial victories in RAF service. As leader of the 148th Aero Squadron, USAS, he was credited with another eleven victories. (Courtesy The Springs Close Family Archives, Fort Mill, SC)

Arthur Bishop wrote:
'Somehow the serious business of preparing 85 Squadron for war continued. Someone pinned the name "Flying Foxes" on the squadron and the pilots asked Bishop's permission to attach fox-tails to their [aeroplanes'] wing struts. Bishop decided to make this a privilege of pilots who shot down two enemy 'planes.

'When Princess Marie Louise heard this [news], she presented 85 Squadron with a mess-table centrepiece in the form of an inscribed silver fox. In a sense the squadron had royal sponsorship.'[31]

Off to France

On Wednesday, 22 May, Billy Bishop led 85 Squadron from Hounslow Heath to Lympne, near the Channel coast in Kent, and then over the water to 1 Aircraft Depot at St. Omer. [32]

That evening he wrote to Margaret:

'We had a delightful Channel crossing … [Then] by flights and I by my lonesome, we proceeded to our aerodrome [at Petite-Synthe]. It is up north, just near the coast … We all landed safely, that is, seventeen of us …' [33]

One of the Americans, First-Lieutenant John McGavock Grider, also wrote home after arriving at Petite-Synthe. He commented on Billy:

'Our trip over the Channel was great … We crossed in fifteen minutes …

'Get the major's new book that is being published in America. I think it's [titled] "Aerial Warfare" or something like that. It will give you some idea of the man I am with, anyway. He is one of the best and we all love him …

'We have a wonderful mess here. A damned stout crowd, as the English say …' [34]

The streamlined LVG C.V was often mistaken for its Albatros counterpart. It served from summer 1917 until the end of the war. The aeroplane seen here is in summer 1918 national markings. (Greg VanWyngarden)

Bishop and his men were eager for combat but, at the moment, were content to settle into their new facilities. Billy noted they found a way to cope with intermittent rain showers: 'Last night we all sat around and sang songs in our new mess after Springs and Grider had mixed us all a pail of egg-nog.' [35]

Two days later, however, Billy got down to business:

'Tonight [26 May] I took Horn and Springs up to look at the lines … I saw four Huns and then one alone. [I] longed to dash over and down him, but I want to study their tactics, so I kept [to] this side. He was just doing the same old things as a year ago … "Grid" Caldwell was down [for a visit] and he says a baby can hit Huns now.' [36]

Caldwell, now commanding 74 Squadron, may have been overly optimistic about the air war in Flanders following the failed German offensive in March, but he noted that the protracted withdrawal of enemy ground forces created opportunities for Allied airmen.

Billy was pleased with the performance of his new S.E.5a (serial number) C.6490. He was eager to test it in combat and, after an opportunity presented itself on the afternoon of Monday, 27 May, he wrote to Margaret:

'This morning I had my guns sighted again and a lot of other things adjusted … This afternoon at 4:00 I went out … and crossed [over the lines] after a big fat two-seater. There were ten scouts up higher, so I came back [over the lines] and got up to 17,500 feet, then went over to worry them from above.

'Suddenly, 200 feet below me, coming toward me appeared a two-seater. He saw me at practically the same moment I saw him, and turned to allow his observer to fire and also to beetle off east. I then … slipped under his tail and he, seeing this, lost his head and put his nose down for all he was worth. So I closed up to 125 yards and let him have ten [rounds] from each gun. I think the first burst killed both [crew-

In various air combats, Billy Bishop fought against diverse Albatros Scouts, including the D.V type seen here. He was never shot down by any German airman. (Dr. Volker Koos)

men]. He sort of went half out of control, skidding to the left, and I closed up to fifty yards and got in thirty-five more [rounds] from each gun. Then his left top [wing], followed by the right, folded back and he fell. In a second the [bottom] wings and tail came off. It was about four miles over [the lines] and I am just waiting to hear if [British anti-aircraft] saw it …'[37]

Billy's combat report noted that his target 'fell east of Passchendaele'.[38] Ambiguously worded German records make it difficult to identify a possible match for Billy's first 1918 victory. The *Nachrichtenblatt* report for the Western Front on 27 May stated losses as: 'Four aeroplanes in aerial combat, seven [flyers] missing, among them Leutnant Windisch.'[39] The report was candid enough to admit losing twenty-two-victory ace and Pour le Mérite recipient Rudolf Windisch, who fell into French captivity and then disappeared without a trace.[40] But it cloaked information about the day's other German casualties. German 6th Army air staff reported no losses for that day and corresponding reports for the 4th and 17th Armies are not available in known archives.

The daily RAF Communiqué, successor to the former RFC publication of the same name, added only that on 27 May Billy 'dived on an EA two-seater over Houthulst Forest' and sent it down.[41]

Pfalz D.IIIa 1370/17 of Jasta 10 shows the sleek look for which the type was known. This particular aeroplane was forced to land within British lines on 27 December 1917 and, as seen here, assigned the captured identification number G 110. The pilot, Vzfw Hecht, was taken prisoner. (Author's Collection)

The following day, 28 May, the Communiqué listed only: 'Major W.A. Bishop, 85 Squadron (two),'[42] shorthand for two victories confirmed. Billy Bishop's 28 May air combats are explained at the beginning of Chapter One in this book, including *Nachrichtenblatt* obfuscation in the daily account. In glaring contrast was the useful information provided by German 4th Army air staff, the personal war diary of Jagdstaffel 7's commanding officer and a post-war German aviation necrology. In this author's view, that day's German air casualty overview is a murky brew that is typical of the inexplicable nature of reporting many aerial combats.

Billy did not fly the following day, but his men made him proud, as he related to Margaret:

'Tonight [29 May] Benbow, Carruthers, Canning, Horn and McGregor went out for a practice patrol and met a lot of Huns, which they attacked. A big fight followed and McGregor got one. So that makes four for the squadron in three days. Not bad for a new squadron which hasn't officially crossed the lines yet, is it?'[43]

During the last week in May 1918, Billy's air victory score rose dramatically, but his success was not without cost. He had recruited Captain Louis Benbow, MC, who had eight confirmed victories to his credit from his time with 40 Squadron.[44] Then, as stated in the letter below, on the 30th he became anguished after Benbow tried his hand at 'lone-wolf' hunting in the manner that worked for Billy:

'I'm too worried to write much tonight. Lobo [Benbow] went out by himself … at 7 o'clock and has not returned. It is now … [9:50] and he has only a little over two hours' petrol. But … we are a long way back and he may easily have had a forced landing …

'For myself, it has been another very lucky day … [This] afternoon I went out and ran into two two-seaters, one of which I shot down. The other I frightened so much that he dived his wings off.

'Tonight I went out again and, sure enough, two Albatroses were waiting to be shot down, so I proceeded to do it. Got one and sent the other down out of control, but I haven't claimed him, as I didn't see the result. That makes my total fifty-three.'[45]

The day's RAF Communiqué stated that Billy was 'attacked by two EA two-seaters. He zoomed and fired at one of them, which fell in flames near Roulers. He then got on the tail of the second one, which, after several bursts had been fired, fell to pieces in the air. [He] also destroyed an Albatros Scout later in the day.'[46]

The *Nachrichtenblatt* summary for 30 May reported: 'Three aeroplanes [lost] in aerial combat, one through ground machine-gun fire, two [flyers] are missing, five captive balloons [sent down].'[47] Once again, German 4th, 6th Army and 17th Armies' air staff reports are not available. Some clarification of the *Nachrichtenblatt* report was found in the unit history of Flieger-Abteilung (A) 221, which reported losing a distinguished pilot-observer team to ground machine-gun fire that day: Vizefeldwebel Heinrich-Ernst Schäfer, who became a posthumous recipient of Prussia's highest enlisted man's award, the Golden Military Merit Cross, and Leutnant der Reserve Wilhelm Paul Schreiber, the only posthumous Pour le Mérite recipient.[48] However, they were brought down two hours before the two-seaters that Billy Bishop claimed and, therefore, cannot be considered as his fifty-first or fifty-second victories. The *Nachrichtenblatt* is too vague to suggest any other German casualty reported that day.

On 31 May, Billy wrote:

'We learned today that poor old Lobo, bless him, was killed last night.[49] He fell just inside our lines.[50] His funeral is tomorrow. I would like to go, but I don't think I shall, and I'm not allowing any of the flying officers to go. It is too upsetting … Three Huns surprised him and fought him for some time, finally shooting his wings off and he fell, of course killed instantly … He died a hero's death.

'We have sworn to get forty Huns to avenge him. Today I got two more, one this afternoon. I sent a Pfalz Scout down out of control, opened fire from twenty yards' range and riddled the damn' pilot. Later I attacked a two-seater and killed the observer, I think. This evening … I caught [a Pfalz] two miles over and he was so terrified he never even attempted a turn. I shot him to pieces from fifty yards … That makes ten for the squadron … My total is fifty-five.'[51]

Billy was credited with one Pfalz Scout and one two-seater, ten minutes apart.[52] Based on existing reports, his victories that day may have included a Pfalz D.IIIa from Jagdstaffel 30.[53] That unit's airfield at Phalempin, south of Lille, was within Billy's operational area; further, a 6th Army report noted that Jasta 30 pilot Ltn Erich Kaus was 'slightly wounded in aerial combat with S.E.5s'.[54] Billy's second victory may have been a Halberstadt Cl.II or Hannover Cl.II from the aerial protection unit Schlachtstaffel 36, which went down over Ronchin, a suburb of Lille. Gefreiter Wilhelm Schoop, the pilot, and Unteroffizier Sindt, the aerial gunner, were described as 'wounded in aerial combat'.[55]

Moreover, the day's RAF Communiqué accorded sparse mention of Billy's latest double victory, including him among twenty-one single- and two-seat airmen who had 'also brought down' enemy aircraft that day.[56] In a style change, the Communiqué now heralded singular achievements of lesser known flyers. In any event, Billy had received enough acclaim and successfully attacked another black Pfalz D.IIIa the following day.

Billy led a patrol to the Lille area on 1 June and raised his score again. That night he wrote:

'This evening I was out alone and ran into Horn, Springs and McGregor. They followed me around for about ten minutes and suddenly we met six black Pfalz Scouts. Into them we waded and I got one [that] crashed. McGregor got two out of control and Springs got one, making my total fifty-six and the squadron's total fourteen.'[57]

Billy's opponent, sent down at 8:10 pm[58] (British time, then an hour behind German time), was undoubtedly Leutnant der Reserve Paul Billik, commander of Jagdstaffel 52, which flew black Pfalz D.IIIa aeroplanes.[59] A German 6th Army air staff report for 1 June indicates that at 9:10 pm (German time) Billik was 'lightly wounded in aerial combat [and was] forced to land east of Estaires',[60] not far from La Gorgue, which Billy identified as the 'crash' site in his combat report. American First-Lieutenant Elliott White Springs reported that at 8:15 pm: 'I saw an EA below, descending in a slow spin, which was the EA [that] Major Bishop shot down.'[61]

Billik was a formidable opponent. Earlier that day, he scored the nineteenth of his thirty-one victories[62] when he shot down and killed Captain William Jameson Cairnes in an S.E.5a of 74 Squadron.[63]

From various sources Billy Bishop knew that Captain James McCudden had attained fifty-seven confirmed victories before he was posted from 56 Squadron in March to become an instructor in England.[64] Consequently, Billy counted his victories carefully, intent on regaining his position as Britain's leading fighter ace. In the area of Armentières, on Sunday, 2 June, he came closer to his goal, as he wrote to Margaret:

Billy Bishop was credited with his fifty-sixth victory after he wounded and sent down Ltn.d.Res Paul Billik, CO of Jasta 52, on the evening of 1 June 1918. Billik returned to fight again and eventually was credited with 31 victories. He was nominated for the Pour le Mérite, but was not considered for the award after he was shot down and taken prisoner on 10 August 1918. (Greg VanWyngarden)

'Tonight I went out … [on] just our side of the lines and I picked up [First-Lieutenant L.K.] Callahan and [Lieutenant H.E.] Thompson. They followed me about the sky until we sighted eight Huns and down at them we went. I got one in pieces and Thompson got one out of control. That gives the squadron sixteen in all and, [for] myself, fifty-seven. The same number as McCudden and still going up.'[65]

Billy's combat report for 2 June stated he 'fired at four different EA, one of which fell out of control for 1,500 feet, then broke up in pieces. This machine was seen and confirmed … by Lieutenant Callahan.'[66] The *Nachrichtenblatt* offered the only report of German casualties available for that day: 'Four aeroplanes [lost], seven missing, three captive balloons [shot down].' It is not possible to make a match with such sketchy information.

CHAPTER TWELVE

What Price Success?

'[Bishop's] value as a moral factor to the Royal Air Force
cannot be over-estimated.'
– Distinguished Flying Cross citation[1]

According to the Royal Air Force War Diary, Tuesday, 4 June 1918 was marked by 'overcast [weather] all day … Enemy activity [was] very slight. One EA was shot down in flames into the sea by Major W.A. Bishop …'[2] In fact, Billy Bishop was credited with two victories that morning. The first was at 11:28 am, over the North Sea coast between Ostend and Nieuport:

'Seeing a formation of eight EA out to sea, I flew towards them from the east and diving [from 14,000 feet, I] attacked a straggler [and], after ten rounds from each gun, he burst into flames and fell burning brightly. I zoomed away and escaped.'[3]

Billy followed the German aeroplanes a few miles south of Ostend to Leffinge and, he reported, nine minutes later:

'I attacked another straggler of the same formation. Diving from the east on them and zooming away, [I] fired thirty rounds from each gun at 75 yards' range. EA, which was a silver Albatros, fell completely out of control and passed through clouds 8,000 feet below still out of control.'[4]

If it were not such a serious matter, the 4 June *Nachrichtenblatt* report would be laughable in asserting there were no German air losses at all across the entire Western Front, stretching from the Dutch border to Switzerland. The Zickerick necrology, mentioned in Chapter One, lists eight German airmen killed and two wounded in combat in that broad area on 4 June.[5] However, none related to the North Sea coast. German land and sea-based naval aviation units operated along the Flanders coast, but a check of their casualty records[6] shows no naval air losses on that date. Hence, after checking all available sources, it can only be said that no matching losses have been found.

As fifteen of Billy Bishop's confirmed victories are considered to have 'no matching German loss' (see Appendix), a certain scepticism arises about his actions during these encounters. If the events he described did not occur, what was he doing at that time, alone and over German-held territory? It is difficult to accept that he was simply 'flying around', expending fuel and ammunition needlessly. Certainly, there was no place in the sky to hide. For these reasons, this author prefers to give Billy the benefit of the doubt – until it can be conclusively proven that the events did not take place as described.

Desk-Bound

For the next ten days Billy's air fighting activities became secondary to his administrative duties as squadron commander. After more than three weeks in France, 85 Squadron was set to move closer to the frontlines and, as Arthur Bishop wrote:

> '[The] new order required a great deal of paper work that kept Bishop at his desk … until [7:30 pm] … It was the part of his duties that irked him most, and he used to say that an hour of administrative time tired him more than several hours in the air …'[7]

Fortunately, Billy could share his frustration about not being able to fly with his wife, as seen in this morning note from Petite-Synthe:

> 'Still no word about moving and, in spite of the fact that the squadron is standing by … we are carrying on with the work. In fact, if we are still here the day after tomorrow, we shall all start doing two [sorties] a day. That is, of course, with the exception of myself. Our work will be escorting bomb raids …' [8]

The same afternoon, he wrote from his new base at St. Omer:

> 'Noon today the order came to move and we … [had to get] the whole squadron off in less than three hours.[9] All machines except for Carruthers', [which] is coming by road. We have moved about twenty-five miles south west, which brings me within six miles of where I was when I came over with 21 Squadron [in 1916].'[10]

Back in the Air

Three days later Billy received a new aeroplane, S.E.5a C.1904, which he boasted to Margaret 'easily does 136 mph [in] level flying, so it will take a good Hun to catch me'.[11] Billy's former mount, S.E.5a C.6490, was passed along to another 85 Squadron pilot, Second-Lieutenant Nelson H. Marshall, who flew it for a month, when it was shot down by Leutnant der Reserve Carl Degelow,[12] commander of Jagdstaffel 40, and the pilot was captured unwounded.[13]

The weather for Friday, 14 June, was overcast, with low clouds and high wind; flying was scant that day.[14] On Saturday, Billy Bishop took advantage of improved conditions and headed out alone toward Lille. At length, he spotted a mixture of Albatros and Pfalz fighters at 17,500 feet, flying high cover for a larger German group below. Billy pounced on one of the higher flying aircraft, a 'Pfalz [with] red fuselage and black wings … [and sent it] down in flames [after firing] from fifty yards' range and behind'.[15] During the fight, however, Billy was nearly undone by a new present from Margaret: a loose-fitting soft zebra-skin flight helmet that slipped about his head and impaired his vision at times.

Unaware of Billy's plight, the other German fighters scattered and he was able to escape.[16] He was credited with his sixtieth victory, thereby extending his lead over Major James McCudden's fifty-seven 'kills' and the forty-nine-victory score of Major Edward ('Mick') Mannock.[17] Billy's achievement on 15 June was mentioned in the RAF Communiqué,[18] but there is no matching German casualty. Without further details, the *Nachrichtenblatt* listed: 'One aeroplane [lost due to] aerial combat, one in a crash, three missing, [and] two captive balloons [downed].'[19] The Pfalz with a 'red fuselage' may have belonged to Jagdstaffel 30,[20] which was based in the 6th Army area; however, none of that unit's aircraft was reported lost or missing on 15 June.[21]

Just when Billy regained the lead among British Empire fighter aces, he received stunning news. He confided his disappointment to Margaret:

'It has been a very exciting day. Horn got a Hun, [as did Larry] Callahan, and [Alec] Cunningham-Reid [shot down] a balloon … I got two Huns, one in flames and one crashed. [Howard] Thompson is missing, he landed under control.[22]

'But here is the awful news. General Webb-Bowen [commander of 2nd Brigade, RAF[23]] rang up tonight to say that I had been recalled to England. Unofficially, he told me it was at the request of the Canadian government. I have never been so furious in my life. McCudden is to take my place …

'The thought of seeing you is wonderful, but it makes me furious to be pulled away just as things are starting [to happen].'[24]

Billy waited until the rain stopped and the sky cleared[25] before setting out alone on the evening of 16 June. First, he attacked a two-seater about 1,800 feet over British lines, pursued it and later reported: 'Getting to 100 yards' range, [I] fired twenty rounds from each gun. EA [began to] smoke, then burst into flames and fell.' Eight minutes later, four Albatros Scouts made a diving run at him – and continued their speedy descent. Billy 'dived onto [the] rear one, opened fire at seventy-five yards … EA went down vertically and crashed on [the] western edge of Armentières.'[26]

Billy received confirmation for his sixty-first and sixty-second victories, as well as passing notice in the daily RAF Communiqué tally[27]. However, it is not possible to match his claims with the considerable but inexplicable German losses reported in the *Nachrichtenblatt*: 'Five aeroplanes in aerial combat, one aeroplane missing, one crashed; furthermore, three pilots or, as the case may be, observers, wounded, [and] one dead.'[28]

Bishop was determined to make his remaining days with 85 Squadron as productive as possible and, within a half hour on 17 June, he claimed three victories. Billy almost made his deadly work seem easy when he described it to Margaret:

'I went out this morning and carefully searched the sky, finding one two-seater at 18,000 feet … [which] I sent down in flames. Then I found a scout … [which] I crashed. Then I found another two-seater and sent him down. He crashed. Cunningham-Reid also got a Hun. Springs, Grider and Canning got one between them. That's five today. Squadron total, thirty; mine, sixty-five.'[29]

Billy noted carefully the times and locations of the fights in the hope they might be confirmed by British ground forces. In the case of the third German aeroplane to fall on the 17th, he noted that it 'crashed between [the village of] Leventie and the main road'. No witness came forward and, again, historians are left with indefinable *Nachrichtenblatt* loss notes. A known casualty in the area that day was the Pfalz D.IIIa flown by Oberleutnant Hans-Georg von der Marwitz of Jagdstaffel 30,[31] a unit with which 85 Squadron had tangled several times. While he 'zoomed into the edge of a cloud'[32] after his adversary, Billy could have mistaken the sleek Pfalz for an equally streamlined and shark-like Albatros. But, while Billy was credited with downing three German aeroplanes, it is not possible to identify the two-seaters he engaged that day.

Members of 85 Squadron C Flight in June 1918. Standing: Capt M.C. McGregor and Lt E.W. Springs. Seated from left: Capt S.B. Horn, Lt H.G. Thompson. Lt L.K. Callahan and Lt J.M. Grider. (Courtesy The Springs Close Family Archives, Fort Mill, SC)

On the morning of 18 June, several patrols from 85 Squadron went out looking for German aeroplanes. Billy Bishop took off a bit late and headed north east toward Ypres to catch up with one of the patrols. Meanwhile, American Lieutenants Elliott White Springs and John McGavock Grider headed farther east to Menin, north of Lille. They shot down a Rumpler two-seater with 'camouflaged wings and fuselage, white tail, circles on [the] wings with small black crosses'. Springs reported he 'saw the EA go down in a vertical dive and crash near Menin Road. Lieutenant Grider was just above where the flight had taken place.'[33]

En route back to St. Omer, the pair flew into clouds and then came under German anti-aircraft fire. After Springs regained his bearings, Grider was not in sight. Springs returned alone and later agonised: 'We never had any word from Mac [Grider].[34] We had already lost Benbow and Thompson and I got hell for losing Mac from Captain Horn, though I wasn't leading.'[35]

Billy Bishop's patrol was more successful. He saw four 'Albatros Scouts [with] natural wood finish' and:

> '… in a gap in the clouds, circling around each other. I dived into the cloud and came out … just above them [and] secured a position on the tail of one. After [a] very short burst, he seemed to explode and went down in flames. At [the] same moment one of the other three spun away; of the remaining two, one attacked me … I fired a long burst in a deflection shot at EA fighting me and he smoked, then burst into flames …' [36]

That day's RAF Communiqué reported: 'Enemy aircraft [were] active in the morning' – when Billy Bishop was credited with downing two German aeroplanes – but 'very slight in the afternoon.'[37] The *Nachrichtenblatt* agreed with that assessment and stated its Western Front losses as: 'One aeroplane in aerial combat, three from crashes … furthermore, three pilots or, as the case may be, observers, wounded in aerial combat.'[38] However, the German 4th Army alone reported four fighter pilot casualties for 18 June, including one fatality during a test flight.[39] Of the three combat-related airmen, two from Jagdstaffel 56 come close to Billy's combat report narrative: Leutnant der Reserve Rudolf Heins and Unteroffizier Koehler. Both pilots were wounded within 85 Squadron's operational area.[40]

Bishop's Last Air Combat

Wednesday, 19 June 1918 was Billy Bishop's last day in combat. Before heading back to England the following day, the hours ahead of him were his last opportunity to add to his

Billy Bishop's seventy-second confirmed victory was reportedly a 'new' Halberstadt two-seater. That would have been a C.V type, illustrated here. Delivered in 1918, this long-range reconnaissance aeroplane was produced by Halberstadt and three licensees. (Author's Collection)

score of aerial victories. It is easy to imagine Billy's disappointment when he arose that morning to a sky filled with 'low clouds and rain … [and to face] Enemy aircraft activity [that was] very slight'.[41] He left his comrades to enjoy a 'dud' day of no flying and had his S.E.5a fuelled and armed. His combat report described his final mission, alone, beginning at 1,000 feet altitude:

'After crossing the [front] lines in the clouds, I came out over Ploegsteert Wood [north of Armentières], saw three Pfalz Scouts which I attacked. Two other Pfalz then approached from the east [and] I fired [a] short burst into one of the original three EA. He went down in [a] vertical dive. Second and Third EA then, while circling about me, collided and fell together. First EA crashed and burst into flames one-and-a-half miles east of Ploegsteert. Remaining two EA turned and flew east. I gave chase and opened fire on one at 200 yards' range. EA spun into [the] ground. Last EA zoomed into [the] clouds and escaped.

'[Then at 900 feet between Neuve Eglise and Ploegsteert] I met a two-seater and attacked from behind and underneath. EA burst into flames. I then fired on a small body of troops on the ground, scattering them. [I] climbed into clouds and flew west.'[42]

Given the day's 'slight activity', the RAF Communiqué carried a six-line paragraph, noting Billy's success with four Pfalz Scouts – including two that reportedly collided – and a two-seater.[43] Numerically, it was the single best day of his air fighting career. But comparing Billy's five credited victories with German losses is an exercise in frustration. The *Nachrichtenblatt* reported only the loss of one captive observation balloon.[44] German 4th Army air staff, however, noted the loss of one Jagdstaffel 7 Pfalz D.IIIa[45] near Bailleul, which is about seven miles west of Ploegsteert. But, as noted in this book's Foreword, that particular Pfalz was without a doubt brought down by Captain Arthur Cobby, DSO, MC, DFC, of 1 Australian Squadron; it was also credited to him in the same Communiqué in which Billy Bishop's five victories appeared. Examination of available records shows no matches for the four Pfalzes and the two-seater that Billy claimed that day.

That evening, Billy's comrades – still uncertain about the fate of Mac Grider – hosted as grand a farewell party as possible under the circumstances. The next morning, 20 June, it was more of the same wet and windy weather[46] as members of 85 Squadron piled into various vehicles and drove to Boulogne[47] to give their old 'boss' a proper send off on his return to England.

Other military leaders did not see Billy in the same warm light, but later appreciated him. Major (later Air Chief Marshal Sir) William Sholto Douglas, MC, DFC, who commanded 84 Squadron when Billy led 85 Squadron, remarked in a memoir:

'I came to see quite a lot of him; but there was something about [Bishop] that left one feeling that he preferred to live as he fought: in a rather brittle, hard world of his own. He has been described as a lone wolf, but I do not think that any of us came to know him or understand his motives well enough to be sure about that …'[48]

After Billy left France, Major-General [later Sir] Edward W. B. Morrison, commander of all Canadian artillery and a former journalist, had a dispassionate and more practical view of his young countryman:

> 'I was particularly interested in meeting Major Bishop and am glad he was selected for an administrative appointment. The more so because Major [J.T.B.] McCudden, VC, was killed yesterday afternoon [9 July 1918]. While Major Bishop's services were invaluable to the army as a fighting man, I believe he can do more good by training others than [to] continue to risk the almost inevitable on the firing line.'[49]

McCudden 'was accidentally killed … while flying to France'[50] to assume command of Billy's old squadron. *Nachrichtenblatt* compilers learned of McCudden's death in the French journal *Petit Parisien* and were quick to state that McCudden had attained fifty-four (instead of fifty-seven) aerial victories – and seemed to suggest an invidious comparison by noting Billy Bishop's latest known score of seventy victories.[51]

More Honours

Billy's name had become so synonymous with aerial victories that the topic was raised during his third meeting with King George V. The monarch asked: 'Bishop, I've been telling everyone that you shot down seventy-two 'planes and now I read in your own book [*Winged Warfare*] that you shot down forty-seven. Are you a liar or am I?' To which Billy responded: 'Neither of us, Sir. When I wrote the book I had forty-seven, [and] since then I have added twenty-five.'[52]

While in London, on 3 August, Billy received a new high decoration, the Distinguished Flying Cross. He was recommended for the award by Brigadier-General T.I. Webb-Bowen, commanding 2nd Brigade, RAF.[53] Billy was honoured for 'signally valuable services in personally destroying twenty-five enemy machines in

Billy Bishop (left) and his older brother, Worth, back in Canada at war's end. Both brothers were lieutenant-colonels. (Billy Bishop Home and Museum)

twelve days – five of which he destroyed on the last day of his service at the front. The total number of machines destroyed by this distinguished officer is seventy-two, and his value as a moral factor to the Royal Air Force cannot be over-estimated.'[54]

Ostensibly, Billy returned to England to become the first commander of the Canadian wing, composed of two squadrons that would support the Canadian Corps in France. He was promoted to 'Lieutenant-Colonel, Canadian Cavalry' and relinquished his RAF

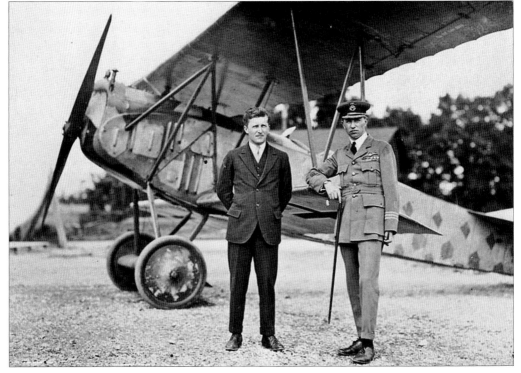

After the war, Billy Bishop and Billy Barker posed in Canada by a captured Fokker D.VII. Bishop never fought against this type, but the last three of Barker's fifty confirmed victories were Fokker D.VIIs. (Greg VanWyngarden)

commission on 5 August.[55] But, with the defeat of Germany and Austria-Hungary now a matter of time, the Allied emphasis was on pressing their enemies to the point of collapse or at least to retreat to within their own borders. Creating other British Empire entities had to wait for calmer times.

With little for them to do in England, Billy and Margaret returned to Canada. Officially, Billy was ordered to report on the Canadian wing's progress to Prime Minister Sir Robert Borden and to help with national recruiting efforts. But, after some weeks at home, Billy was ordered to return to England. He was halfway across the Atlantic Ocean when the ship's wireless operator reported the war had ended.

Billy remained in England long enough to collect two significant French decorations for his efforts to liberate France from German aggression: Chevalier (Knight) of the Legion of Honour and the Croix de Guerre (Cross of War) with a Palme in lieu of a second award.[56] Then he came back to Canada, where, as one account reported: 'Many of the heroes of [World War I], who had been household names in the days of fighting, slipped into

Between the world wars, Billy Bishop, third from left, made several visits to the Aero Club of Berlin, where he was hosted by former German ace Hermann Göring, fourth from left. The other former combat pilots in the photograph are not identified. (DHH/DND photo RE 22066-5)

obscurity in peacetime. [But] Bishop was much too active to keep out of the public eye.'[57]

Indeed, he easily stepped out of uniform and on to the lecture circuit, regaling audiences with his war tales, some of which took on grander proportions. Plus, his book did quite well for a while and provided income.

When the lecture audiences eventually dwindled, Billy tried his hand at a business venture with Canada's other Victoria Cross-winning fighter pilot, Major William George ('Billy') Barker. The victor in fifty air fights, Barker had more medals than Bishop, boasting the VC, DSO and Bar, MC and two Bars, (French) Croix de Guerre and (Italian) Silver Medal for Military Valour. The two 'Billies' formed the Barker-Bishop Company to sell aeroplanes and, eventually, to carry passengers to various water destinations in war surplus seaplanes they bought for $1,000 apiece. Eventually, the business failed and Barker joined the fledgling Royal Canadian Air Force.[58]

Billy Bishop went on to other ventures and he and Margaret raised a family: Arthur Christian William Avery Bishop, born in 1923, and Margaret Marise Bishop, born in 1926. Billy also remained in contact with many World War I flyers – one was Ernst Udet, then the highest-scoring living German fighter ace, with sixty-two confirmed aerial victories to his credit. Another was Hermann Göring, the last wartime commander of the fighter wing once led by Manfred von Richthofen. In March 1928, both men hosted Billy at the Aero Club of Berlin.

Turning some humour on himself, Billy told his now-friendly but slightly mystified

While in London during World War II, Air Marshal Billy Bishop, VC, DSO and Bar, MC, DFC admired a new Supermarine Spitfire. It was a far cry from the wooden and fabric aeroplanes he flew into combat. (via Clayton Knight, OBE)

German colleagues: 'You honour me for having shot down more German 'planes than any other Allied airman. But I now ask you to honour me as Germany's great ace. I personally destroyed more Allied 'planes by my own method of landing than all of you combined!'[59]

Good relations with Billy's German friends lasted another decade, but by 1939 the British Empire and the German Reich were again at great odds. In 1935, Billy Bishop was elevated to air vice-marshal in the RCAF and, as turmoil in Europe grew, he maintained contact with old friends such as Winston Churchill. On 10 August 1938, Billy was appointed 'honorary air marshal, the highest rank in the country at the time … [and] became head of the Air Advisory Committee'.[60]

When war broke out in 1939, Billy Bishop became involved in RCAF recruitment, an important resource for the RAF, which was nearly alone in opposing Hermann Göring's Luftwaffe. Through his old 85 Squadron friend Elliott White Springs, Billy knew most of the Americans who flew with the RAF in World War I. One was prominent aviation artist Clayton Knight, who Billy enlisted to set up a covert group to help US citizens travel to Canada to train for RAF service – in violation of official US neutrality. Called the Clayton

Knight Committee, it arranged for over 2,000 Americans to join the RAF – and most of them later transferred to the US Army Air Service, which badly needed experienced combat pilots. Small wonder that US President Franklin D. Roosevelt sent Billy a photo with the warm inscription: 'To my great friend Air Marshal Bishop'.[61]

Billy's role in World War II was noted in print:

'As a liaison officer between the RCAF and RAF, Bishop flew back and forth between Canada and England – reporting to the Canadian cabinet at one end and to King George VI and Winston Churchill at the other. Early in 1944 he was made a Companion of the Order of the Bath ...'[62]

Facing Reality

Upon Billy's retirement from the RCAF, Canadian Air Minister Charles Gavan Power said:

'The services performed by the air marshal extended far beyond the requirements of his position as director of recruiting. This country, already deeply indebted to ... [him] for his service in [World War I], has cause to be even more grateful for his contribution to the development of the RCAF.' [63]

Billy had a long affiliation with McColl-Frontenac Oil Company, a grouping of several petroleum companies headquartered in Montreal. He was vice president for sales promotion and he retired from the company in 1949 due to ill health. He spent more and more time at his winter home in West Palm Beach, Florida, where he passed away quietly on 10 September 1956. Billy's mortal remains were returned to Canada and his ashes were interred with military honours in his home town of Owen Sound.

One lingering question is: How many German aeroplanes did Billy Bishop actually shoot down? Due to the various circumstances covered in this book, there can be no definitive answer. To be sure, some of his opponents slipped away after feigning being mortally wounded and others, who may have died some time later, were not listed on the days they fell; still other victory claims were witnessed by Allied sources, but not acknowledged in German reports. It also needs to be remembered that, during an aerial encounter, a combat airman – whether pilot or observer – needed to be aware of his location, altitude, time of day and other in-flight details. Very importantly, he also had to keep track of the ammunition he expended, to avoid running out at a crucial moment. Hence, with all of these factors to be borne in mind, detail errors in combat reports were not unusual and most probably happened when Bishop filed some of his reports.

The situation of Billy Bishop and many other aces was well covered by the World War II RCAF pilot and eminent Canadian history professor Sydney F. Wise:

'Despite their inflated claims and credits, the "aces" of the air war – the Vosses, von Richthofens, Bishops, Barkers, and Collishaws – were anything but fakes. They earned and held the respect of their peers, as well as that of the public by their fighting, shooting and tactical skills ... But the compilation of lists of scores and the many rankings of Allied and German pilots [which were] so plentiful in the … literature which has been built up since [World War I] often rest upon assumptions which will not bear critical scrutiny. At least as far as 1918 is concerned, claims of air victories by either side should be reduced by at least one-third.'[64]

Indeed, perhaps Billy Bishop had his own doubts about his success. As reported in his Toronto obituary, in later years, Billy called his memoir *Winged Warfare* 'a terrible book. It is so terrible, [that] I cannot read it today. It turns my stomach. It was headline stuff, whoop-de-doop, red-hot, hurray-for-our-side stuff. Yet the public loved it.'[65]

Crucially, the internationally known figure of Bishop the air hero was created for and by the crowds that applauded his achievements. As one of his Canadian biographers noted:

'Billy Bishop was in many ways a product of his own success and, often through his own embellishments, a victim of his own success. However he was a skilled and resourceful warrior, possessed of uncommon valour, who served his nation with great distinction. Canada should take great reflected pride for his tenacity and daring. He richly deserves that measure of respect and recognition.'[66]

Appendix

Aerial Victory List of William A. Bishop

[Author's note: The following victory list was compiled from William A. Bishop's own accounts, RFC/RAF combat reports and other sources, as well as official German daily, weekly and monthly reports. Time, air combat locations and German aircraft type designators appear as noted in Bishop's combat reports. Credits were granted for aircraft: destroyed = DES; destroyed and set on fire = DES(F); and sent down out of control = OOC. Assumptions about downed German aircraft are based on the author's research. In determining which German units and airmen were involved in these aerial combats, several factors were considered: dates, times, places of the victory/loss, as well as proximity of the opposing air units' airfields. Other more recent research provided additional corresponding casualty information to determine the most likely identities of Bishop's victims. Dates are stated in the military style (day and month) and times are expressed in military time, with sub-headings to clarify whether a victory claim was an hour ahead of British/ French time, or matched it. In two-seater claims, pilots are listed first, observers second. Condition of the aircrew is indicated by the abbreviations: WiA = Wounded in Action; DoW = Died of Wounds; KiA = Killed in Action; PoW = Prisoner of War.]

e	Time	Location	Aircraft Type		Victor & Aircraft	Vic. No	Crew / Disposition
1917							
ar		Allied time synchronised with German time					
ar	1700	between St. Leger and Arras	Albatros Scout (G 16)	DES	Lt W.A. Bishop Nieuport 17 A.306	1	Gefr Berkling, Jasta 22, WiA
ar	0730	north east of Arras	Albatros Scout	DES	Lt W.A. Bishop Nieuport 23 A.6769	2	Confirmed by AA, but no matching loss found
ril	0935	north east of Chérisy /Biache-Saint-Vaast	Albatros D.II 510/16		Lt W.A. Bishop Nieuport 23 A.6769	n/c	Possibly Uffz L. Weber, Jasta 3, WiA
	1710	near Arras	Albatros Scout or Rumpler C.I 2600/16	OOC	Lt W.A. Bishop Nieuport 23 A.6769	3	Possibly Gefr W. Schoop, Schusta 7 & Ltn Hupe. Fl.-Abt (A) 233
	1710	Vis-en-Artois	Balloon	DES	Lt W.A. Bishop Nieuport 23 A.6769	4	Unit unknown

Date	Time	Location	Aircraft Type		Victor & Aircraft	Vic. No	Crew / Disposition
8 Apr	0930	between Douai and Flesquières	two-seater	DES	Lt W.A. Bishop Nieuport 23 A.6769	5	No matching loss fo
	0930	north east of Arras	Albatros Scout	OOC	Lt W.A. Bishop Nieuport 23 A.6769	6	Possibly Vzfw S. Fe Jasta 11 (forced to la
	1010	near Vitry-en-Artois	Albatros Scout	OOC	Lt W.A. Bishop Nieuport 23 A.6769	7	No matching loss fou
17 April	German time one hour ahead of Allied time						
20 Apr	1458	Biache-Saint-Vaast	two-seater (possibly Aviatik C.V)	DES(F)	Lt W.A. Bishop Nieuport 23 B.1566	8	German records incomplete
22 Apr	1120	Vis-en-Artois	single-seater	OOC	Lt W.A. Bishop Nieuport 23 B.1566	9	German records incomplete
23 Apr	1530	between Vitry-en-Artois and Évin-Malmaison	two-seater	DES	Lt W.A. Bishop Nieuport 23 B.1566	10	Ltn.d.Res Möbius & Ltn.d.Res Goldamn Fl.Abt. (A) 211, KiA
	1559	east of Vitry	Albatros Scout	DES	Lt W.A. Bishop Nieuport 23 B.1566	11	German records incomplete
27 Apr	0855	north west of Vitry-en-Artois	Balloon	DES	Lt W.A. Bishop Nieuport 23 B.1566	12	Unit unknown
29 Apr	1155	east of Épinoy	Albatros C.VII	DES(F)	Capt W.A. Bishop Nieuport 23 B.1566	13	Ltn B. Kittel & Ltn Waldschmidt, Fl.-Ab KiA
30 Apr	1115	south of Lens	DFW CV 4874/16	DES	Capt W.A. Bishop Nieuport 23 B.1566	14	Ltn.d.Res A. Rodenb Fl.-Abt (A) 233, Wi DoW
2 May	1010	east of Drocourt-Quéant line	DFW C.V 5866/16 (G 31)	DES	Capt W.A. Bishop Nieuport 23 B.1566	15	Gefr K. Prill, PoW & Ltn.d.Res P. Reichel, Fl.-Abt 26, KiA
	1012	east of Drocourt-Quéant line	DFW C.V 5178/16	OOC	Capt W.A. Bishop Nieuport 23 B.1566	16	Vzfw Seifert, WiA & Uffz W. Niess, Schus KiA
4 May	1336	west of Brebières	AEG C.IV	DES	Capt W.A. Bishop Nieuport 23 B.1566	17	possibly Ltns.d.Res K. Leidreiter & K. Böt Fl.-Abt. (A) 210, KiA
7 May	0950	Hénin-Liétard	Albatros Scout	OOC	Capt W.A. Bishop Nieuport 23 B.1566	18	German records incomplete
	1500	south of Brebières	Albatros Scout	OOC	Capt W.A. Bishop Nieuport 23 B.1566	19	German records incomplete

APPENDIX

Date	Time	Location	Aircraft Type		Victor & Aircraft	Vic. No	Crew / Disposition
26 May	1016	Izel-lès-Équerchin	single-seater	OOC	Capt W.A. Bishop Nieuport 23 B.1566	19½	German records incomplete
27 May	0940	Dourges	two-seater	DES	Capt W.A. Bishop Nieuport 23 B.1566	20½	Uffz F. Johänniges & G. von Roebern, Fl.-Abt. (A) 256, KiA
31 May	1911	Épinoy	Albatros Scout	DES	Capt W.A. Bishop Nieuport 23 B.1566	21½	German records incomplete
2 June	0430	uncertain, possibly Émerchicourt	Albatros Scout or Albatros C.VII	DES	Capt W.A. Bishop Nieuport 23 B.1566	22½	possibly Vzfw Delesse & Ltn Heinz, Fl.-Abt 26, WiA
	0435	uncertain	Albatros Scout	DES	Capt W.A. Bishop Nieuport 23 B.1566	23½	No matching loss found
	0440	uncertain	Albatros Scout	DES	Capt W.A. Bishop Nieuport 23 B.1566	24½	No matching loss found
3 June	1210	north of Lille, over Wytschaete bend	Albatros D.III	DES	Capt W.A. Bishop Nieuport 23 B.1566	25½	Vzfw F. Bucher, Jasta 30, KiA
4 June	1125	north of Beaumont	red Albatros Scout	DES(F)	Capt W.A. Bishop Nieuport 23 B.1566	26½	German records incomplete
5 June	1025	Dury, east of Arras	Albatros Scout	OOC	Capt W.A. Bishop Nieuport 23 B.1566	27½	No matching loss found
5 June	1055	Annay	scout	DES(F)	Capt W.A. Bishop Nieuport 23 B.1566	28½	German records incomplete
	1056	Annay	scout	OOC	Capt W.A. Bishop Nieuport 23 B.1566	29½	German records incomplete
8 June	1230	south of La Bassée Canal	Albatros D.III	DES	Capt W.A. Bishop Nieuport 23 B.1566	30½	German records incomplete
1 July	2010	Quiéry-la-Motte	scout	OOC	Capt W.A. Bishop Nieuport 23 B.1566	31½	No matching loss found
July	1340	Vitry-en-Artois	Enemy Aeroplane	DES	Capt W.A. Bishop Nieuport 23 B.1566	32½	Witnessed, but no matching loss found
July	1945	Havrincourt Wood	Enemy Aeroplane	DES(F)	Capt W.A. Bishop Nieuport 23 B.1566	33½	Witnessed, but no matching loss found
	1955	Marquion	Enemy Aeroplane	DES	Capt W.A. Bishop Nieuport 23 B.1566	35	Witnessed, but no matching loss found
July	1205	south east of Havrincourt Wood	Enemy Aeroplane	OOC	Capt W.A. Bishop Nieuport 23 B.1566	36	No matching loss found

Date	Time	Location	Aircraft Type		Victor & Aircraft	Vic. No	Crew / Disposition
28 July	1810	Phalempin	Enemy Aeroplane DES(F)		Capt W.A. Bishop S.E.5 A.8936	37	No matching loss found
29 July	0700	Beaumont	Enemy Aeroplane OOC		Capt W.A. Bishop S.E.5 A.8936	38	No matching loss found
5 Aug	2000	north of Hendecourt-lès-Cagnicourt	Albatros D.III	DES(F)	Capt W.A. Bishop S.E.5 A.8936	39	Ltn B. Lehmann, Jasta 12, KiA
	2000	north of Hendecourt-lès-Cagnicourt	Albatros D.III	OOC	Capt W.A. Bishop S.E.5 A.8936	40	German records incomplete
6 Aug	1545	north west of Brebières	Albatros D.III	DES	Capt W.A. Bishop S.E.5 A.8936	41	Witnessed, but no matching loss found
9 Aug	0900	north of Écourt-St.-Quentin	two-seater	DES	Capt W.A. Bishop S.E.5 A.8936	42	No matching loss found
13 Aug	1902	south of Douai	Albatros Scout	DES(F)	Capt W.A. Bishop S.E.5 A.8936	43	German records incomplete
	1902	south of Douai	Albatros Scout	DES(F)	Capt W.A. Bishop S.E.5 A.8936	44	German records incomplete
15 Aug	2020	north east of Hénin-Liétard	Enemy Aeroplane OOC		Capt W.A. Bishop S.E.5 A.8936	45	possibly Ltn.d.Res W. Merschmann & Ltn.d.Res W. Liebert, Fl.-Abt 5, KiA
16 Aug	1903	north east of Harnes	two-seater	DES	Capt W.A. Bishop S.E.5 A.8936	46	No matching loss found
	1906	north east of Harnes	Albatros	DES	Capt W.A. Bishop S.E.5 A.8936	47	No matching loss found

1918

Date	Time	Location	Aircraft Type		Victor & Aircraft	Vic. No	Crew / Disposition
16 April		German time one hour ahead of Allied time					
27 May	1632	east of Passchendaele	two-seater	DES	Major W.A. Bishop S.E.5a C.6490	48	German records incomplete
28 May	1555	south west of Courtemarck	Albatros D.V	DES	Major W.A. Bishop S.E.5a C.6490	49	German records inexplicable
	1555	south west of Courtemarck	Albatros D.V	DES	Major W.A. Bishop S.E.5a C.6490	50	German records inexplicable
30 May	1542	Roulers	two-seater	DES(F)	Major W.A. Bishop S.E.5a C.6490	51	German records incomplete

Date	Time	Location	Aircraft Type		Victor & Aircraft	Vic. No	Crew / Disposition
	1545	Roulers	two-seater	DES	Major W.A. Bishop S.E.5a C.6490	52	German records incomplete
	1953	north of Armentières	Albatros D.V	DES	Major W.A. Bishop S.E.5a C.6490	53	German records incomplete
May	1505	Quesnoy	Pfalz Scout	DES	Major W.A. Bishop S.E.5a C.6490	54	Possibly Ltn. E. Kaus, Jasta 30, WiA
	1515	south west of Lille	two-seater	DES	Major W.A. Bishop S.E.5a C.6490	55	Possibly Gefr. W. Schoop & Uffz. Sindt, Schlasta 36, WiA
June	2010	La Gorgue	Pfalz D.III	DES	Major W.A. Bishop S.E.5a C.6490	56	Ltn.d.Res P. Billik, Jasta 52, WiA
June	2015	south of Armentières	EA Scout	DES	Major W.A. Bishop S.E.5a C.6490	57	Witnessed, but no matching loss found
June	1128	3 miles off coast between Nieuport and Ostend	Albatros Scout	DES(F)	Major W.A. Bishop S.E.5a C.6490	58	No matching loss found
	1137	Leffinghe	silver Albatros Scout	OOC	Major W.A. Bishop S.E.5a C.6490	59	No matching loss found
June	1855	east of Estaires	red and black Pfalz Scout	DES	Major W.A. Bishop S.E.5a C.1904	60	No matching loss found
June	2020	east of Armentières	two-seater	DES	Major W.A. Bishop S.E.5a C.1904	61	German records inexplicable
	2025	over Armentières	Albatros Scout	DES	Major W.A. Bishop S.E.5a C.1904	62	German records inexplicable
June	1025	between Staden and Hooglede	two-seater	DES(F)	Major W.A. Bishop S.E.5a C.1904	63	German records inexplicable
	1050	over Sailly-sur-la-Lys	Albatros Scout (or Pfalz)	DES	Major W.A. Bishop S.E.5a C.1904	64	Possibly Oblt H-G von der Marwitz, Jasta 30, WiA
	1055	near Leventie	two-seater	DES	Major W.A. Bishop S.E.5a C.1904	65	German records inexplicable
June	1045	north east of Ypres	Albatros Scout	DES	Major W.A. Bishop S.E.5a C.1904	66	Possibly Ltn.d.Res R. Heins, Jasta 56, WiA
	1045	north east of Ypres	Albatros Scout	DES	Major W.A. Bishop S.E.5a C.1904	67	Possibly Uffz Koehler, Jasta 56, WiA
June	0958	east of Ploegsteert	Pfalz Scout	DES	Major W.A. Bishop S.E.5a C.1904	68	German records incomplete, no matching loss found

Date	Time	Location	Aircraft Type		Victor & Aircraft	Vic. No	Crew / Dispositi
	0958	east of Ploegsteert	Pfalz Scout	DES	Major W.A. Bishop S.E.5a C.1904	69	Reported collided, K but no matching loss found
	0958	east of Ploegsteert	Pfalz Scout	DES	Major W.A. Bishop S.E.5a C.1904	70	Reported collided, K no matching loss fou
	0958	east of Ploegsteert	Pfalz Scout	DES	Major W.A. Bishop S.E.5a C.1904	71	German records incomplete, no matching loss fou
	1010	between Neuve Eglise and Ploegsteert	Halberstadt	DES(F)	Major W.A. Bishop S.E.5a C.1904	72	German records incomplete, no matching loss fou

Bibliography and Sources

Books

Bashow, D. *Knights of the Air – Canadian Fighter Pilots in the First World War*, McArthur & Co. (Toronto, 2000)

Bishop, A. *The Courage of the Early Morning*, David McKay Co., Inc. (New York, 1966)

Bishop, W. *Winged Warfare – Hunting the Huns in the Air*, Hodder and Stoughton (London, 1918)

----. *Winged Peace*, Viking Press (New York, 1944)

Bowyer, C. *Albert Ball, VC*, William Kimber & Co. Ltd. (London, 1977)

----. *For Valour - The Air V.C.s*, William Kimber & Co. Ltd. (London, 1978)

Bronnenkant, L. *The Blue Max Airmen – German Airmen Awarded the Pour le Mérite, Vol. 3*, Aeronaut Books (Indio, CA, 2013)

Bruce, J. *British Aeroplanes 1914-1918*, Putnam & Co. Ltd. (London, 2nd ed., 1969)

Chadderton, H. *Hanging a Legend: The National Film Board's Shameful Attempt to Discredit Billy Bishop, VC*, The War Amputations of Canada (Ottawa, 1986)

Creagh, O. & Humphris, E. (eds.). *The V.C. and D.S.O., Vol. II,* Standard Art Book Co. Ltd. (London, ca. 1923)

Cross & Cockade International. *Nieuports in RNAS, RFC and RAF Service,* The First World War Aviation Historical Society (London, 2007)

Cunningham, *G. Mac's Memoirs – The Flying Life of Squadron-Leader McGregor*, A.H. & A.W. Reed (Dunedin, New Zealand, 1937)

Davilla, J. & Soltan, A. *French Aircraft of the First World War*, Flying Machines Press (Stratford, CT, 1997)

Degelow, C. *Mit dem weissen Hirsch durch dick und dünn*, Verlag von Chr. Adolff (Altona-Ottensen, 1920)

Deutscher Offizier-Bund, *Ehren-Rangliste des ehemaligen Deutschen Heeres* (Berlin, 1926)

Douglas, S. *Years of Combat*, Collins (London, 1963)

Duckers, P. *British Gallantry Awards 1855 - 2000*, Shire Publications (Oxford, 2010)

Duiven, R. & Abbott, D. *Schlachtflieger! Germany and the Origins of Air/Ground Support 1916-1918,* Schiffer Military History (Altglen, PA, 2006)

Franks, N. & Bailey, F. *Over the Front – A Complete Record of the Fighter Aces and Units of the United States and French Air Services 1914-1918*, Grub Street (London, 1992)

Franks, N., Bailey, F. & Duiven, R. *The Jasta Pilots,* Grub Street (London, 1996)

----. *Casualties of the German Air Service 1914-1920*, Grub Street (London, 1999)

Franks, N., Bailey F. & Guest, R. *Above the Lines – The Aces and Fighter Units of the German Air Service, Naval Air Service and Flanders Marine Corps 1914-1918*, Grub Street (London, 1993)

Fry, W. *Air of Battle*, William Kimber & Co. Ltd. (London, 1974)

Gibbons, F. *The Red Knight of Germany – The Story of Baron von Richthofen*, Doubleday, Page & Co,. (New York, 1927)

Greenhous, B. *The Making of Billy Bishop – The First World War Exploits of Billy Bishop, VC*, Dundurn Group (Toronto, 2002)

Henshaw, T. *The Sky Their Battlefield*, Grub Street (London, 1995)

Hervey, H. *Cage-Birds*, Penguin Books Ltd. (London, 1940)

Hobson, C. *Airmen Died in the Great War*, J.B. Hayward & Son (Suffolk, 1995)

Humphries, M. & Maker, J. (ed.). *Germany's Western Front – Translations from the German Official History of the Great War - 1914 - Part 1*, Wilfred Laurier University Press (Waterloo, Ontario, 2013)

Jones, H. *The War in the Air, Vol. II,* Oxford University Press (London, 1928)

----. *The War in the Air, Vol. III*, Oxford University Press (London, 1931)

----. *The War in the Air, Vol. IV*, Oxford University Press (London, 1934)

----. *The War in the Air, Vol. VI*, Oxford University Press (London, 1937)

Jones, I. *Tiger Squadron: The Story of 74 Squadron, R.A.F. in Two World Wars*, W.H. Allen & Co. Ltd. (London, 1955)

Kilduff, P. *Richthofen – Beyond the Legend of the Red Baron*, Arms and Armour Press (London, 1993)

Koch, A. *Die Flieger-Abteilung (A) 221 - Nach den Kriegstagebüchern und Flugmeldungen der Abteilung bearbeitet*, Druck und Verlag von Gerhard Stalling (Oldenburg, 1925)

Lamberton, W. *Fighter Aircraft of the 1914-1918 War,* Harleyford Publications Ltd. (Letchworth, Herts., 1960)

----. *Reconnaissance & Bomber Aircraft of the 1914-1918 War,* Harleyford Publications Ltd. (Letchworth, Herts., 1962)

Lee, A. *No Parachute – A Fighter Pilot in World War I*, Harper & Row Publishers (New York, 1st US ed., 1970). Reprinted by Grub Street (London, 2013)

Lewis, P. *Squadron Histories: RFC, RNAS & RAF Since 1912*, Putnam & Co. Ltd. (London, 2nd ed., 1968)

Liddell Hart, B. *The Real War 1914-1918*, Little, Brown and Co. (New York, re-issued US ed., 1964)

Mathieson, W. *Billy Bishop, VC*, Fitzhenry & Whiteside Ltd. (Markham, Ontario, 1989)

McCaffery, D. *Billy Bishop, Canadian Hero*, James Lorimer & Co. (Toronto, 2nd ed., 2002)

Morris, A. *Bloody April*, Jarrolds Publishers Ltd. (London, 1967)

O'Connor, N. *Aviation Awards of Imperial Germany and the Men Who Earned Them, Vol. I - The Aviation Awards of the Kingdom of Bavaria*, Foundation for Aviation World War I (Princeton, NJ, 1988)

----. *Aviation Awards of Imperial Germany and the Men Who Earned Them, Vol. II - The Aviation Awards of the Kingdom of Prussia*, Foundation for Aviation World War I (Princeton, NJ, 1990)

Pengelly, C. *Albert Ball, VC - The Fighter Pilot Hero of World War One*, Pen & Sword Aviation (Barnsley, South Yorkshire, 2010)

Platt, F. (ed.). *Great Battles of World War I: In the Air*, Signet Books (New York, 1966)

Preston, R. *Canada's RMC - A History of the Royal Military College*, University of Toronto Press (Toronto, 1969)

Raleigh, W. *The War in the Air, Vol. I*, Oxford University Press (London, 1922)

Revell, A. *No. 60 Sqn RFC/RAF*, Osprey Publishing (Botley, Oxford, 2011)

Richthofen, M. von. *Der rote Kampfflieger*, Verlag Ullstein & Co. (Berlin, 1917)

Robertson, B. *British Military Aircraft Serials 1911-1971*, Ian Allan Ltd. (London, 4th revised ed., 1971)

Robinson, D. *The Zeppelin in Combat – A History of the German Naval Airship Division 1912-1918*, Schiffer Military/Aviation History (Altglen, PA, 1994)

Rogers, L. *British Aviation Squadron Markings of World War I*, Schiffer Military History (Altglen, PA, 2001)

Schmeelke, M. *Das Kriegstagebuch der Jagdstaffel 12*, VDM Heinz Nickel (Zweibrücken, 2004)

Scott, A. *Sixty Squadron, R.A.F. 1916-1919*, William Heinemann Ltd. (London, 1920)

Shirer, W. *The Collapse of the Third Republic, an inquiry into the fall of France in 1940*, Simon & Schuster (New York, 1969)

Shores, C., Franks, N. & Guest, R. *Above the Trenches*, Grub Street (London, 1990)

Sloan, J. *Wings of Honor – American Airmen in World War I*, Schiffer Military/Aviation History (Altglen, PA, 1994)

Sturtivant, R. & Page, G. *The S.E.5 File*, Air Britain Historians Ltd. (Tunbridge Wells, Kent, 1996)

VanWyngarden, G. *Pfalz Scout Aces of World War I*, Osprey Publishing (Oxford, 2006)

Vaughan, D. *Letters from a War Bird - The World War I Correspondence of Elliott White Springs*, University of South Carolina Press (Columbia, SC, 2012)

Welkoborsky, N. (ed.). *Die Flieger-Abteilung (A) 211 im Weltkriege*, Bernhard Sporn Verlag (Zeuelenroda, 1938)

Wise, S. *Canadian Airmen and the First World War – The Official History of the Royal Canadian Air Force, Vol. I*, University of Toronto Press (Toronto, 1980)

Woodman, H. *Early Aircraft Armament – The Aeroplane and the Gun up to 1918*, Arms and Armour Press (London, 1989)

Zuerl, W. *Pour le Mérite-Flieger – Heldentaten und Erlebnisse unserer Kriegsflieger*, Curt Pechstein Verlag (Munich, 1938)

Documents

Anonymous, *Lewis Machine Gun (Airplane Type)* manual, Savage Arms Corporation (Utica, NY, undated)

Bishop, W.A. *Military Service Record*, The [UK] National Archive, File Air 76/40/143

Canadian Directorate of History and Heritage, Department of National Defence, *W.A. Bishop Collection* (combat and other reports, letters, flight logbooks, miscellaneous documents), 1915-1919

Gruppenführer der Flieger 4 (Grufl 4), *Gefechtstätigkeit-Berichte*, in the field, 1917

Kommandeur der Flieger der 2. Armee (Kofl 2). *Wochenberichte*, in the field, 1918

Kommandeur der Flieger der 4. Armee (Kofl 4). *Tagesbefehle,* in the field, 1917

----. *Wochenberichte über die Tätigkeit*, in the field, 1917

----. *Meldungen über die Tätigkeit*, in the field, 1917

Kommandeur der Flieger der 6. Armee (Kofl 6). *Meldungen*, in the field, 1917, 1918

Kommandierende General der Luftstreitkräfte (Kogenluft). *Nachrichtenblatt der Luftstreitkräfte*, Vol. I, in the field, 1917

----. *Nachrichtenblatt der Luftstreitkräfte*, Vol. II, in the field, 1918

Marinefeldflugchef. *Mitteilungen aus dem Gebiete des Luftkrieges*, in the field, 1918

Royal Flying Corps/Royal Air Force. Communiqués, in the field, 1917 (File Air 1/2097/207/14/1)

----. Pilot and Observer Casualties, indexed in the field, March-May 1917 (File Air 1/968/204/5/1099)

----. 11 Squadron, RFC/RAF, Combat Reports, in the field, 1917-1918 (File Air 1/1219/204/5/2634/11 Sqdn)

----. 60 Squadron, RFC/RAF, Combat Reports, in the field, 1917 (File Air 1/1225/204/5/2634/60 Sqdn)

----. 60 Squadron, RFC/RAF, Officers' Record Book, July 1916-May 1917, in the field (File Air 1/1554/204/79/56)

----. 60 Squadron, RFC/RAF, Officers' Record Book, June 1917-September 1918, in the field (File Air 1/1554/204/79/57)

----. 85 Squadron, RAF, Combat Reports, in the field, 1918 (File Air 1/1227/204/5/2634/85 Sqdn)

----. 2nd Brigade, Honours and awards: all ranks, in the field April 1918-May 1919 (File Air 1/1580/204/81/83)

----. 3rd Brigade, Recommendations for honours and awards, in the field (Air 1/1515/204/58/50)

----. 3rd Brigade, Reports from Wings on excellent work performed by individuals, in the field (Air 1/1516/204/58/58)

----. 3rd Brigade, Daily Summary, June 1917, in the field (Air 1/2239/42/6)

----. 13th Wing, Flight Returns and Messages, 1917, in the field (DHH/DND, 2001-9 File 3A3)

----. War Diary, in the field, November 1915 - May 1916 (File Air 1/1184/204/5/2595)

----. War Diary, in the field, January - September 1917 (File Air 1/1185/204/5/2595)

----. War Diary, in the field, June 1918 - April 1919 (File Air 1/1187/204/5/2595)

Royal Naval Air Service, Daily Summaries, in the field, June 1917 (File Air 1/54/15/9/45)

Articles, Monographs, Periodicals and Texts

Anonymous. 'The Flying Corps Spirit' in *Flying*, Vol. 2, No. 34, London, 1917

Bashow, D. 'The Incomparable Billy Bishop: The Man and the Myths' in *Canadian Military Journal*, Vol. 3, No. 3, Kingston, Ontario, 2002

Bishop, W. 'Tales of the British Air Service' in *National Geographic*, Vol. 23, No. 1, Washington, DC, 1918

Bock, G. *Königl. Preuss. Jagdstaffel 7*, research notes, Bad Homburg v.d.H., undated

----. *Königl. Preuss. Jagdstaffel 11*, research notes, Bad Homburg v.d.H., undated

----. *Königl. Preuss. Jagdstaffel 29*, research notes, Bad Homburg v.d.H., undated

----. *Königl. Preuss. Jagdstaffel 30*, research notes, Bad Homburg v.d.H., undated

----. *Königl. Preuss. Jagdstaffel 56*, research notes, Bad Homburg v.d.H., undated

----. *Kofl 4 Wochenberichte summaries*, research notes, Bad Homburg v.d.H., undated

----. *Kofl 6 Casualty summaries*, research notes, Bad Homburg v.d.H., undated

Bruce, J. Nieuport Fighters, Vol. 1, Albatros Productions Ltd., Berkhamsted, Herts., 1993

Doyle, R. 'They Called Bishop Hell's Handmaiden and said he was Half the Air Force' in Toronto *Globe and Mail*, 12 September 1956

Flight magazine, Royal Aero Club, various issues, London, 1916-1918

Fry, W. & Revell, A. '"The Bishop Affair" – A Previously Unpublished Document by Wing Commander William Mays Fry, MC' in *Cross & Cockade International Journal*, Vol. 32 No. 1, Farnborough, 2001

Grosz, P. *Albatros D.III Windsock Datafile Special,* Albatros Productions Ltd., Berkhamsted, Herts., 2003

Markham, P. 'The Early Morning Hours of 2 June 1917' in *Over the Front*, Vol. 10, No. 3, Dallas, TX, 1995

---- & VanWyngarden, G. 'Bishop's Aircraft – Colors and Markings No. 60 Squadron, RFC' in *Over the Front*, Vol. 10, No. 3, Dallas, TX, 1995

Molesworth, W. 'Memories of 60 Squadron R.F.C.' in *Popular Flying*, Vol. 5, No. 5, 1934

Mortane, J. '*L'autre As des As: Bishop*' in *La Guerre Aérienne Illustrée,*' Vol. 1 No 47, Paris, 1917

Nicod, A. 'Memories of 60 Squadron R.F.C.' in *Popular Flying*, Vol. 3, No. 10, 1934

Puglisi, W. 'Jacobs of Jasta 7 – Highest Ranking Living German Ace of World War I' in *Cross & Cockade Journal*, Vol. 6, No. 4, Whittier, CA, 1965

----. 'German Aircraft Down in British Lines - RFC/RAF "G" Numbers, Part 1' in *Cross & Cockade Journal*, Vol. 10, No. 2, Whittier, CA, 1969

Rabe, H. 'Observers and Fighter Pilots in the First World War' in *Cross & Cockade Journal*, Vol. 9, No. 3, Whittier, CA, 1968

Russell, H. & Puglisi, W. '"Grid" Caldwell of 74 [Squadron]' in *Cross & Cockade Journal*, Vol. 10, No. 3, Whittier, CA, 1969

Skelton, M. 'John McGavock Grider - War Bird' in *Cross & Cockade Great Britain Journal*, Vol. 11 No. 1, Farnborough, 1980

Smith, F. 'Jack Scott, Cripple Hero of the Air' in *The Times,* 17 January 1922

The Times, Times Newspapers, various issues, London, 1917-1922

Warne, J. '60 Squadron: A Detailed History, Part 2' in Cross & *Cockade Great Britain Journal,* Vol. 11 No. 2, Farnborough, 1980

Zickerick, W. 'Verlustliste der deutschen Luftstreitkräfte im Weltkriege' in Eberhardt, W. von (ed.). *Unsere Luftstreitkräfte 1914-18 - Ein Denkmal deutschen Heldentums*, Vaterländischer Verlag C.A. Weller, Berlin, 1930

On-line Resources
Airship Heritage Trust, 'Submarine Scout Class' airships, 2014, http://www.airshiponline.com/airships/ss/

Cummins, T. Family Trees – Nicod, (n.d.), http://terrycummins.co.uk/fam/nc3/alfnic3.htm

Graves, E. World War I service memorial (n.d.), http://www.hambo.org/lancing/view_man.php?id=68

McKenzie, R. 'The Real Case of No. 943 - William Avery Bishop,' occasional paper presented at the [Canadian] Royal Military College Historical Convention, 1990. http://www.rmcclubkingston.com/History%20Articles/Billy%20Bishop/Bishop-%20article%20by%20J.R.%20McKenzie.pdf

Naval Warfare blog, *SS Caledonia*, June 4, 2013, http://navalwarfare.blogspot.com/2013/06/ss-caledonia.html

U.S. Naval Observatory Astronomical Applications Department. http://aa.usno.navy.mil/data/docs/RS_OneDay.php

Weaver, H. 'Billy Bishop's Loyalist Roots' in Branches, United Empire Loyalists' Association, Grand River Branch, Vol.5 No.1, 1993. http://www.grandriveruel.ca/Newsletter_Reprints/93v5n1Billy_Bishop.htm

Wings Over Cambridge: Keith Logan "Grid" Caldwell, (n.d.). http://www.cambridgeairforce.org.nz/World%20War%20One%20Airmen.htm;http://www.cambridgeairforce.org.nz/Keith%20Caldwell.htm

Other Sources

Library and Archives of Canada. William Avery Bishop fonds [textual record, graphic material], (n.d.). http://collectionscanada.gc.ca/pam_archives/index.php?fuseaction=genitem.displayItem&lang=eng&rec_nbr=102606

Soldiers of the First World War, Personnel Records: W.A. Bishop, Ottawa (n.d.).

Endnotes

Foreword Endnotes

1. Shirer, *The Collapse of the Third Republic*, an inquiry into the fall of France in 1940, p.15.
2. 'Honours' listing for Distinguished Flying Cross award in *Flight* magazine, 8 August 1918, p. 878 reads: 'The total number of machines destroyed by this distinguished officer is 72, and his value as a moral factor to the Royal Air Force cannot be over-estimated.'
3. Noted in considerable detail in Humphries & Maker, *Germany's Western Front – Translations from the German Official History of the Great War – 1914 – Part 1*, p. 1.
4. Shores, Franks & Guest, *Above the Trenches*, pp. 216-217.
5. Jones, *Tiger Squadron: The Story of 74 Squadron, RAF in Two World Wars*, p. 255.
6. Ibid., pp. 255-256.
7. Shores, Franks & Guest, op.cit., p. 110.
8. Zickerick, 'Verlustliste der deutschen Luftstreitkräfte im Weltkriege'.
9. Franks, Bailey & Duiven, *Casualties of the German Air Service 1914-1920*.
10. Ibid., pp. 280-281.
11. RAF, War Diary, 19 June 1918, p. 37.
12. Shores, Franks & Guest, op.cit., pp. 78, 110, 179.
13. Police Research Group, *Crime Prevention Unit Series: Paper No. 37*, London: Home Office Police Department, 1992
14. 11 Squadron, RFC/RAF, Combat Reports, archival cover note.
15. Greenhous, *The Making of Billy Bishop – The First World War Exploits of Billy Bishop, VC*, p. 10.
16. Shirer, op.cit.

Chapter One Endnotes

1. Bishop, W., *Winged Warfare*, p. 105.
2. According to one German report that day: 'Western Front: During good weather, very heavy deployment of air forces by both sides. Activity of enemy aeroplanes in the northern battle zone was very brisk' [Ref: Kogenluft, *Nachrichtenblatt der Luftstreitkräfte*, Vol. 2 Nr. 15, 6 June 1918, p. 207]. A British report for the day stated: 'On the 28th instant, fine weather enabled our aeroplanes and balloons to accomplish a full day's work …' [Ref: GHQ Report in Flight magazine, 6 June 1918, p. 631].
3. Rabe, 'Comments and Reminiscences: Flying as an Observer in Flieger-Abteilung (A) 253,' (based on an interview with this author on 10 September 1984), pp.296-297.
4. Ibid., p. 297.
5. Author's interview with H-G. Rabe, 10 September 1984.
6. Directorate of History and Heritage, Department of National Defence, W. A. Bishop letter to Margaret, 28 May 1918 (typed copies of this and other Bishop letters are stored in Canada's DHH/DND).
7. Shores, Franks & Guest, *Above the Trenches*, p. 77.
8. Royal Air Force, War Diary, 28 May 1918, p. 213-214.
9. Kogenluft, op.cit.
10. Zickerick, 'Verlustliste der deutschen Luftstreitkräfte im Weltkriege' and, in English, Franks, Bailey & Duiven, *Casualties of the German Air Service 1914-1920*.
11. Ibid., p. 274.
12. Kommandeur der Flieger der 4. Armee, *Wochenbericht, Nr. Ia 1559* op., 31 May 1918, p. 5.
13. Puglisi, 'Jacobs of Jasta 7 – Highest Ranking Living German Ace of World War I', p. 325.
14. Ibid.
15. Weaver, 'Billy Bishop's Loyalist Roots', p. 10.
16. Ibid., p. 11.
17. Ibid., p. 12.
18. Bishop, A., *The Courage of the Early Morning*, p. 10.
19. Ibid., pp. 11-12.
20. Ibid., p. 12.
21. R.W. Bishop obituary, *Owen Sound Sun*, 28 November 1957.
22. The entire rhyme is: 'Monday's child is fair of face / Tuesday's child is full of grace / Wednesday's child is full of woe / Thursday's child has far to go / Friday's child is loving and giving / Saturday's child works hard for a living / But the child who is born on the Sabbath Day / Is bonny and blithe and good and gay.'
23. Bishop, A., op.cit.
24. M. (Bishop) McKay obituary, *Owen Sound Sun*, 29 October 1974.
25. W.A. Bishop obituary, *Toronto Globe*, undated.

26. Mathieson, *Billy Bishop, VC*, p. 6.
27. Bishop, A., op.cit.
28. Bashow, *Knights of the Air – Canadian Fighter Pilots in the First World War*, p. 101.
29. Quoted in Mathieson, op.cit., p. 3.
30. Bishop, A., op.cit.
31. Hynd, 'Flying to Kill' in Platt, *Great Battles of World War I: In the Air*, p. 27.
32. A, Bishop, op.cit.
33. McCaffery, *Billy Bishop, Canadian Hero*, p. 28.
34. Quoted in Bishop, A., op.cit., p. 13.
35. McKenzie, 'The Real Case of No. 943 – William Avery Bishop'.
36. Bishop, A., op.cit., pp. 15-16.
37. McKenzie, op.cit., p. 4.
38. Ibid.
39. Library & Archives Canada, *W.A. Bishop Fonds, Enlistment Form,* 30 September 1914.
40. Bishop, A., op.cit., p. 16.
41. McKenzie, op.cit.
42. Mathieson, op.cit., p. 7.
43. Preston, *Canada's RMC – A History of the Royal Military College*, p. 196.
44. McKenzie, op.cit., pp. 4, 5.
45. Ibid.
46. Bishop, A., op.cit., p. 17.
47. McKenzie, op.cit., p. 5.
48. Bishop, A., op.cit., p. 17.
49. McKenzie, op.cit., p. 8.
50. Ibid.
51. Ibid.
52. Creagh & Humphris, *The V.C. and D.S.O., Vol. II*, p. 266.
53. LAC, *W.A. Bishop Fonds, Application for Discharge [of] Gent.Cadet W.A. Bishop*, 28 September 1914.
54. LAC, *W.A. Bishop Fonds, Certificate of Discharge of a Gentleman Cadet*, 30 September 1914.
55. McKenzie, op.cit., pp. 8-9.
56. Bishop, A., op.cit., p. 19.
57. LAC, *W.A. Bishop Fonds, Record of Service*, ca. 1919; Toronto-area indigenous people and their descendants are called Mississaugas.

Chapter Two Endnotes

1. Directorate of History and Heritage, Department of National Defence, W. A. Bishop letter to Margaret, 17 June 1915.
2. Quoted in Hynd, 'Flying to Kill' in Platt, *Great Battles of World War I: In the Air*, p. 28.
3. The First Contingent of the Canadian Expeditionary Force set out for England in early October.
4. Bishop, A., *The Courage of the Early Morning*, p. 23.
5. Quoted in McCaffery, *Billy Bishop, Canadian Hero*, p, 35.
6. Quoted in ibid., pp. 38-39.
7. WAB letter to Margaret, 7 April 1915.
8. WAB letter to Margaret, 15 April 1915.
9. Bishop, A., op.cit., p. 23.
10. Naval Warfare blog, *SS Caledonia*, 4 June 2013; Billy Bishop later wrote that *SS Caledonia* was 'an old-time cattle-boat' that carried '700 horses' [Ref: Bishop, W., *Winged Warfare*, p. 3].
11. WAB letter to Margaret, 9 June 1915.
12. WAB letter to Margaret, 17 June 1915.
13. WAB letter to Margaret, 23 June 1915.
14. WAB letter to Margaret, 14 July 1915.
15. WAB letter to Margaret, 25 July 1915.
16. Bishop, W., op.cit., pp. 1-2.
17. WAB letter to Margaret, 6 August 1915.
18. Bishop, A. op.cit., pp. 25-26.
19. WAB letter to Margaret, 7 August 1915.
20. Bishop, A., op.cit.
21. WAB letter to Margaret, 8 August 1915.
22. Robinson, *The Zeppelin in Combat*, p. 121.
23. WAB letter to Margaret, 13 August 1915.
24. Robinson, op.cit., p. 124.
25. WAB letter to Margaret, 18 August 1915.
26. WAB letter to Margaret, 22 August 1915.
27. Bishop, W., op.cit., p. 33.
28. Bruce, *British Aeroplanes 1914-1918*, p. 39.
29. No. 21 Squadron, RFC was formed at Netheravon on 23 July 1915 [Ref: Lewis, *Squadron Histories: RFC, RNAS & RAF Since 1912*, p. 20].
30. WAB letter to Margaret, 3 September 1915.
31. WAB letter to Margaret, 4 September 1915.
32. WAB letter to Margaret, 5 September 1915.
33. WAB letter to Margaret, 6 September 1915.
34. WAB letter to Margaret, 6 September 1915.
35. WAB letter to Margaret, 10 September 1915.
36. WAB letter to Margaret, 14 September 1915.
37. Bruce, ibid., p. 357.
38. WAB letter to Margaret, 1 October 1915.
39. WAB letter to Margaret, 7 October 1915.
40. WAB letter to Margaret, 29 October 1915.
41. WAB letter to Margaret, 11 November 1915.
42. WAB letter to Margaret, 13 November 1915.
43. More likely the officer was Major F.W. Richey, Commanding Officer of 21 Squadron, RFC.
44. WAB letter to Margaret, 17 November 1915.
45. WAB letter to Margaret, 24 November 1915.
46. Commercial pilot James F. Miller informs the author that, in a tail-slide, the pilot pulls the aeroplane up vertically until the thrust of the engine's power can no longer overcome gravity, or he reduces power to enable the aeroplane to 'hang' in mid-air. As the airspeed dissipates, the pilot holds the aeroplane in the nose-up attitude and, instead of descending nose-first, the aero-

plane 'slides' backwards tail-first until the nose falls forward in a downward direction and the pilot recovers control of the aeroplane. A good view of a tail-slide can be seen at this link: http://www.youtube.com/watch?v=HCMaSWuh-4o

47. Commercial pilot James F. Miller informs the author that a vertical bank or, in pilots' parlance, flying 'knife edge', involves rolling the wings 90 degrees so they go from horizontally level to vertically up and down – one wing pointing at the sky, the other at the ground. A slip enables the pilot to lose altitude without gaining much airspeed – rather than simply pushing the nose over. Pilots of aircraft without flaps use a slip for this purpose. The difference between sideslip and forward slip is demonstrated in the link: http://www.youtube.com/watch?v=G0DTjW-lafkw

48. WAB letter to Margaret, 27 November 1915.

49. Lamberton, *Reconnaissance & Bomber Aircraft of the 1914-1918 War*, p. 42; and the test aircraft was probably not, as suggested elsewhere, a Sopwith Two-Seater (so-called 1½ Strutter), which was not available at this time [Ref: Bruce, op.cit., p. 541].

Chapter Three Endnotes

1. Directorate of History and Heritage, Department of National Defence, W. A. Bishop letter to Margaret, 21 December 1915.

2. R.E.7 deliveries began late in 1915 [Ref: Bruce, British Aeroplanes 1914-1918, pp. 421-422].

3. WAB letter to Margaret, 13 December 1915.

4. Jones, *The War in the Air, Vol. II*, p. 144.

5. Bruce, op.ci., p. 422.

6. Ibid., p. 425.

7. Major Richey had been promoted from flight commander to squadron commander on 12 October 1915 [Ref: 'The British Air Services', *Flight* magazine, 19 November 1915, p. 891].

8. WAB letter to Margaret, 21 December 1915.

9. WAB letter to Margaret, 25 December 1915; according to Arthur Bishop (op.cit., p. 31), the letter went to Billy's parents, but one must wonder whether the twenty-year-old would have been so open to them in describing the London party scene of the day.

10. Library & Archives Canada, *W.A. Bishop Fonds, Record of Service*, 1919.

11. WAB letter to Margaret, 9 January 1916.

12. WAB letters to Margaret, 12 and 16 January 1916.

13. WAB letter to Margaret, 18 January 1916.

14. Bruce, op.cit.

15. Royal Flying Corps, War Diary, Operation Order No. 358, 21 January 1916, p. 108.

16. WAB letter to Margaret, 23 January 1916.

17. Jones, op.cit., p. 148.

18. WAB letter to Margaret, 25 January 1916.

19. Lewis, *Squadron Histories: RFC, RNAS & RAF Since 1912*, p. 16.

20. Henshaw, *The Sky Their Battlefield*, p. 66.

21. RFC, War Diary, 12 January 1916, p. 86; R.E.7 2287 crewed by 2/Lt Leonard Kingdon (KiA) and Lt K.W. Grey (WiA/PoW).

22. Jones, op.cit., p. 156.

23. Ibid., pp. 156-157.

24. WAB letter to Margaret, 27 January 1916.

25. Shores, Franks & Guest, *Above the Trenches*, p. 290.

26. WAB letter to Margaret, 29 January 1916.

27. Bishop, W., Winged Peace, p. 35.

28. Bruce, op.cit., p. 425.

29. Quoted in McCaffery, *Billy Bishop, Canadian Hero*, p. 51.

30. Bishop, W., op.cit., pp. 35-36.

31. WAB letter to Margaret, 30 January 1916.

32. WAB letter to Margaret, 2 February 1916.

33. Raleigh, *The War in the Air, Vol. I*, p. 343; The song's lyrics and music were composed in 1909 by John L. St John & Alfred Glover [Ref: http://monologues.co.uk/musichall/Songs-A/Archibald-Certainly-Not.htm].

34. RFC, War Diary, 2 February 1916, p. 117.

35. WAB letter to Margaret, 8 February 1916.

36. RFC, War Diary, 8 February 1916, p. 125.

37. WAB letter to Margaret, 9 February 1916.

38. 'Boches' was a disparaging French term for Germans.

39. WAB letter to Margaret, 15 February 1916.

40. RFC, War Diary, 15 February 1916, p. 131.

41. Ibid.

42. WAB letter to Margaret, 16 February 1916.

43. Quoted in McCaffery, op.cit., p. 55.

44. Bishop, W., op.cit., pp. 36.

45. RFC, War Diary, 9 March 1916, p. 165; in fact, 21 Squadron's first air-related casualty did not occur until 31 March 1916, when R.E.7 (serial number) 2290 was hit by German anti-aircraft fire and Captain D.C. Ware was wounded [Ref: Henshaw, *The Sky Their Battlefield*, p. 78].

46. WAB letter to Margaret, 9 March 1916.

47. Bishop, A., *The Courage of the Early Morning*, p. 37.

48. Ibid.

49. Ibid.

50. Ibid., p. 38.

51. LAC, W.A. Bishop Fonds, War Office Form B.9, 26 May 1916.

Chapter Four Endnotes

1. Bishop, W., *Winged Peace*, p. 38.
2. Library & Archives Canada, *W.A. Bishop Fonds, Record of Service*, 1919.
3. Quoted in Bishop, A., *The Courage of the Early Morning*, p. 38.
4. Bishop, W., op.cit.
5. Born and recorded as Susan Mary Elizabeth Stewart-Mackenzie circa 1845.
6. 'The Royal Flying Corps Hospital,' *Flight* magazine, 27 April 1916, p. 348 noted: 'The splendid work which is being done by the Royal Flying Corps [Hospital] will benefit greatly by the beneficence of the Lady Tredegar, who has lent her beautiful house at 37, Bryanston Square, W., to the hospital … Lady Tredegar has given twelve beds, and is also contributing liberally to the maintenance fund ... and Lady St. Helier has also presented some beds, together with some other practical gifts, besides obtaining financial assistance.'
7. Bishop, op.cit., A., p. 39.
8. Today, Epsom and St Helier University Hospitals provide a range of medical services to inhabitants of southwest London and northeast Surrey.
9. Lady St. Helier obituary, *The Times*, 26 January 1931, p. 12.
10. Quoted in Bishop, A., op.cit., p. 41.
11. Quoted in ibid.
12. Ibid.
13. *The Times*, op.cit.
14. Bishop, A., op.cit., pp. 41-42.
15. Ibid., p. 42.
16. Ibid.
17. Ibid., p. 43.
18. Bishop, A., op.cit., p. 44.
19. Quoted in ibid.
20. Bishop, W., op.cit., p. 38.
21. Davila & Soltan, *French Aircraft of the First World War*, p. 231,
22. DHH/DND, W.A. Bishop Collection, personal flight logbook, 2001-9 File 3A6, 4 November 1916.
23. Robertson, *British Military Aircraft Serials 1911-1971*, p. 35.
24. Bishop, W., op.cit., p. 39.
25. LAC, *W.A. Bishop Fonds, Record of Service*, 1919.
26. DHH/DND, personal flight logbook, op.cit.
27. Bishop, W., op.cit.
28. Ibid., p. 40.
29. Ibid.
30. WAB letter to Margaret, 29 November 1916.
31. Robinson, *The Zeppelin in Combat*, pp. 217-223.
32. DHH/DND, personal flight logbook, op.cit.
33. The name that appears in a rubber stamped entry in Bishop's flight logbook.
34. Jones, *The War in the Air, Vol. III*, p. 169.
35. Bishop, A., op.cit., p. 48.
36. DHH/DND, personal flight logbook, op.cit.
37. Bruce, *British Aeroplanes 1914-1918*, p. 373.
38. 'Correspondence', *Flight* magazine, 6 April 1916, p. 302.
39. Bishop, A., op.cit.
40. Ibid., p. 49.
41. UK National Archives, Bishop, W.A. Military Service Record, p. 3.
42. Jones, op.cit., the other units were 39, 50, 75, 76 and 77 Squadrons.
43. Ibid.
44. Bruce, op.cit., pp. 357, 380.
45. Lewis, *Squadron Histories: RFC, RNAS & RAF Since 1912*, p. 27.
46. Jones, op.cit., p. 169.
47. Ibid., p. 42,
48. 'Rewards for Zepp. Wreckers', *Flight* magazine, 5 October 1916, p. 855.
49. *The London Gazette, No. 11042*, 14 November 1916.
50. *The London Gazette, No. 4930*, 16 May 1916.
51. Flight magazine, op.cit.
52. WAB letter to Margaret, 19 January 1917.
53. Robinson, op.cit., pp. 222-223.
54. WAB letter to Margaret, 22 January 1917.
55. WAB letter to Margaret, 28 February 1917.
56. Woodman, *Early Aircraft Armament - The Aeroplane and the Gun up to 1918*, p. 37
57. Bishop, W., op.cit., p. 43.

Chapter Five Endnotes

1. Directorate of History and Heritage, Department of National Defence, W.A. Bishop letter to Margaret, 4 March 1917.
2. DHH/DND, W.A. Bishop Collection, personal flight logbook, 2001-9 File 3A6, 30 December 1916.
3. Ibid., 3 March 1917.
4. More precisely, Captain Ball was made a Companion of the Distinguished Service Order and later received two Bars in lieu of subsequent awards; Ball also received the Military Cross and Bar, the latter honour in lieu of a subsequent award [Ref: Bowyer, C. *Albert Ball,* VC, pp. 184, 185].
5. Imperial Russia's Order of St. George the Triumphant, 4th Class [Ref: Ibid., p. 185].
6. WAB letter to Margaret, op.cit.
7. Pengelly, *Albert Ball, VC – The Fighter Pilot Hero of World War One*, p. 7.
8. WAB letter to Margaret, 6 March 1917.

9. Bishop, A., *The Courage of the Early Morning*, p. 56

10. Bishop, W., *Winged Warfare*, pp. 29-30.

11. Jones, *The War in the Air, Vol. III*, App. xii, p. 3.

12. Lee, *No Parachute*, p. 122.

13. Ibid.

14. Royal Flying Corps, War Diary, Locations of RFC Units, 17 February 1917, p. 62.

15. Bishop, W., *Winged Peace*, p. 7.

16. During the Boxer Rebellion in China, Kaiser Wilhelm II told his troops: "Mercy will not be shown … Just as a thousand years ago, the Huns under Attila won a reputation of might that lives on … so may the name of Germany in China, be such that no Chinese will even again dare so much as to look askance at a German" [Ref: *Encyclopedia Americana 1918, Vol. 4*, p. 374].

17. WAB letter to Margaret, 10 March 1917.

18. Smith, 'Jack Scott, Cripple Hero of the Air', p. 11.

19. Bishop, W., *Winged Warfare*, op.cit., pp. 32-33.

20. Scott, *Sixty Squadron, R.A.F. 1916-1919*, p. 28.

21. Lamberton, *Fighter Aircraft of the 1914-1918 War*, p. 216.

22. WAB letter to Margaret, 12 March 1917.

23. Lt Arthur D. Whitehead in Nieuport Scout A.279 [Ref: RFC, *Pilot and Observer Casualties*, 11 March 1917].

24. Kogenluft, *Nachrichtenblatt der Luftstreitkräfte, Vol. 1 No. 7*, 12 April 1917, p. 14.

25. Russell & Puglisi, '"Grid" Caldwell of 74 [Squadron]', p. 198.

26. *Wings Over Cambridge: Keith Logan "Grid" Caldwell*, p. 3.

27. WAB letter to Margaret, 14 March 1917.

28. DHH/DND, W.A. Bishop Collection, personal flight logbook, op.cit., 14 March 1917.

29. Bruce, *Nieuport Fighters*, Vol. 1, p. 8.

30. Liddell Hart, *The Real War 1914-1918*, pp. 299-300.

31. 60 Squadron, RFC, *Officers' Record Book*, Flight Log, 17 March 1917.

32. Cross & Cockade International, *Nieuports in RNAS, RFC and RAF Service*, p. 101.

33. Ibid.

34. In fact, Bishop made the flight on 17 March (not 18 March, as the letter infers) [Ref: RFC, *Officers' Record Book*, op.cit.].

35. WAB letter to Margaret, 19 March 1917.

36. Apparently the repaired Nieuport 17 A.274 [Ref: RFC, *Officers' Record Book*, op.cit.].

37. WAB letter to Margaret, 22 March 1917.

38. Woodman, *Early Aircraft Armament – The Aeroplane and the Gun up to 1918*, p.37.

39. Scott, op.cit., pp. 28-29.

40. Grosz, *Albatros D.III Windsock Datafile Special*, p. 1.

41. Lamberton, op.cit., pp. 216, 218.

42. Woodman, op.cit., p. 242.

43. RFC, War Diary, 25 March 1917, p. 100.

44. Ibid.

45. *Cross & Cockade International*, op.cit., p. 102.

46. 60 Squadron, RFC, Combat Report No. 286 by Lt W.A. Bishop, 25 March 1917.

47. Shores, Franks & Guest, *Above the Trenches*, p. 7.

48. WAB letter to his mother, 25 March 1917; RFA = Royal Field Artillery.

49. WAB letter to Margaret, 29 March 1917.

50. RFC, War Diary, op.cit.

51. Mallinckrodt began his service with 8th Rheinisches Infanterie-Regiment Nr. 70 and later transferred to the Luftstreitkräfte [Ref: Deutscher Offizier-Bund, *Ehren-Rangliste des ehemaligen Deutschen Heeres*, p. 239].

52. Kogenluft, *Nachrichtenblatt der Luftstreitkräfte, Vol. 1 No. 5*, 29 March 1917, p. 2.

53. Franks, Bailey & Duiven, *Casualties of the German Air Service 1914-1920*, p. 345.

54. Puglisi, 'German Aircraft Down in British Lines – RFC/RAF "G" Numbers, Part 1', p. 155.

55. Ibid.

56. RFC, *Pilot and Observer Casualties*, 28 March 1917; Hobson, *Airmen Died in the Great War*, p. 30.

57. Lt William Patrick Garnett, 22, in Nieuport Scout A.273 'Last seen over Fampoux. Death accepted [26/7/17] by the Army Council on 30/3/17 on evidence of reports of other officer prisoners of war in Germany' [Ref: RFC, *Pilot and Observer Casualties*, 30 March 1917].

58. 2/Lt Frank. Bower, 22, in Nieuport Scout A.6774 [Ref: RFC, *Pilot and Observer Casualties*, 30 March 1917].

59. 60 Squadron, RFC, Combat Report No. 291 by Lt W.A. Bishop, 31 March 1917

60. WAB letter to Margaret, 31 March 1917.

61. Henshaw, *The Sky Their Battlefield*, p. 148.

62. Kogenluft, op.cit., Vol. 1 No. 7, 12 April 1917, p. 15; Kommandeur der Flieger der 6. Armee, *Wochentlicher Tätigkeitsbericht Nr 25500*, Teil 11, 7 April 1917, p. 4.

63. Kofl 6, *Wochentlicher Tätigkeitsbericht Nr 25500*, Teil 14, 30 March 1917, p. 3

64. 2/Lt Leckie's addendum to 60 Squadron, RFC, Combat Report No.291, op.cit.

65. Kogenluft, op.cit., Vol. 1 No. 6, 5 April 1917, p. 2.

66. Kofl 6, *Wochentlicher Tätigkeitsbericht Nr 25500*, Teil 11, 7 April 1917, p. 4.

67. RFC, Communiqué No. 81, 1 April 1917, p. 2.

Chapter Six Endnotes

1. Directorate of History and Heritage, Depart-

ment of National Defence, W.A. Bishop letter to Margaret, 7 April 1917.

2. A figure gleaned from German Luftstreitkräfte tallies for the month's two bi-weekly aerial victory summaries: Kogenluft, *Nachrichtenblatt der Luftstreitkräfte, Vol. 1 Nr. 11*, 10 May 1917, pp. 12-15; Kogenluft, Nachrichtenblatt der Luftstreitkräfte, Vol. 1 Nr. 12, 17 May 1917, pp. 10-12.

3. Morris, *Bloody April,* p. 15.

4. Kilduff, *Richthofen – Beyond the Legend of the Red Baron,* p. 87.

5. Liddell Hart, *The Real War 1914-1918*, pp. 321-325.

6. Jones, *The War in the Air, Vol. III*, p. 334.

7. Ibid., pp. 334-335.

8. 2/Lt Vaughn Floyer Williams, 18, in Nieuport 23 A.6763 [Ref: RFC, *Pilot and Observer Casualties*, 2 April 1917]; he was most likely shot down by Leutnant Otto Bernert of Jagdstaffel 2, who claimed a Nieuport over Quéant as his tenth aerial victory [Ref: Kogenluft, *Nachrichtenblatt der Luftstreitkräfte*, Nr. 11, op.cit., p. 12].

9. WAB letter to Margaret, 3 April 1917.

10. 60 Squadron, RFC, *Officers' Record Book*, Flight Log, 17 March 1917.

11. Royal Flying Corps, War Diary, Locations of RFC Units, 31 March 1917, p. 108.

12. Lt [later Air Commodore] Ernest John Dennis Townesend, 21, in Nieuport 17 A.6693, subsequently listed as 'a prisoner and severely wounded' [Ref: RFC, *Pilot and Observer Casualties*, 5 April 1917].

13. WAB letter to Margaret, 5 April 1917.

14. RFC, 3rd Brigade, Recommendations for honours and awards, 2 April 1917.

15. 60 Squadron, RFC, Combat Report No. 312 by Lt W.A. Bishop, 6 April 1917.

16. Ibid.

17. Kofl 6, Nr 25500, op.cit.

18. Franks, Bailey & Duiven, *The Jasta Pilots*, p. 290.

19. Hervey flew Nieuport 17 B.1517, which was damaged in the fight [Ref: Henshaw, op.cit., p. 154].

20. Warne, '60 Squadron: A Detailed History, Part 2', p. 56.

21. 60 Squadron, RFC, Combat Report No. 314 by Lt W.A. Bishop, 7 April 1917.

22. WAB letter to Margaret, 7 April 1917.

23. Kofl 6, *Wochentlicher Tätigkeitsbericht Nr 50150, Teil 10,* 13 April 1917, p. 3.

24. Scott, *Sixty Squadron, R.A.F. 1916-1919*, p. 41; 2/Lt George Orme Smart, 31, in Nieuport 17 A.6645, later 'found at N.7.d.53 burnt. The pilot had been burnt to death. He has been buried in a shell hole near his machine and a cross is being erected by his squadron' [Ref: RFC, *Pilot and Observer Casualties*, 7 April 1917].

25. Kofl 6, Nr 50150, op.cit.

26. 2/Lt Charles Sidney Hall, 18, in Nieuport 23 A.6766 [Ref: RFC, op.cit.].

27. Kofl 6, Nr 50150, op.cit.

28. Capt Maurice B. Knowles, in Nieuport 23 A.6773 [Ref: RFC, op.cit.].

29. Kofl 6, Nr 50150, op.cit.

30. RFC, op.cit

31. Shores, Franks & Guest, *Above the Trenches*, p. 7.

32. Jones, op.cit., p. 383.

33. 60 Squadron, RFC, Combat Report No. 314 by Lt W.A. Bishop, 7 April 1917.

34. RFC, Communiqué No. 82, 8 April 1917, p. 5.

35. Kogenluft, *Nachrichtenblatt der Luftstreitkräfte, Vol. 1 Nr. 7*, 12 April 1917, p. 2.

36. Kofl 6, Nr 50150, op.cit., p. 4.

37. RFC, War Diary, Weather Report, 8 April 1917, p. 128.

38. Scott, op.cit., p. 45.

39. 60 Squadron, RFC, *Officers' Record Book*, Flight Log, 8 April 1917.

40. Major J. Adelard Adrien MIlot, 34, in Nieuport 23 B.6764; 'Report by 5th Canadian F.A. states that an unknown major RFC is buried at T.20.d.Central alongside the remains of his aeroplane which has been identified as Nieuport Scout No. A.6764' [Ref: RFC, *Pilot and Observer Casualties*, 8 April 1917].

41. Hobson, *Airmen Died in the Great War*, p, 73.

42. Bishop, A., *The Courage of the Early Morning*, p. 56.

43. Hervey, in Nieuport 17 A.311, became 'an unwounded prisoner of war' [Ref: RFC, *Pilot and Observer Casualties*, 8 April 1917]; He later wrote that, after he had been hit, 'I had a faint hope that I should be able to glide back over our lines, but I had not sufficient height, and eventually finished up on top of a well-camouflaged German artillery dugout' [Ref: Hervey, *Cage-Birds*, p. 8].

44. Henshaw, *The Sky Their Battlefield*, p. 155.

45. Bock, *Königl. Preuss. Jagdstaffel 11, research notes*, 8 April 1917.

46. The manufacturer's number of Festner's aeroplane, as seen here, was not copied correctly – either by Richthofen or Gibbons – as 223/16 does not appear in the known listing of Albatros fighters [Ref: Grosz, *Albatros D.III Windsock Datafile Special*, p. 55].

47. Gibbons, *The Red Knight of Germany – The Story of Baron von Richthofen*, p. 206.

48. 60 Squadron, RFC, Combat Report No. 322 by Lt W.A. Bishop, 8 April 1917.

49. Reported in Gibbons, op.cit.

50. Grosz, op.cit., p. 11.

51. Major Scott's addendum to 60 Squadron, RFC, Combat Report No. 322.

52. Ibid.

53. Very likely Brigadier-General John F.A. Higgins, Commander of 3rd Brigade.

54. WAB letter to his mother, 9 April 1917.

55. WAB letter to Margaret, 9 April 1917.

56. Shores, Franks & Guest, op.cit., pp. 333 and 77, respectively.

57. RFC, Communiqué No. 83, 15 April 1917, p. 1.

58. Kogenluft, *Nachrichtenblatt, Nr. 7*, op.cit., p. 66.

59. Franks, Bailey & Guest, *Above the Lines*, pp, 108-109.

60. O'Connor, *Aviation Awards of Imperial Germany and the Men Who Earned Them, Vol. II – The Aviation Awards of the Kingdom of Prussia*, p. 71; Bronnenkant, *The Blue Max Airmen – German Airmen Awarded the Pour le Mérite, Vol. 3*, p. 94.

61. Kofl 6, Nr 50150, op.cit., p. 4.

62. Bronnenkant, ibid.

63. Franks, Bailey & Duiven, op.cit., p.21.

64. 'The Struggle for Air Supremacy', *The Times*, 3 April 1917, p. 7.

65. That day, A Flight was led by Lt Alan Binnie [Ref: Scott, op.cit., p. 44] in Nieuport 23 A.6772, sent down badly wounded, captured, and his left arm had to be amputated. Lt William Oswald Russell in Nieuport 23 A.6796, shot down, unwounded, and taken prisoner. 2/Lt Lewis Carlton Chapman, 32, in Nieuport 23 B.1523, sent down badly wounded and died. And Lt John Herbert Cock, 23, in Nieuport 23 B.1511, shot down and killed [Ref: RFC, *Pilot and Observer Casualties*, 14 April 1917].

66. WAB letter to Margaret, 15 April 1917.

67. Scott, op.cit.

68. Kogenluft, *Nachrichtenblatt, Nr. 11*, op.cit., p. 14 lists these German victories and directly links (by the Nieuport serial numbers) Manfred von Richthofen 's and Kurt Wolff's claims; Kofl 6, *Wöchentlicher Tätigkeitsbericht Nr 50369, Teil 10*, 20 April 1917, p. 3 provides time and locations for the four Jasta 11 claims. Also see endnote 53 above.

69. RFC, War Diary, Weather Report, 15 April 1917, p. 149.

70. Jones, op.ci., p. 356.

71. Scott, op.ci., p. 45.

72. Ibid., pp. 45-46.

73. Davilla & Soltan, *French Aircraft of the First World War*, p. 390.

74. *Cross & Cockade International. Nieuports in RNAS, RFC and RAF Service*, p. 51.

75. RFC, War Diary, Weather Report, 17 April 1917, p. 154.

76. WAB letter to Margaret, 18 April 1917.

77. The weather may have favoured Billy, but not his adversary, according to the day's weather report: 'Mist and low clouds made aerial [reconnaissance] work very difficult' [Ref: RFC, *War Diary*, Weather Report, 20 April 1917, p. 155].

78. 60 Squadron, RFC, Combat Report No. 329 by Lt W.A. Bishop, 20 April 1917.

79. WAB letter to his mother, 21 April 1917.

80. Bruce, *Nieuport Fighters, Vol. 1*, p. 41.

81. Major Scott's addendum to 60 Squadron, RFC, Combat Report No. 329, op.cit.

82. Flying in Nieuport 23 B.1513, Atkinson crashed and 'sustained broke nose, cuts about the face and injured knee [Ref: RFC, *Pilot and Observer Casualties*, 20 April 1917].

83. RFC, Communiqué No. 84, 22 April 1917, p. 2.

84. Kogenluft, *Nachrichtenblatt der Luftstreitkräfte, Vol. 1 Nr. 9*, 26 April 1917, p. 1.

85. Kofl 6, *Wochentlicher Tätigkeitsbericht Nr 50570, Teil 11*, 28 April 1917, p. 5.

86. 60 Squadron, RFC, Combat Report No. 336 by Lt W.A. Bishop, 22 April 1917.

87. 60 Squadron, RFC, Combat Report No. 346 by Lt W.A. Bishop, 23 April 1917.

88. WAB letter to Margaret, 25 April 1917.

89. RFC, Communiqué No. 85, 29 April 1917, p. 2.

90. Ibid., p. 3.

91. Jones, op.cit., pp. 362-363.

92. Welkoborsky, *Die Flieger-Abteilung (A) 211 im Weltkriege*, p. 62.

93. 60 Squadron, RFC, *Officers' Record Book*, Flight Log, 23 April 1917.

94. 2/Lt Reginald Burton Clarke, in Nieuport 23 A.6777, 'Reported by 50th Divn. To have been brought down on fire by 3 H.A. Pilot sustained fractured leg and burns' [Ref: RFC, *Pilot and Observer Casualties*, 24 April 1917]. He died of his wounds on 1 May 1917 [Ref: Hobson, op.cit., p. 33].

95. 2/Lt N.P. Henderson, in Nieuport 23 B.1549, 'was brought down by AA fire and landed in a lake. Pilot slightly injured' [Ref: RFC, *Pilot and Observer Casualties*, 26 April 1917].

96. 2/Lt F. Stedman, in Nieuport 23 B.1570, became, according to a 'German message … is [a PoW but] unwounded' [Ref: RFC, *Pilot and Observer Casualties*, 27 April 1917].

97. WAB letter to Margaret, 27 April 1917.

98. 60 Squadron, RFC, Combat Report No. 354 by Lt W.A. Bishop, 27 April 1917.

99. RFC, Communiqué No. 85, op.cit., p. 7.

100. Library & Archives Canada, *W.A. Bishop Fonds, Record of Service*, 1919.

101. WAB letter to Margaret, 30 April 1917.

102. Kofl 6, *Wochentlicher Tätigkeitsbericht Nr 50790, Teil 12*, 4 May 1917, p. 7.

103. Gruppenführer der Flieger 4, *Gefechtstätig-keit-Bericht*, 29 April 1917.
104. 60 Squadron, RFC, Combat Report No. 358 by Lt W.A. Bishop, 29 April 1917.
105. Jones, op.cit., p. 367.
106. 60 Squadron, RFC, Combat Report, op.cit.
107. 60 Squadron, RFC, Combat Report No. 362 by Lt W.A. Bishop, 30 April 1917.
108. Kofl 6, op.cit.
109. RFC, Communiqué No. 86, 6 May 1917, p. 1.
110. Ibid., p. 2.

Chapter Seven Endnotes

1. Directorate of History and Heritage, Department of National Defence, W.A. Bishop letter to his father, 26 May 1917.
2. Royal Flying Corps, War Diary, Weather Reports, 29 and 30 April 1917, pp. 183, 191.
3. Ibid., 1 May 1917, p. 197.
4. Richthofen, *Der rote Kampfflieger*, p. 155.
5. Jones, *The War in the Air, Vol. III*, p. 370.
6. Ibid.
7. WAB letter to Margaret, 2 May 1917.
8. 60 Squadron, RFC, Combat Report No. 370 by Capt W.A. Bishop, 2 May 1917.
9. Kommandeur der Flieger der 6. Armee, *Wochentlicher Tätigkeitsbericht Nr 469 I*, 8 June 1917, *Muster A*, 7 June 1917, p. 1.
10. Puglisi, 'German Aircraft Down in British Lines – RFC/RAF "G" Numbers, Part 1,' p. 156.
11. Ibid.
12. RFC, Communiqué No. 86, 6 May 1917, p. 5.
13. Kofl 6. Armee, *Muster A*, op.cit.
14. Ibid.
15. WAB letter to his sister, 5 May 1917.
16. Rogers, *British Aviation Squadron Markings of World War I*, p. 118.
17. 60 Squadron, RFC, *Officers' Record Book*, Flight Log, 1 May 1917.
18. 60 Squadron, RFC, Combat Report No. 382 by Capt W.A. Bishop, 3 May 1917.
19. Revell, *No. 60 Sqn RFC/RAF*, p. 45.
20. 60 Squadron, RFC, Combat Report No. 388 by Capt W.A. Bishop, 4 May 1917.
21. Lt Fry's addendum to ibid.
22. RFC, Communiqué, op.cit., p. 6.
23. More correct examples, as shared victories, are found in Shores, Franks & Guest, *Above the Trenches*, pp. 77 and 161.
24. Franks, Bailey & Duiven, *Casualties of the German Air Service 1914-1920*, p. 210.
25. Kogenluft, *Nachrichtenblatt der Luftstreitkräfte, Vol. 1 Nr. 12*, 17 May 1917, p. 1.
26. RFC, War Diary, Weather Report, 7 May 1917, p. 221.
27. 60 Squadron, RFC, Combat Report No. 395 by Capt W.A. Bishop, 7 May 1917.
28. 60 Squadron, RFC, Combat Report No. 396 by Capt W.A. Bishop, 7 May 1917.
29. Major Scott's addendum to ibid.
30. RFC, Communiqué No. 87, 13 May 1917, p. 3.
31. Shores, Franks & Guest, op.cit., p. 6.
32. DFW C.VI 5177/16 from Fl.-Abt (A) 202 crewed by Uffz Kurt Schnell (pilot) and Ltn Georg Prätorius (observer), both killed in a fight over Arras [Ref: Kofl 6. Armee, *Muster A*, op.cit.].
33. RFC, *Pilot and Observer Casualties*, 7 May 1917.
34. Pengelly, *Albert Ball, VC – The Fighter Pilot Hero of World War One*, pp. 195-199.
35. Kilduff, *Richthofen – Beyond the Legend of the Red Baron*, p. 63.
36. Pengelly, op.cit., p. 203.
37. RFC, War Diary, Report on Hostile Aircraft, 9 May 1917, p. 230.
38. WAB letter to Margaret, 9 May 1917.
39. WAB letter to Margaret, 11 May 1917.
40. Shores, Franks & Guest, op.cit., pp. 92-93.
41. WAB letter, op.cit.
42. RFC, 13th Wing, Flight Returns and Messages, 15 May 1917.
43. WAB letter to Margaret, 19 May 1917.
44. WAB letter to Margaret, 24 May 1917.
45. Shores, Franks & Guest, op.cit., p. 8.
46. WAB letter to his parents, 26 May 1917.
47. 60 Squadron, RFC, Combat Report No. 435 by Capt W.A. Bishop, 26 May 1917.
48. RFC, Communiqué No. 90, 13 May 1917, p. 1.
49. Kogenluft, *Nachrichtenblatt der Luftstreitkräfte, Vol. 1 Nr. 14*, 31 May 1917, p. 2.
50. Kofl 6, *Wochentlicher Tätigkeitsbericht Nr 380/I*, 1 June 1917, Teil 12, p. 6.
51. 13th Wing, Flight Returns and Messages, 26 May 1917.
52. WAB letter to Margaret, 28 May 1917.
53. RFC, War Diary, Locations of RFC Units, 1 June 1917, p. 302.
54. 60 Squadron, RFC, Combat Report No. 440 by Capt W.A. Bishop, 27 May 1917.
55. Kogenluft, *Nachrichtenblatt*, op.cit., p. 154.
56. Kofl 6, op.cit.
57. 60 Squadron, RFC, Combat Report No. 448 by Capt W.A. Bishop, 30 May 1917.
58. 60 Squadron, RFC, Combat Report No. 449 by Capt W.A. Bishop, 31 May 1917.
59. Kogenluft, *Nachrichtenblatt der Luftstreitkräfte*, Vol. 1 Nr. 15, 7 June 1917, p. 2.
60. Kofl 6, op.cit.
61. Kommandeur der Flieger der 4. Armee, *Wochenbericht Nr. 19798/19*, 2 June 1917, Teil 3f, p. 5.
62. RFC, Communiqué No. 90, op.cit., p. 6.
63. 'Honours', *Flight* magazine, 31 May 1917, p. 527.

64. RFC, War Diary, Locations of RFC Units, op.cit.
65. WAB letter to Margaret, 31 May 1917.

Chapter Eight Endnotes

1. Quoted in Directorate of History and Heritage, Department of National Defence, W.A. Bishop letter to Margaret, 7 June 1917.
2. Jones, *The War in the Air, Vol. IV*, p. 109.
3. Liddell Hart, *The Real War 1914-1918*, pp. 330-331.
4. Quoted in Jones, op.cit., p. 129.
5. Bishop, W. *Winged Warfare*, p. 194.
6. Major Scott's addendum to 60 Squadron, RFC, Combat Report No. 456 by Capt W.A. Bishop, 2 June 1917.
7. Royal Flying Corps, War Diary, Weather Report, 1 June 1917, p. 303.
8. 60 Squadron, RFC, *Officers' Record Book*, Flight Log, 1 June 1917.
9. 60 Squadron, RFC, Combat Report No. 450 by Capt W.A. Bishop, 1 June 1917.
10. Fry, *Air of Battle*, p. 135.
11. RFC, War Diary, Weather Report, 2 June 1917, p. 307.
12. As noted above, surely the two friends were Lt W.H. Fry and Capt K.L. Caldwell; Billy Bishop worked closely with both men and held them in high esteem.
13. Bishop, W., op.cit., pp. 197-199.
14. 60 Squadron, RFC, Combat Report No. 456 by Capt W.A. Bishop, 2 June 1917.
15. Major Scott's addendum to Combat Report No. 456, op.cit.
16. Markham, 'The Early Morning Hours of 2 June 1917', p. 244.
17. 60 Squadron, RFC, *Officers' Record Book*, Correspondence, 2 June 1917.
18. Fry, op.cit.
19. Ibid., p. 136.
20. WAB letter to Margaret, 3 June 1917.
21. 60 Squadron, RFC, *Officers' Record Book*, Correspondence, 3 June 1917.
22. RFC, 3rd Brigade, Daily Summary, 2 June 1917,
23. 60 Squadron, RFC, Combat Report No. 456, op.cit.
24. Bishop, W., op.cit., p. 199.
25. RFC, 3rd Brigade, Recommendations for honours and awards, 4 June 1917.
26. Fry, op.cit., p. 116.
27. 'Official Information', *Flight* magazine, 7 June 1917, p. 569.
28. Kogenluft, *Nachrichtenblatt der Luftstreitkräfte*, Vol. 1 Nr. 15, 7 June 1917, p. 165.
29. Royal Naval Air Service, Daily Summaries, 2-3 June 1917, p. 2.
30. 'German Bases Again Attacked', *The Times*, 4 June 1917, p. 8.
31. 'Raids on Zeebrugge, Ostend and Bruges', *Flight* magazine, 7 June 1917, p. 560.
32. Kommandeur der Flieger der 4. Armee, *Wochenbericht Nr. 20652/19*, 9 June 1917, p. 7.
33. Kommandeur der Flieger der 2. Armee, *Wochenbericht Nr. 3702*, 7 June 1917, p. 3.
34. Kommandeur der Flieger der 6. Armee, *Wöchentlicher Tätigkeits-Bericht Nr. 469 I*, 8 June 1917, p. 7.
35. On-line references: http://www.timeanddate.com/calendar/aboutmoonphases.html and http://aa.usno.navy.mil/data/docs/RS_OneDay.php
36. 'Final Report of the Committee on the Administration and Command of the Royal Flying Corps', *Flight* magazine, 11 January 1917, p. 40.
37. Markham, op.cit., pp. 240-259; see also www.overthefront.com
38. Bashow, 'The Incomparable Billy Bishop: The Man and the Myths', p. 58.
39. Nicod, 'Memories of 60 Squadron RFC' in *Popular Flying*, December 1934, reprinted in Chadderton, *Hanging a Legend: The National Film Board's Shameful Attempt to Discredit Billy Bishop, VC*, p. 322.
40. Fry, op.cit., p. 136.
41. Anonymous, *Lewis Machine Gun (Airplane Type)* manual, p. 9.
42. Fry, op.cit., p. 135.
43. Bishop, A., *The Courage of the Early Morning*, p. 102.
44. Anonymous, *Lewis Machine Gun*, op.cit.
45. Greenhous, *The Making of Billy Bishop*, p. 123.
46. Bashow, 'The Incomparable Billy Bishop: The Man and the Myths', pp. 58-59.
47. RFC, Communiqué No. 91, 9 June 1917, p. 2.
48. RFC, War Diary, Hostile Aircraft Report, 2 June 1917, p. 308.
49. RFC, 3rd Brigade, Recommendations for honours and awards, 1 July 1917.
50. WAB letter to Margaret, 7 June 1917.
51. 2/Lt Ronald Milton Harris, 19, in Nieuport 17 B.1503 [Ref: Hobson, *Airmen Died in the Great War*, p. 54; RFC, *Pilot and Observer Casualties,* 7 June 1917].
52. WAB letter to Margaret, 9 June 1917.
53. Bishop, W., op.cit., p.209.
54. Kogenluft, *Nachrichtenblatt der Luftstreitkräfte*, Vol. 1 Nr. 20, 12 July 1917, p. 80-81.
55. RFC, War Diary, Weather Report, 8 June 1917, p. 334.
56. 60 Squadron, RFC, Combat Report No. 475 by Capt W.A. Bishop, 8 June 1917.
57. Kogenluft, *Nachrichtenblatt der Luftstreitkräfte,*

Vol. 1 Nr. 16, 14 June 1917, p. 16.

58. Kofl 6, *Wöchentlicher Tätigkeits-Bericht Nr. 561 I*, 15 June 1917, p. 4.

59. RFC, Communiqué No. 92, 17 June 1917, p. 2.

60. 'The Victoria Cross. 29 Officers and Men Decorated', *The Times*, 9 June 1917, p. 4.

61. Bowyer, *For Valour – The Air V.C.s, p. 20.*

62. *The London Gazette, 30122*, 8 June 1917, p. 5702.

63. Ibid., p. 5703.

64. Bowyer, op.cit., p. 84.

65. 'Honours. Two New VCs', *Flight* magazine, 14 June 1917, p. 579.

66. RFC, 13th Wing, Flight Returns and Messages, 9 June 1917.

67. 60 Squadron, RFC, *Officers' Record Book*, Flight Log, 10, 11, 12, 13 June 1917.

68. Fry, op.cit., p. 137.

69. Ibid.

70. Fry & Revell, '"The Bishop Affair" – A Previously Unpublished Document by Wing Commander William Mays Fry, MC', p. 42.

71. UK Ministry of Defence letter to Markham (1986) quoted in his *Over the Front* article, op.cit., p. 242.

72. Ibid., p. 243.

73. *The London Gazette*, No. 30135, 18 June 1917.

74. Quoted in 'Honours', *Flight* magazine, 21 June 1917, p. 613.

75. WAB letter to Margaret, 21 June 1917.

Chapter Nine Endnotes

1. Directorate of History and Heritage, Department of National Defence, W.A. Bishop letter to Margaret, 24 June 1917.

2. Kogenluft, *Nachrichtenblatt der Luftstreitkräfte, Vol. 1 Nr. 18*, 28 June 1917, p. 54.

3. 60 Squadron, RFC, Combat Report No. 456 by Capt W.A. Bishop, 2 June 1917.

4. Ref: 60 Squadron, RFC, Combat Report No. 503 by Capt W.A. Bishop, 24 June 1917.

5. Bishop, W., Winged Warfare, p. 238.

6. Ibid, p. 238.

7. Nieuport 23 B.1610 [Ref: RFC, *Pilot and Observer Casualties*, 16 June 1917; also 'Personals', *Flight* magazine, 7 June 1917, p. 1145].

8. The German pilot was Vizefeldwebel Robert Riessinger, age 24 [Ref: Schmeelke, M. *Das Kriegstagebuch der Jagdstaffel 12*, pp. 32-33].

9. 'Victory in Death', *The Times*, 3 July 1917, p. 8.

10. WAB letter to Margaret, 24 June 1917.

11. 60 Squadron, RFC, Combat Report No. 504 by Capt W.A. Bishop, 24 June 1917.

12. RFC, Communiqué No. 94, 1 July 1917, p. 2.

13. Kogenluft, *Nachrichtenblatt Nr. 18*, op.cit., p. 46.

14. Kommandeur der Flieger der 4. Armee, *Meldung Nr. 22816*, 29 June 1917, p. 6.

15. Franks, Bailey & Duiven, *The Jasta Pilots*, p. 238.

16. WAB letter to Margaret, 26 June 1917.

17. 60 Squadron, RFC, Combat Report No. 509 by Capt W.A. Bishop, 25 June 1917

18. RFC, Communiqué, op.cit., p. 3.

19. Kogenluft, *Nachrichtenblatt*, op.cit.

20. 60 Squadron, RFC, Combat Report No. 510 by Capt W.A. Bishop, 26 June 1917.

21. Ibid.

22. RFC, Communiqué, op.cit., p. 4.

23. Kogenluft, *Nachrichtenblatt*, op.cit., p. 47.

24. 60 Squadron, RFC, Combat Report No. 514 by Capt W.A. Bishop, 27 June 1917.

25. 60 Squadron, RFC, Combat Report No. 520 by Capt W.A. Bishop, 27 June 1917.

26. WAB letter to Margaret, 28 June 1917.

27. 60 Squadron, RFC, Combat Report No. 522 by Capt W.A. Bishop, 28 June 1917.

28. Ibid,

29. RFC, Communiqué, op.cit., p. 5.

30. Kogenluft, *Nachrichtenblatt der Luftstreitkräfte, Vol. 1 Nr. 19*, 5 July 1917, p. 58.

31. 13th Wing, RFC, Flight Returns and Messages, 30 June 1917.

32. Ibid.

33. WAB letter to Margaret, 4 July 1917.

34. WAB letter to Margaret, 5 July 1917.

35. Kogenluft, *Nachrichtenblatt Nr. 19*, op.cit., p. 65.

36. Kogenluft, *Nachrichtenblatt der Luftstreitkräfte, Vol. 1 Nr. 23*, 2 August 1917, p. 115.

37. Kogenluft, *Nachrichtenblatt der Luftstreitkräfte, Vol. 1 Nr. 28,* 6 September 1917, p. 203.

38. Kogenluft, *Nachrichtenblatt der Luftstreitkräfte, Vol. 1 Nr. 37*, 8 November 1917, p. 379.

39. Kogenluft, *Nachrichtenblatt der Luftstreitkräfte, Vol. 1 Nr. 15*, 7 June 1917, p. 2.

40. Kommandeur der Flieger der 6. Armee, *Wöchentlicher Tätigkeits-Bericht Nr. 469 I*, 8 June 1917, p. 7.

41. Scott, *Sixty Squadron, R.A.F. 1916-1919*, p. 65.

42. Bruce, *British Aeroplanes 1914-1918,* p. 448.

43. Warne, '60 Squadron: A Detailed History, Part 2', p. 60.

44. WAB letter to Margaret, 7 July 1917.

45. 60 Squadron, RFC, Combat Report No. 544 by Capt W.A. Bishop, 7 July 1917.

46. Twenty-eight according to Shores, Franks & Guest, *Above the Trenches*, p. 240.

47. Thirty-two according to Ibid., p. 77.

48. WAB letter to Margaret, 12 July 1917.

49. RFC, Communiqué No. 96, 15 July 1917, p. 3.

50. Scott, op.cit.

51. 60 Squadron, RFC, Combat Report No. 553 by Capt W.A. Bishop, 12 July 1917.

52. RFC, Communiqué, op.cit., p. 4.

53. Ibid., p. 5.
54. Little and Mowle addenda to combat report, op.cit.
55. Kogenluft, *Nachrichtenblatt der Luftstreitkräfte, Vol. 1 Nr. 21*, 19 July 1917, p. 86.
56. Kommandeur der Flieger der 6. Armee, *Wöchentlicher Tätigkeits-Bericht Nr. 835 I*, 13 July 1917, p. 6.
57. Bock, *Königl. Preuss. Jagdstaffel 29*, entry for 12 July 1917.
58. 60 Squadron, RFC, Combat Report No. 564 by Capt W.A. Bishop, 12 July 1917.
59. WAB letter to Margaret, 14 July 1917.
60. 13th Wing, RFC, Flight Returns and Messages, 14 July 1917.
61. RFC, War Diary, Weather Report, 14, 15 and 16 July 1917, pp. 446, 450, 452.
62. WAB letter to Margaret, 17 July 1917.
63. Shores, Franks & Guest, op.cit., p77.
64. RFC, Communiqué No. 97, 22 July 1917, p. 4.
65. 11 Squadron, RFC notation on 60 Squadron, RFC, Combat Report No. 566 by Capt W.A. Bishop, 17 July 1917.
66. Kogenluft, *Nachrichtenblatt Nr. 21*, op.cit., p. 87.
67. Kofl 4, *Meldung Nr.25300/19*, 20 July 1917, p. 9.
68. WAB letter to Margaret, 19 July 1917.
69. 60 Squadron, RFC, Combat Report No. 569 by Capt W.A. Bishop, 20 July 1917.
70. Ibid.
71. RFC, Communiqué, op.cit., p. 6.
72. Kogenluft, *Nachrichtenblatt der Luftstreitkräfte, Vol. 1 Nr. 22*, 26 July 1917, p. 97.
73. Kofl 6, *Wöchentlicher Tätigkeits-Bericht Nr. 965 I*, 27 July 1917, p. 4.

Chapter Ten Endnotes

1. Directorate of History and Heritage, Department of National Defence, W.A. Bishop letter to his mother, 29 July 1917.
2. Shores, Franks & Guest, *Above the Trenches*, pp. 110-111.
3. Capt Cochran-Patrick's addendum to 60 Squadron, RFC, Combat Report No. 573 by Capt W.A. Bishop, 21 July 1917.
4. WAB letter to Margaret, 22 July 1917.
5. Bruce, *British Aeroplanes 1914–1918*, p. 447.
6. 60 Squadron, RFC, Combat Report No. 574 by Capt W.A. Bishop, 23 July 1917.
7. 60 Squadron, RFC, Combat Report No. 578 by Capt W.A. Bishop, 23 July 1917.
8. Robertson, *British Military Aircraft Serials 1911-1971*, p. 52.
9. Warne, '60 Squadron: A Detailed History, Part 2', p. 62.
10. 60 Squadron, RFC, *Officers' Record Book*, Flight Log, 24 July 1917.
11. *Cross & Cockade International. Nieuports in RNAS, RFC and RAF Service*, p. 118.
12. WAB letter to Margaret, 26 July 1917.
13. WAB letter to Margaret, 28 July 1917.
14. Bruce, op.cit., p. 454.
15. WAB letter to his mother, 29 July 1917.
16. 60 Squadron, RFC, Combat Report No. 581 by Capt W.A. Bishop, 28 July 1917.
17. Kogenluft, *Nachrichtenblatt der Luftstreitkräfte, Vol. 1 Nr. 23*, 2 August 1917, p. 110.
18. RFC, Communiqué No. 99, 5 August 1917, p. 3.
19. 60 Squadron, RFC, Combat Report No. 582 by Capt W.A. Bishop, 29 July 1917.
20. Russell & Puglisi, '"Grid" Caldwell of 74 [Squadron]', p. 201.
21. Bishop, W., *Winged Warfare*, pp. 233-234.
22. While an infantry Leutnant [Second-Lieutenant] Adolf Tutschek was awarded the Kingdom of Bavaria's highest bravery award, the Knight's Cross [Ritterkreuz] of the Military Max-Joseph Order, which carried with it personal (non-hereditary] nobility and the title 'Ritter von', which was part of his name when he was in the aviation service [Ref: O'Connor, *Aviation Awards of Imperial Germany and the Men Who Earned Them, Vol. I – The Aviation Awards of the Kingdom of Bavaria*, pp. 9, 94].
23. Kommandeur der Flieger der 6. Armee, *Wöchentlicher Tätigkeits-Bericht Nr. 1015/I*, 3 August 1917, p. 4.
24. 2/Lt William Henry Gunner, MC, age 26, was killed in S.E.5 A.8937 after being 'last seen over Douai above an enemy formation' [Ref: RFC, *Pilot and Observer Casualties*, 29 July 1917; Hobson, *Airmen Died in the Great War*, p. 51].
25. 60 Squadron, RFC, Combat Report, op.cit.
26. RFC, Communiqué No. 99, op.cit., p. 4.
27. Schmeelke, *Das Kriegstagebuch der Jagdstaffel 12*, p. 37.
28. 13th Wing, RFC, RFC, Flight Returns and Messages, 28 July 1917.
29. 3rd Brigade, RFC, Recommendations for honours and awards, 2 June 1917 [date of record, more likely sent later].
30. WAB letter to Margaret, 2 August 1917.
31. Liddell Hart, *The Real War 1914-1918*, p. 337.
32. WAB letter to Margaret, 2 August 1917.
33. 60 Squadron, RFC, Combat Report No. 584 by Capt W.A. Bishop, 5 August 1917.
34. RFC, Communiqué No. 100, 12 August 1917, p. 1.
35. 60 Squadron, RFC, Combat Report No. 585 by Capt W.A. Bishop, 5 August 1917.
36. Schmeelke, op.cit., p. 39.
37. Kogenluft, *Nachrichtenblatt der Luftstreitkräfte,*

Vol. 1 Nr. 24, 9 August 1917, p. 126.

38. Kofl 6, *Wöchentlicher Tätigkeits-Bericht Nr. 1065/I*, 10 August 1917, p. 2.

39. 60 Squadron, RFC, Combat Report No. 586 by Capt W.A. Bishop, 6 August 1917.

40. The original RFC Communiqué No. 100 identified the F.2B unit as 'No. 11 Squadron', with which 60 Squadron had worked in the past; however, the hard-working and distinguished crew of Captain C.M. Clement and Lieutenant R.B. Carter flew with 22 Squadron; hence, the inadvertent typographical error is corrected in this book's use of the historical account.

41. Ibid., p. 2

42. 60 Squadron, RFC, Combat Report No. 591 by Capt W.A. Bishop, 9 August 1917.

43. RFC, Communiqué No. 100, op.cit., p. 4.

44. Kogenluft, *Nachrichtenblatt der Luftstreitkräfte, Vol. 1 Nr. 25*, 16 August 1917, p. 143.

45. Kofl 6, op.cit.

46. WAB letter to Margaret, 10 August 1917.

47. Molesworth, quoted in Scott, *Sixty Squadron, R.A.F. 1916-1919*, pp. 104-105.

48. 60 Squadron, RFC, *Officers' Record Book,* Flight Log, 11 August 1917.

49. 'An Airman V.C. – Single-handed Attack on an Aerodrome', *The Times*, 13 August 1917, p. 6.

50. 'Honours, A Canadian V.C.', *Flight* magazine, 16 August 1917, p. 834.

51. WAB letter to Margaret, 14 August 1917.

52. RFC, Communiqué No. 101, 19 August 1917, p. 4.

53. 60 Squadron, RFC, Combat Report No. 598 by Capt W.A. Bishop, 13 August 1917.

54. Kogenluft, *Nachrichtenblatt Nr. 25*, op.cit., p. 145.

55. Bock, *Kofl 4 Wochenberichte summaries*, 13 August 1917.

56. Kofl 6, Wöchentlicher Tätigkeits-Bericht Nr. 1120/I, 17 August 1917, p. 4.

57. 60 Squadron, RFC, *Officers' Record Book*, Flight Log, 15 August 1917.

58. 60 Squadron, RFC, Combat Report No. 599 by Capt W.A. Bishop, 15 August 1917.

59. RFC, Communiqué No. 101, op.cit., p. 7.

60. Kogenluft, *Nachrichtenblatt der Luftstreitkräfte, Vol. 1 Nr. 26*, 23 August 1917, p. 159.

61. Kofl 6, op.cit.

62. 60 Squadron, RFC, Combat Report No. 600 by Capt W.A. Bishop, 16 August 1917.

63. Ibid.

64. RFC, Communiqué No. 101, op.cit., p. 8.

65. Kogenluft, *Nachrichtenblatt Nr. 26*, op.cit., p. 160.

66. Bock, *Kofl 4 Wochenberichte summaries*, 16 August 1917.

67. Bishop, A. *The Courage of the Early Morning*, p. 124.

68. Shores, Franks & Guest, op.cit., p. 77,

69. Ibid., p. 60.

70. WAB letter to Margaret, 14 August 1917.

71. Quoted in Bishop, A., op.cit., p. 125.

72. Promotion to temporary major was recorded in Billy's service record, following promulgation in London Gazette No. 30279, 28 August 1917 [Ref: Library & Archives Canada, *W.A. Bishop Fonds, Record of Service*, 1919].

73. WAB letter to Margaret, 30 August 1917.

74. WAB letter to Margaret, 22 August 1917.

75. Bishop, A., op.cit., p. 126.

76. A noted sculptor and cousin of Winston Churchill

77. WAB letter to Margaret, 10 September 1917.

78. Quoted in Bishop, A. op.cit., p. 127.

79. 3rd Brigade, RFC, Recommendations, op.cit., 27 August 1917.

80. Kogenluft, *Nachrichtenblatt der Luftstreitkräfte, Vol. 1 Nr. 30*, 20 September 1917, p. 244.

81. Franks & Bailey, *Over the Front*, p. 171.

82. Anonymous. 'The Flying Corps Spirit', p. 1.

83. 'Airisms to the Four Winds,' *Flight* magazine, 20 September 1917, p. 976.

84. Quoted in Bishop, A. op.cit., p. 129.

Chapter Eleven Endnotes

1. *Illustrated London News*, 14 January 1911.

2. Bishop, A. *The Courage of the Early Morning*, p. 129.

3. McCaffery, Billy Bishop, *Canadian Hero*, pp. 168-169.

4. Quoted in Bishop, A., op.cit., p. 130.

5. Kogenluft, *Nachrichtenblatt der Luftstreitkräfte, Vol. 1 Nr. 32*, 4 October 1917, p. 279.

6. *La Guerre Aérienne Illustrée*, 4 October 1917, p. 748.

7. Kogenluft, *Nachrichtenblatt der Luftstreitkräfte, Vol. 1 Nr. 37*, 8 November 1917, p. 380.

8. Bishop, A., op.cit.

9. Ibid., p. 131.

10. Library & Archives Canada, *W.A. Bishop Fonds, Record of Service*, 1919; honour published in *The London Gazette* 30308, 29 September 1917.

11. 'Personals', *Flight* magazine, 25 October 1917, p. 1117.

12. Bishop, A., op.cit., pp. 131-132.

13. Bowyer, *For Valour – The Air V.C.s*, pp. 65-67.

14. Bishop, A., op.cit., p. 132.

15. Bishop, W., 'Tales of the British Air Service', pp. 27-35.

16. LAC, *W.A. Bishop Fonds, Record of Service*, 1919; honour published in *The London Gazette* 30421,

11 December 1917.

17. Duckers, *British Gallantry Awards 1855-2000*, p. 54.

18. Bishop, A., op.cit., p. 131.

19. Ibid., p. 135.

20. Ibid, p. 136.

21. Quoted in Bishop, A., op.cit., p. 138.

22. 'Honours,' *Flight* magazine, 17 January 1918, p. 60; *The London Gazette*, No. 30466, 9 January 1918.

23. Bishop, A., op.cit., p. 136.

24. Sloan, *Wings of Honor – American Airmen in World War I*, pp. 194-195.

25. Bishop, A., op.cit.

26. Quoted in ibid., p. 137.

27. Bruce, *British Aeroplanes 1914-1918*, pp. 603-604.

28. Ibid., p. 451.

29. Jones, *The War in the Air, Vol. VI*, p. 25.

30. Royal Air Force, Communiqué No. 3, 24 April 1918, p. 3.

31. Bishop, A., op.cit., p. 141.

32. RAF, War Diary, Locations of RAF Units, 23 April 1918, p. 87.

33. Directorate of History and Heritage, Department of National Defence, W.A. Bishop letter to Margaret, 22 May 1918.

34. Quoted in Skelton, 'John McGavock Grider – War Bird', p. 14.

35. WAB letter to Margaret, 24 May 1918.

36. WAB letter to Margaret, 26 May 1918.

37. WAB letter to Margaret, 27 May 1918.

38. 85 Squadron, RAF, Combat Report by Major W.A. Bishop, 27 May 1918.

39. Kogenluft, *Nachrichtenblatt der Luftstreitkräfte, Vol. 2 Nr. 14*, 30 May 1918, p. 196.

40. Zuerl, *Pour le Mérite-Flieger*, p. 477.

41. RAF, Communiqué No. 9, 4 June 1918, p. 1.

42. Ibid.

43. WAB letter to Margaret, 29 May 1918.

44. Shores, Franks & Guest, *Above the Trenches*, p. 73.

45. WAB letter to Margaret, 30 May 1918.

46. RAF, Communiqué No. 9, op.cit., p. 2.

47. Kogenluft, *Nachrichtenblatt der Luftstreitkräfte, Vol. 2 Nr. 15*, 6 June 1918, p. 207.

48. O'Connor, *Aviation Awards of Imperial Germany and the Men Who Earned Them, Vol. II - The Aviation Awards of the Kingdom of Prussia*, p. 122.

49. Reportedly the eighth victory of Oberflugmeister Kurt Schönfelder, a naval pilot assigned to Jagdstaffel 7 [Ref: Shores, Franks & Guest, op.cit.].

50. Captain Edwin Louis Benbow, age 22, flying in S.E.5a C.1862, was reported 'Killed in combat'

[Ref: RFC, *Pilot and Observer Casualties*, 30 May 1918; Hobson, *Airmen Died in the Great War*, p. 117].

51. WAB letter to Margaret, 31 May 1918.

52. 85 Squadron, RAF, Combat Report by Major W.A. Bishop, 3:15 p.m., 31 May 1918

53. VanWyngarden, *Pfalz Scout Aces of World War I*, pp. 70-75.

54. Bock, *Kommandeur der Flieger der 6. Armee casualty summary*, 31 May 1918.

55. Duiven & Abbott, *Schlachtflieger! Germany and the Origins of Air/Ground Support 1916-1918*, p. 359

56. RAF, Communiqué No. 9, op.cit.

57. WAB letter to Margaret, 1 June 1918.

58. 85 Squadron, RAF, Combat Report by Major W.A. Bishop, 1 June 1918.

59. VanWyngarden, op.cit., pp. 67-68.

60. Bock, op.cit.

61. 85 Squadron, RAF, Combat Report by 1st-Lt E.W. Springs, 1 June 1918.

62. Franks, Bailey & Guest, *Above the Lines*, p. 74.

63. Shores, Franks & Guest, op.cit., p. 94.

64. Ibid., pp. 268-269.

65. WAB letter to Margaret, 2 June 1918.

66. 85 Squadron, RAF, Combat Report by Major W.A. Bishop, 2 June 1918.

67. Kogenluft, *Nachrichtenblatt Nr. 15*, op.cit., p. 208.

Chapter Twelve Endnotes

1. *The London Gazette*, No. 30827, 3 August 1918.

2. Royal Air Force, War Diary, Enemy Aircraft, 4 June 1918, p. 7.

3. 85 Squadron, RAF, Combat Report by Major W.A. Bishop, 4 June 1918.

4. Ibid.

5. Franks, Bailey & Duiven, *Casualties of the German Air Service 1914-1920*, pp. 277, 370.

6. Marinefeldflugchef, *Mitteilungen aus dem Gebiete des Luftkrieges, Verluste im Monat Juni 1918*, 13 July 1918, p. 242

7. Bishop, A., *The Courage of the Early Morning*, p. 156.

8. Directorate of History and Heritage, Department of National Defence, W.A. Bishop morning letter to Margaret, 10 June 1918.

9. 85 Squadron move from Petite-Synthe to St. Omer [Ref: RAF, War Diary, Movements, 11 June 1918, p. 22].

10. WAB afternoon letter to Margaret, 10 June 1918.

11. WAB letter to Margaret, 13 June 1918.

12. Degelow, *Mit dem weissen Hirsch durch dick und dünn*, p. 97.

13. Sturtivant & Page, *The S.E.5 File*, p. 70.

14. RAF, War Diary, Weather Report, 14 June 1918, p. 28.
15. 85 Squadron, RAF, Combat Report by Major W.A. Bishop, 15 June 1918.
16. Bishop, A., op.cit., pp. 157-158.
17. Shores, Franks & Guest, *Above the Trenches*, pp. 268-269 and 255-156, respectively.
18. Royal Air Force, Communiqué No. 11, 19 June 1918, p.3.
19. Kogenluft, *Nachrichtenblatt der Luftstreitkräfte, Vol. 2 Nr. 17*, 20 June 1918, p. 236.
20. VanWyngarden, *Pfalz Scout Aces of World War I*, p. 39.
21. Bock, *Kommandeur der Flieger der 6. Armee Casualty Summary*, 15 June 1918.
22. According to RFC, *Pilot and Observer Casualties*, 16 June 1918: '2/Lt Howard Grant Thompson [in] S.E.5a D.6876 [was] last seen 12:45 pm at Kruiseecke by Lt Trapp to land in an uncertain way and turn over. MG fire from ground was intense. German message received 23.7.18 states that this officer is unwounded.'
23. Jones, *The War in the Air, Vol. VI*, p. 512.
24. WAB letter to Margaret, 16 June 1918.
25. RAF, War Diary, Weather Report, 16 June 1918, p. 31.
26. 85 Squadron, RAF, Combat Report by Major W.A. Bishop, 16 June 1918.
27. RAF, Communiqué No. 11, op.cit.
28. Kogenluft, *Nachrichtenblatt Nr. 17*, op.cit.
29. WAB letter to Margaret, 17 June 1918.
30. 85 Squadron, RAF, Combat Report by Major W.A. Bishop, 17 June 1918.
31. Bock, *Kofl 6 Casualty summary*, 17 June 1918.
32. 85 Squadron, RAF, Combat Report by Major W.A. Bishop, op.cit.
33. 85 Squadron, RAF, Combat Report by Lieutenant E.W. Springs, 18 June 1918.
34. 'Captain G.M. [*sic*] Grider [in] S.E.5a C.1883 … [reported] last seen near Menin in engagement with EA at 1:50 pm' [Ref: RFC, *Pilot and Observer Casualties*, 18 June 1918].
35. Quoted in Vaughan, *Letters from a War Bird – The World War I Correspondence of Elliott White Springs*, p. 161.
36. 85 Squadron, RAF, Combat Report by Major W.A. Bishop, 18 June 1918.
37. RAF, Communiqué No. 12, 26 June 1918, pp. 1-2.
38. Kogenluft, *Nachrichtenblatt der Luftstreitkräfte, Vol. 2 Nr. 18*, 27 June 1918, p. 253.
39. Kommandeur der Flieger der 4. Armee, *Wöchenbericht Nr. 1716* op, 20 June 1918, p. 4.
40. Bock, *Königl. Preuss. Jagdstaffel 56, research notes*, 18 June 1918.
41. RAF, War Diary, Weather [and] Enemy Aircraft Reports, 19 June 1918, p. 37.
42. 85 Squadron, RAF, Combat Report by Major W.A. Bishop, 19 June 1918.
43. RAF, Communiqué No. 11, op.cit., p. 2.
44. Kogenluft, *Nachrichtenblatt Nr. 18*, op.cit.
45. Kofl 4, op.cit.
46. RAF, War Diary, Weather Report, 20 June 1918, p. 39.
47. Vaughan, op.cit.
48. Douglas, *Years of Combat*, p. 195.
49. Quoted in Bishop, A., op.cit., p. 164.
50. 'The Death of Major McCudden, VC' in *Flight* magazine, 18 July 1918, p. 807.
51. Kogenluft, *Nachrichtenblatt der Luftstreitkräfte, Vol. 2 Nr. 22*, 25 July 1918, p. 326.
52. Quoted in Bishop, A., op.cit., p. 165.
53. Jones, op.cit., p. 532.
54. *The London Gazette*, No. 30827, 3 August 1918.
55. 5 August 1918 [Ref: Library & Archives Canada, *W.A. Bishop Fonds, Record of Service*].
56. Awarded 2 November 1918 [Ref: LAC, *W.A. Bishop Fonds, Record of Service*, 1919].
57. Doyle, 'They Called Bishop Hell's Handmaiden and Said He Was Half the Air Force', p. 8.
58. Bishop, A., op.cit., pp. 166-171.
59. Quoted in ibid., p. 174.
60. Ibid., p. 185.
61. Ibid., p. 186.
62. Doyle, op.cit.
63. Quoted in ibid.
64. Wise, *Canadian Airmen and the First World War – The Official History of the Royal Canadian Air Force, Vol. I*, p. 574,
65. Doyle, op.cit.
66. Bashow, *Knights of the Air – Canadian Fighter Pilots in the First World War*, p. 127.

Maps

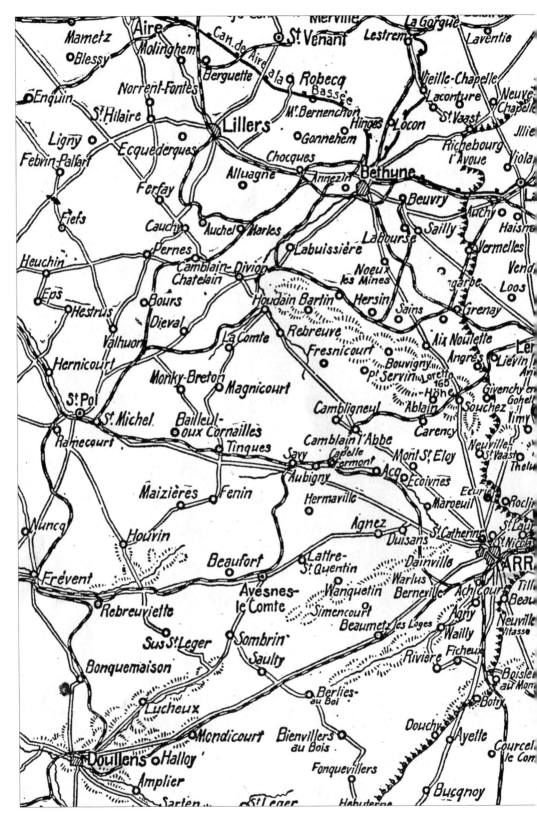

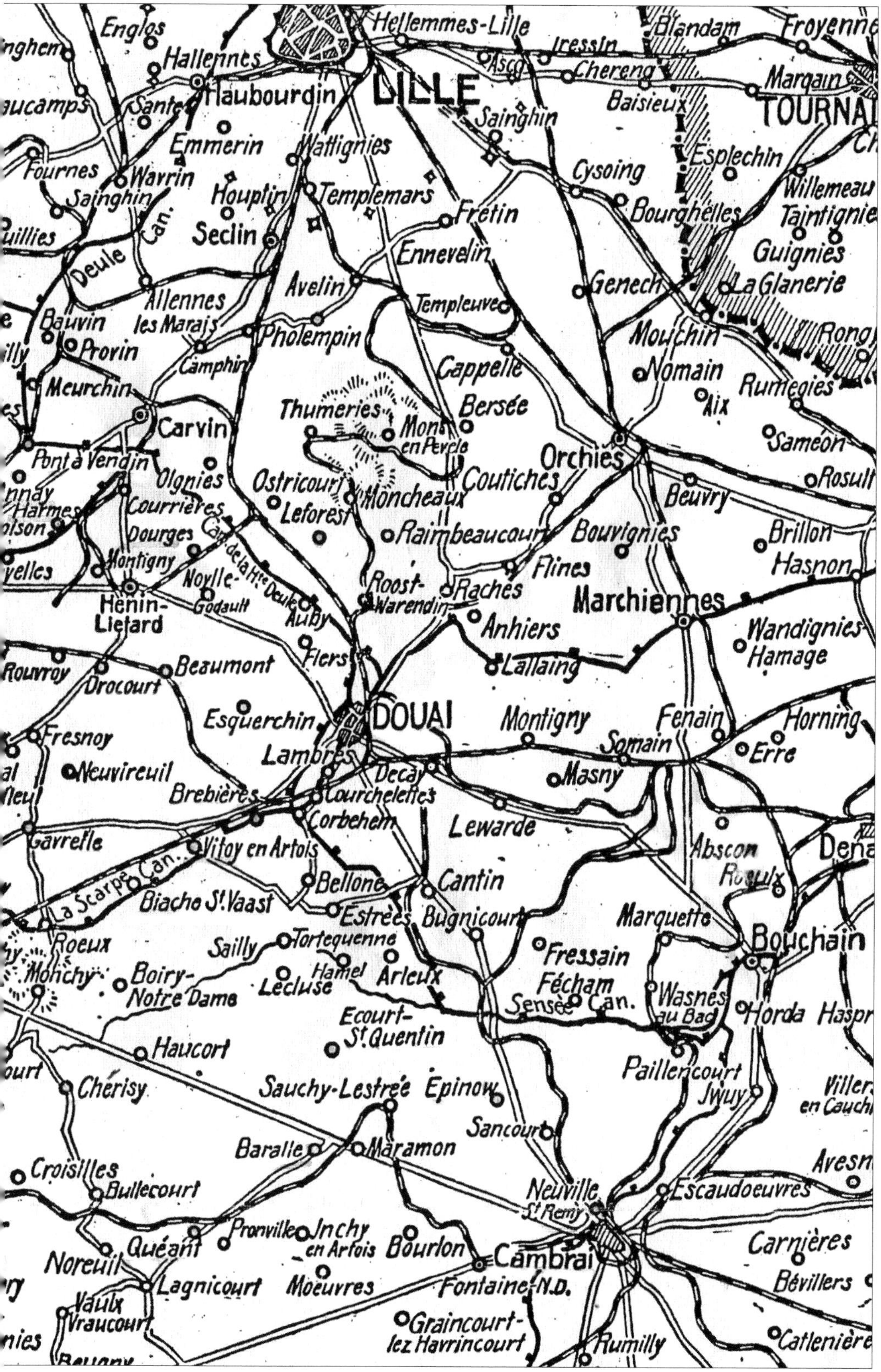

60 SQUADRON SECTOR IN 1917

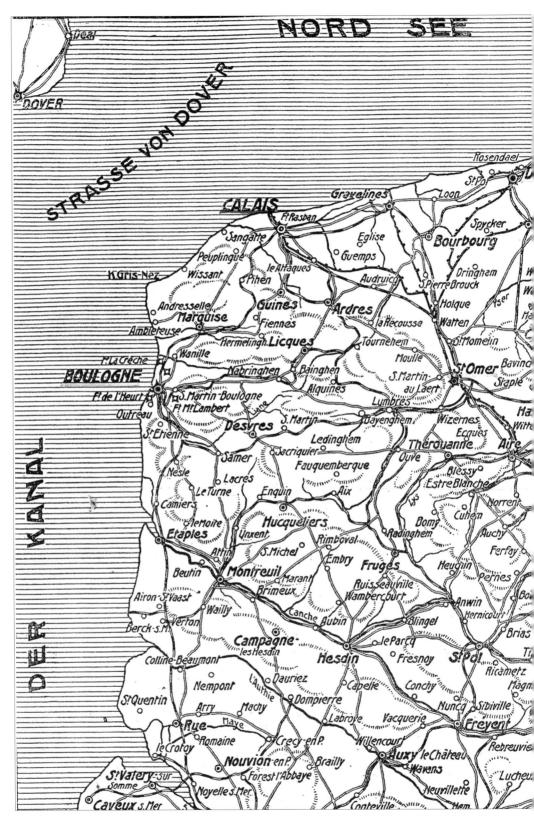

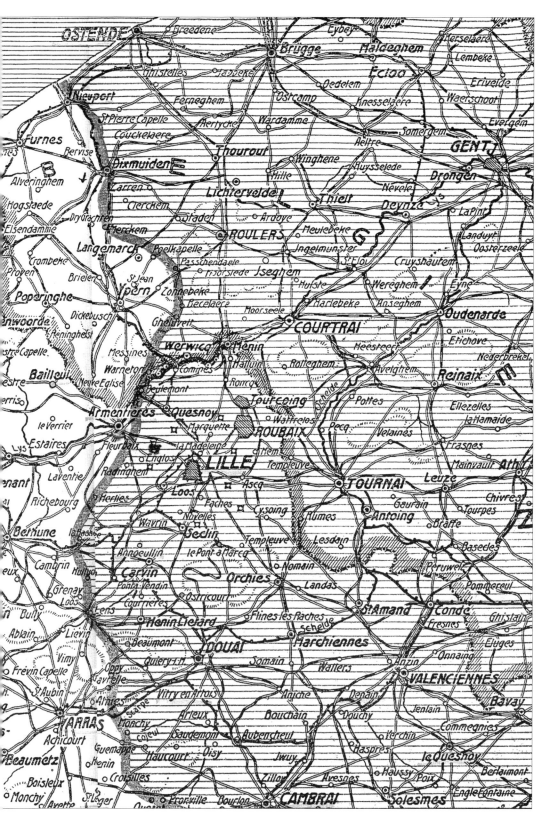

85 SQUADRON SECTOR IN 1918

INDEX

I. MILITARY FORMATIONS

II. PERSONNEL

FURTHER INFORMATION
Readers interested in obtaining additional information about World War I military aviation history may wish to contact websites of research-oriented, non-profit organizations, including:

The Aerodrome
URL: http://www.theaerodrome.com/

Australian Society of World War I Aero Historians
URL: http://asww1ah.0catch.com

Cross & Cockade International (UK)
URL: http://www.crossandcockade.com

League of World War I Aviation Historians (USA)
URL: http://www.overthefront.com

Das Propellerblatt (Germany)
URL: www.Propellerblatt.de

World War One Aeroplanes (USA)
URL: http://www.avation-history.com/ww1aero.htm